Guidance for Women in Twelfth-Century Convents

Library of Medieval Women

Series Editor: Jane Chance

The Library of Medieval Women aims to make available, in an English translation, significant works by, for, and about medieval women, from the age of the Church Fathers to the fifteenth century. The series encompasses many forms of writing, from poetry, visions, biography and autobiography, and letters to sermons, treatises and encyclopedias; the subject matter is equally diverse: theology and mysticism, classical mythology, medicine and science, history, hagiography, and instructions for anchoresses. Each text is presented with an introduction setting the material in context, a guide to further reading, and an interpretive essay.

We welcome suggestions for future titles in the series. Proposals or queries may be sent directly to the editor or publisher at the addresses given below; all submissions will receive prompt and informed consideration.

Professor Jane Chance, Department of English, MS 30, Rice University, PO Box 1892, Houston, TX 77251–1892, USA. E-mail: jchance@rice.edu

Boydell & Brewer Limited, PO Box 9, Woodbridge, Suffolk, IP12 3DF, UK. E-mail: boydell@boydell.co.uk. Website: www.boydell.co.uk

Previously published titles in this series appear at the back of this book

Guidance for Women in Twelfth-Century Convents

Translated by Vera Morton

**with an Interpretive Essay
by Jocelyn Wogan-Browne
(Fordham University)**

D.S. BREWER

First published 2003
D. S. Brewer, Cambridge

ISBN 0 85991 825 4

BX
4210
.G828
2003

D. S. Brewer is an imprint of Boydell & Brewer Ltd
PO Box 9, Woodbridge, Suffolk IP12 3DF, UK
and of Boydell & Brewer Inc.
PO Box 41026, Rochester, NY 14604–4126, USA
website: www.boydell.co.uk

A catalogue record for this book is available
from the British Library

Library of Congress Cataloging-in-Publication Data
Guidance for women in twelfth-century convents /translated
by Vera Morton ; with an interpretive essay by Jocelyn Wogan-Browne.
        p. cm. – (Library of medieval women)
Includes bibliographical references and index.
    ISBN 0–85991–825–4 (alk. paper)
1. Monastic and religious life of women – History – Middle Ages, 600–1500 –
Sources.   2. Virginity – Religious aspects – Christianity – History of doctrines
– Middle Ages, 600–1500 – Sources.   3. Chastity – History of doctrines –
Middle Ages, 600–1500 – Sources.   I. Morton, Vera Petch, 1923–   II. Series.
    BX4210G828 2003
    248.8'943 – dc21   2003006521

This publication is printed on acid-free paper

Printed in Great Britain by
St. Edmundsbury Press, Bury St. Edmunds, Suffolk

Contents

Preface

Letters composed by women in the High Middle Ages survive relatively rarely, but many of the letters written to queens, noblewomen, abbesses and nuns are extant. This volume presents a selection from twelfth-century letters written to women in the female communities of England and Northern France. Although it is male clerics who speak in the letters, what they write is strongly conditioned by an awareness of the status and requirements of their female audiences. The most renowned letter from a churchman to an abbess included here was composed by Abelard at the request of Heloise to aid her in her work as abbess of the Paraclete. This letter's account of the role and achievements of women in Christian history is deservedly famous, though it has not been readily available in modern translation. A second letter by Abelard on the education of Heloise's nuns, also translated here, provides invaluable evidence for how women living professed Christian lives might be educated in communities.

The relationship of Abelard and Heloise, exceptional and celebrated as it is, is in this volume placed against a background of other epistolary relations in North West France and England. Selected letters from Osbert of Clare, Prior of Westminster, and Peter the Venerable of Cluny to abbesses and to young women in convents are translated here for the first time. These less well-known letters have their own considerable interest as well as providing a context for the correspondence of Abelard and Heloise.

In addition, this volume includes extracts from biographies of abbesses commissioned by their successors at the abbey of Barking. These extracts show medieval women administrators using the traditions of institutionalised female virginity and chastity in their own projects and responsibilities. The literary conventions of virginity and chastity writing could shape and express the working lives and ambitions of women as well as men in the twelfth-century church. Letters and biographical texts such as the ones translated here suggest that a richer literary and social history of medieval female communities in England and Northern France can be written than has been sometimes thought.

Acknowledgements

Grateful thanks are due to Dr Constant Mews for generously reading the translation of Abelard Letter 7, recommending the inclusion of Letter 9, and offering many helpful observations and suggestions. His encouragement was of the greatest value to the volume. Dr Gillian Clark solved some knotty problems in Abelard's Letter 9. Phyllis Kon typed the first draft of the manuscript with great competence and unfailing good humour. With infinite patience Simon Mandelkow gave advice and instruction in word processing, and responded to frequent cries for help; his kindness was greatly valued. At a later stage Marynna Mews gave valuable help with copy-editing. Jane Chance, editor of this series, and Caroline Palmer of Boydell & Brewer have been models of patience and helpfulness throughout.

I find it difficult to express the depth of my gratitude to my teacher, Jocelyn Wogan-Browne; anything of value in this book is due to her guidance and rigorous standards of scholarship; that I kept on through all difficulties is due to her kindness and encouragement.

Vera Morton

Abbreviations

ANTS   Anglo-Norman Text Society
AV   The Holy Bible: Authorised King James Version.
Bede   *Historia Ecclesiastica Gentis Anglorum* (A History of the English Church and People), trans. B. Colgrave and R. A. B. Mynors (Oxford: Oxford University Press, 1969).
CCCM   Corpus Christianorum Continuatio Mediaeualis (Turnhout: Brepols, 1966–).
CCSL   Corpus Christianorum Series Latina (Turnhout: Brepols, 1954–).
Cross   *The Oxford Dictionary of the Christian Church*, ed. F. L. Cross, 3rd edn (London: Oxford University Press, 1997).
CSEL   Corpus Scriptorum Ecclesiasticorum Latinorum (Vienna-Leipzig: Teubner, 1866–).
EETS   Early English Text Society
Farmer   *The Oxford Dictionary of Saints*, ed. David Farmer, 4th edn (Oxford: Oxford University Press, 1997).
FMLS   *Forum for Modern Language Studies*
Harvey   *The Oxford Companion to Classical Literature*, ed. Paul Harvey (Oxford: Oxford University Press, 1966).
HBS   Henry Bradshaw Society
Latham   *Revised Mediaeval Latin Word-List*, ed. R. E. Latham (London: Oxford University Press for the British Academy, 1980).
PL   *Patrologia Latina*, ed. J.-P. Migne (Paris: Garnier Frères, 1844–).
SCH   *Studies in Church History*

Introduction

Medieval letters on virginity and chastity

Even when addressed to a single individual, and to someone personally known to the writer, medieval literary letters were designed for copying and circulation among a wider public. Some of them are in effect treatises in epistolary form, meant not only to address particular people, but to be exemplary and useful to further audiences. The correspondence of churchmen was often copied into model collections.[1] Handbooks in the art of composition, the *ars dictandi*, taught the conventions for composing letters (the physical writing of letters was frequently done by secretaries working to dictation) and provided model examples. The twelfth century witnessed a great flowering of letters as literature and of letter collections. The correspondence of churchmen and women in the eleventh and early twelfth centuries often took the form of elaborate Latin verse love-letters in a particular development of the traditions of spiritual friendship more widely used between men in the monastic life.[2] While few women are known personally to have composed Latin letters after the twelfth century, current research suggests that there are more women Latin letter writers than has been thought.[3] (Elite women could of course command their clerks to write letters for them, whether for business and administrative

---

1 On medieval letter collections see Giles Constable, *Letters and Letter-Collections*, Typologie des sources du moyen âge occidental, fasc. 17 (Turnhout: Brepols, 1976) and *The Letters of Peter the Venerable*, ed. Giles Constable, 2 vols. (Cambridge, Mass., Harvard University Press, 1967), 2: 1–44.

2 See Gerald A. Bond, *The Loving Subject: Desire, Eloquence, and Power in Romanesque France* (Philadelphia: University of Pennsylvania Press, 1995), esp. chs. 2 and 5 and for an example from England (Muriel of Wilton), p. 141: Joan M. Ferrante, *To the Glory of Her Sex: Women's Roles in the Composition of Medieval Texts* (Bloomington and Indianapolis: Indiana University Press, 1997), ch. 1.

3 See Alexandra Barratt, 'Small Latin? The Post-Conquest Learning of English Religious Women', in *Anglo-Latin and Its Heritage: Essays in Honour of A. G. Rigg*, ed. Siân Echard and Gernot R. Wieland (Turnhout: Brepols, 2000), pp. 51–65; Laurie J. Churchill, Phyllis R. Brown and Jane E. Jeffrey, eds., *Women Writing in Latin*, 3 vols. (London and New York: Routledge, Taylor and Francis, 2001), vol. 2.

concerns such as the management of their estates, or for more
personal or literary letters).

Twelfth-century churchmen writing to women under their pastoral
care or spiritual direction drew on a substantial literature of virginity
and chastity from the early Christian centuries, as does Abelard in his
letter to Heloise on the teaching and learning of nuns (see V below)
and Peter the Venerable in his letter to his nieces (III below). The
Fathers of the early Church, such as Cyprian, Tertullian, Ambrose,
Augustine and above all Jerome, wrote letters and rules for women
living religious lives in which an ideal of virginity and chastity as a
difficult and superior spiritual state is articulated. Unmarried women
could be consecrated to God as virgins and women who had been
married could at least be his chaste if not virgin servants. By
renouncing marriage and childbirth in order to undertake a life of
vowed chastity or virginity in these ways, women could become
more nearly like men, more *vir*ile (the Latin for 'man' is *vir*). At the
same time, they could lead a modest and decorous life as women,
veiled and enclosed.

While a modern view of virginity and chastity might well regard
them as dead and fruitless states of mind, medieval views were more
positive. Incorporating and further elaborating the patristic ideals of
the early Church, dedicated medieval virginity and chastity did not
signal a life empty of emotional ties so much as a life where all
desires and preoccupations were focussed on God, in relation to
whom women were encouraged to view themselves as brides and
daughters.[4] Duty might call to service in convents, but quite as
important was the engagement of emotion and desire. The idea of
Christ as bridegroom is frequently offered as an ideal romance and
marriage, consoling and encouraging the female reader, informing
her reading and meditation with vivid spiritual relationships and
providing a powerful representation of ardour and aspiration.
Virginity is seen as a particularly demanding and much respected
form of spiritual life, a superior version of the romance heroine's
courtly existence.[5]

---

[4]   For important and subtle accounts of gendering in these works, see Barbara
Newman, 'Flaws in the Golden Bowl', *Traditio* 45 (1989–90), 1–46, repr. in her
From Virile Woman to WomanChrist (Philadelphia: University of Pennsylvania
Press, 1995); Constant J. Mews, ed., *Listen, Daughter: The Speculum Virginum
and the Formation of Religious Women in the Middle Ages* (New York: Palgrave,
2001).

[5]   See further Kim M. Phillips, 'Virginity as the Perfect Age of Women's Life', in

Concern with the emotional state and aspirations of their audiences was not incompatible with systematic thought and analysis in virginity and chastity literature. At this period letters and texts specifically shaped for women could draw on a rich language of desire common to many genres of theological exegesis and commentary. Relations between the divine and the human were frequently expressed and understood by the tropes and figures of love discourse: twelfth-century treatments of the biblical Song of Songs for instance, built on Origen (185–c. 254) and other early commentators to present the Song allegorically as the love song of the soul, the bride of Christ, and the rewards of her love for him. The influential cycle of sermons on the Song by St Bernard of Clairvaux (d. 1153) is one of a number of such commentaries.[6] Emotion was not necessarily opposed to reason: human feeling and desire was, potentially, a microcosmic version of God's creativity and love. As such it could be a source of knowledge of God.[7]

Medieval ideals of virginity included much more than the notion of technical intactness, supposedly physically verifiable in women's bodies, which has often been the first meaning for 'virginity' in modern definitions.[8] The literature of virginity and chastity also had much to say to audiences who were neither young, virgin, or unmarried. The powerful ideal of virginity was continually modified and adapted, both by churchmen and by their female audiences, so as not to exclude widows and wives. Women in these roles tended to have greater socio-economic power and were an important source of patronage for the church. They were frequently seen as honorary virgins, and encouraged to feel that their fleshly condition of chastity, necessarily humbled as it was by not being the higher-ranking state of virginity, could equal the spiritual condition of a virgin. A virgin both technically intact and consecrated to God would potentially have higher rank in heaven than a widow or wife, but might

Young Medieval Women, ed. Katherine J. Lewis, Noel James Menuge and Kim M. Phillips (Gloucester: Sutton, 1999), pp. 25–46.

6 E. Ann Matter, *The Voice of My Beloved: The Song of Songs in Western Medieval Christianity* (Philadelphia: University of Pennyslvania Press, 1990).

7 Colin Morris, *The Discovery of the Individual 1050–1200* (London: SPCK, 1972); Jean Leclercq, *The Love of Learning and the Desire for God*, tr. Catherine Misrahi (New York: Fordham University Press, 1961).

8 Kathleen Coyne Kelly, *Performing Virginity and Testing Chastity in the Middle Ages* (London and New York: Routledge, 2000); Sarah Salih, *Versions of Virginity in Late Medieval England* (Cambridge: D. S. Brewer, 2001), ch. 1.

well be open to the temptation of pride in her condition.[9] Across the range of monastic and secular households, as well as within convents, the ideal of virginity addressed and affected the lives of women of all ages and aspirations.

In addition to positive arguments for virginity and chastity, arguments on the disadvantages of marriage are a common topic of virginity and chastity letters. The pains and dangers of childbirth are emphasised (and were indeed considerable in any case) and the wife's relationship to her husband is suggested as unworthily servile in comparison with the nun's to Christ. Thus Osbert of Clare, writing to Adelidis, abbess of Barking, sees her as a 'mother' of the convent, but a mother for whom the act of giving birth is without the 'corruption' and the dangers of childbirth in the flesh (I, pp. 22–3 below). Although virginity and chastity writings usually recommend one form of union (spiritual) over another (being wedded to an earthly man) without encouraging women to think outside the idea of marriage as such, analyses of the problems of earthly marriage in these writings can offer women a latent critique of female subordination in marriage.[10]

Chastity and virginity were also seen as heroic states that empowered women beyond the limits of gender. Women's capacity for suffering is the focus of many stories of saints, and though actual martyrdom might not be an option, nuns and pious laywomen were encouraged to think of asceticism and self-discipline as versions of martyrdom, less spectacular but still heroic. Nuns of the High Middle Ages were often of noble families. The idea of combating evil on her knees may have offered consolation to a young woman envious of the achievements of her knightly brothers. At all events writing on virginity offered ways of imagining the self that incorporated a range of roles. Heroic women of various kinds are offered as role models in all the texts represented here, whether their recipients are virgin brides of Christ or 'holy mothers', i.e. abbesses. The range of these figures goes well beyond the traditional virgin martyr

---

9   On virginity, chastity, and honorary virginity, see further Cindy L. Carlson and Angela J. Weisl, eds., *Constructions of Widowhood and Virginity in the Later Middle Ages* (New York: St Martin's Press, 1999); Jocelyn Wogan-Browne, *Saints' Lives and Women's Literary Culture c. 1150–1300: Virginity and its Authorizations* (Oxford: Oxford University Press, 2001), chs. 1, 4.

10   Jocelyn Wogan-Browne, 'Saints' Lives and the Female Reader', *FMLS* 27 (1991), 314–32.

heroines of the church, though it does include them. Peter the Venerable and Osbert of Clare, for instance, encourage their nieces with examples from among the great (and semi-legendary) virgin martyrs, saints Agatha, Agnes, Cecilia (III and IV). Abelard, writing a history of women in the church for Heloise (II), includes a much wider range of women. He discusses pagan Roman forerunners such as the Vestal Virgins and the prophetess Sibyl; the women of the Gospels; and biblical figures of heroic intervention or achievement such as Judith, Esther, Deborah, and the mother of the Maccabees. Women of the early church are also present as exemplary and historically important figures, whether as early deaconesses or as the correspondents and allies of St Jerome. In Abelard's letter on education (V), such women again appear, both as useful precedents and as part of the history of women's learning. Osbert of Clare presents the biblical figure of Judith, heroic widow and decisive leader, to abbess Adelidis of Barking (I) in a very different series of examples from those offered in his letters to his nieces in the convent (IV). In Goscelin of St Bertin's portrait of abbess Elfgiva, rebuilder of the Barking Abbey shrines, the abbess is compared (much to her advantage as a Christian builder) with Semiramis and Dido, legendary foundresses and builders of Babylon and Carthage (VI).

Often the authors update their selections of traditional or historical figures by making exemplary heroines of people closer to the women for whom they are writing. Peter the Venerable makes his nieces' grandmother Raingard a figure to be lived up to (III); Osbert discusses Ethelburga, famous foundress of Adelidis' own abbey of Barking (I), a figure with whose legacy of leadership Adelidis must have been deeply familiar. In his biographies for Barking Abbey, Goscelin also portrays Ethelburga, together with many other inspirational figures from among this house's women leaders (VI). Abelard, having already drawn heavily on the figure of Jerome 'the great doctor' and his writings for women in his letter 'On educating virgins' (V), goes on to offer their own abbess as ideal example and teacher to the nuns of the Paraclete: Heloise herself is the modern day equivalent not only of the women of the early church but almost of Jerome himself. The chronological range and variety of virginity and chastity models drawn on in this small selection of texts suggests how important these ideals and the literary genres deploying them have been in women's lives and literature.

Convents and women's lives

The earlier twelfth century saw a period of intense growth in women's foundations in England and Northern France.[11] Convents were often both founded and patronised by the families of the leading women in them. The income from a property might be devoted, for instance, to supporting a succession of female members of a family in a nunnery over the generations. A woman undertaking vowed chastity or virginity in a religious community did not give up all human ties. Apart from the community within which she lived, her duties of prayer and intercession maintained spiritual links with her family of birth.

The reasons why women entered nunneries varied; sometimes a girl might seek refuge from a repulsive marriage: not infrequently postulants were offered to the nunnery for family convenience (the dowry for a nun could often be less than for a secular marriage). Child oblates were less frequently accepted in the twelfth century, but girls of between twelve and fifteen years were admitted; widows might choose to retire to a nunnery as might women separated or divorced from their husbands. So too, could women who actively sought and chose religious careers, such as Christina of Markyate, one of the few twelfth-century women in religion in England for whom a medieval biography is extant.[12]

Although women's religious careers and aspirations are under-represented in the extant records, there seems to have been demand from women for more places in religious houses than were available. In the late twelfth century, organised monasticism declared itself unable to cope with the numbers of women seeking places in religious houses: the major monastic orders refused to affiliate any more female houses, and the provision of resources for female religious lives became more than ever dependent on the interests of founders and foundresses from wealthy families. There were also smaller scale communities of recluses, and less expensive and more informal arrangements made by groups of (mostly) urban women for themselves, living lives of social work and religious devotion in communal houses.[13]

---

[11] On the distinctive patterns of growth in female monasticism see Bruce L. Venarde, *Women's Monasticism and Medieval Society: Nunneries in France and England 890–1215* (Ithaca and London: Cornell University Press, 1997).

[12] C. H. Talbot (ed. and trans.), *The Life of Christina of Markyate* (Oxford: Clarendon Press, 1959, repr. 1987).

[13] For the varieties of religious orders and lives in post-Conquest England see Ann

The social composition and the history of female communities in the middle ages can be seen from a range of viewpoints: a nunnery might be both a place for confining surplus women but also (and perhaps, simultaneously for some women) a place of female aspiration and opportunity. Nunneries included women of all ages, and, though usually run by women of high rank, might also include women from other classes, both among the nuns and the lay sisters who did the bulk of the physical and domestic labour within the convent.[14] The life of a nunnery, strictly ordered though it was by the Benedictine Rule and its derivations and variants, was not as different from that of the larger medieval households as modern conceptions of the private family may suggest. The religious life offered the opportunity of various female careers, much as women's schools and hospitals have done in later periods.[15] Goscelin's account of the building operations at Barking Abbey (see VI below) and the numerous properties from which Barking drew its revenues conform to the baronial status of abbesses in leading nunneries. Such abbesses commanded large estates and complex institutions and had to be prepared to defend their house's rights and revenues against encroachments from the crown, from other magnates, and sometimes from bishops or abbots. For such duties, women who had been married and were accustomed to managerial roles were often

K. Warren, *Anchorites and Their Patrons in Medieval England* (Berkeley: University of California Press, 1985); Sharon K. Elkins, *Holy Women of Twelfth-Century England* (Chapel Hill and London: University of North Carolina Press, 1988); Sally Thompson, *Women Religious: The Founding of English Nunneries after the Norman Conquest* (Oxford: Clarendon Press, 1991); Berenice M. Kerr, *Religious Life for Women c. 1100–c. 1350: Fontevraud in England* (Oxford: Oxford University Press, 1999). On women in French houses, see Penelope D. Johnson, *Equal in Monastic Profession: Religious Women in Medieval France* (Chicago and London: University of Chicago Press, 1991).

14 On the socio-economic composition of nunneries, see Kathleen Cooke, 'Donors and Daughters: Shaftesbury Abbey's Benefactors, Endowments and Nuns c.1086–1130', *Anglo-Norman Studies* 12 (1989), 29–45. The classic work by Eileen Power, *Medieval English Nunneries 1275–1535* (Cambridge: Cambridge University Press, 1922) remains informative, though principally concerned with later medieval foundations. On meritocracy in nunneries, see Marilyn Oliva, 'Aristocracy or Meritocracy: Office-Holding Patterns in late Medieval Nunneries', in *Women in the Church*, ed. W. J. Sheils and Diana Wood, *SCH* 27 (1990), 197–208.

15 Roberta Gilchrist, *Contemplation and Action: The Other Monasticism* (London and New York: Leicester University Press, 1995); Martha Vicinus, *Independent Women: Work and Community for Single Women 1850–1920* (London: Virago, 1985).

preferred: many upper-class medieval widows entered convents, sometimes convents of their own foundation, and such women were often important patronesses or associates of female communities.[16]

Women's languages and learning

The range of duties, occupations and opportunities available in convent life was potentially large, especially in wealthier convents, and a nun might well have no less social work, administration, household duties than women in secular households – and rather greater opportunities for learning and for reading, the latter being an institutional part of the religious day. Nunneries were also one of the few places where women wrote, both as scribes and composers of texts. Peter the Venerable, for instance, explicitly states that he is replying to a letter from his nieces (see III below).

Like male communities, female religious houses could have both strong local and territorial affiliations through their patrons and ecclesiastical supporters and also share in the international dimensions of their orders. Abbesses dealt with Rome as well as with their local bishops and archbishops, and some nunneries, as in the case of the Fontevrault houses established by Henry II (d. 1189), were affiliated with mother houses in other countries.[17] However strictly enclosed they might be, women's houses were part of the wider community of Western Christendom: Osbert of Clare's letters (see I, IV below), like those of many other churchmen, recount news from his travels, and particularly news from Rome.

Partly because of the international nature of the Roman Church as the principal institution of the Western European Latin world, there are striking similarities between northern French conventual lives and those of insular Britain. For many purposes letters about virginity and chastity from either side of the Channel can be treated as products of the same North West European culture. Not only the Latin language, but the images of piety and female chastity presented in Osbert of Clare's letters to Barking would have been recognized by the inhabitants of Peter the Venerable's Marcigny and vice versa. Barking's mid twelfth-century abbess, Adelidis, and Heloise, successful head not only of her own convent of the Paraclete

---

16   Thompson, *Women Religious*, ch. 9; Kerr, *Religious Life for Women* and Elkins, *Holy Women, passim.*

17   Kerr, *Religious Life for Women*; Elkins, *Holy Women*, 146–7.

but of a number of daughter houses, would have had much to say to each other.

They would have said it, perhaps, in Latin. Heloise's was excellent: there is no direct evidence for Adelidis', but Osbert of Clare speaks of her having read a life of St Cecilia (I, p. 24 below) and there certainly were some good Latinists among the nuns of Barking in the late twelfth century.[18] If Adelidis herself read the elaborate letter written to her by Osbert, her knowledge of the language and the classical and Christian literature written in it will not have been mean. A second common language would have been French, for all the developing shades of difference between insular and continental versions of that language. Contacts between England and Normandy pre-dated the Norman Conquest: Edward the Confessor, the last Anglo-Saxon king, spent a period of exile in the Normandy of some of his relatives; the Normans who became landholders in England after 1066 kept up their contacts with France, and many high-ranking families owned lands on both sides of the Channel until the loss of Normandy in 1204. Foreign-born churchmen such as Archbishops Lanfranc and Anselm became significant prelates in England after 1066; Goscelin, writer of institutional biographies for the abbesses of Barking, travelled widely in England and was originally from St Bertin in Flanders.

In spite of the stricter enclosure practised on female communities, women in them had information about and some opportunities of participation in an international culture of learning, administration, law, politics and literature. Unusually accomplished though Heloise was, she should be seen against a background of Latin-literate female monasticism[19] and a culture common to the great nunneries of France and England (see further Interpretative Essay, below).

[18] On Barking as a literary milieu, see Jocelyn Wogan-Browne and Glyn S. Burgess (trans.), *Virgin Lives and Holy Deaths: Two Exemplary Biographies for Anglo-Norman Women* (London: Dent, 1996), Introduction, pp. xxiv–vi: for extant books owned by Barking, see David N. Bell, *What Nuns Read: Books and Libraries in Medieval English Nunneries* (Kalamazoo, MI: Cistercian Publications, 1995), *s.v.* Barking.

[19] Mary Martin McLaughlin, 'Heloise the Abbess: The Expansion of the Paraclete', in Bonnie Wheeler (ed.), *Listening to Heloise: The Voice of a Twelfth-Century Woman* (New York: St Martin's Press, 2000), 1–17.

The present volume

Since the focus of this volume is letters for women, the selection of letters is ordered in accordance with their recipients rather than their writers. Two abbesses, Adelidis of Barking and Heloise of the Paraclete, from England and France respectively, are addressed in the first two letter-treatises, each being offered a historical account of their own profession and allied ways of life, together with accounts of illustrious predecessors. Abelard offers a history of women's activities and roles in the church (II), Osbert a more allegorical and typologically organized account (I), but both are concerned to supply precedents and encouragement. The next grouping of letters concerns young women in convent life and the varying strategies of exhortation and encouragement adopted by their relatives among senior churchmen. Peter the Venerable in France and Osbert of Clare in England address personally tailored letters to their nieces, respectively Margaret and Pontia in Marcigny (III), and Margaret and Cecilia in Barking (IV). The final pair of texts in the volume again involves abbesses, this time not so much for the intellectual justification and history of their way of life as for accounts and precepts for specific aspects of their responsibilities. Abelard writes to Heloise on the education of nuns (V), while the selections from Goscelin of St Bertin's lives of the abbesses of Barking (VI) illustrate their concern for the nunnery cemetery, both as a practical matter and more generally as part of their custody of the community's collective memory as expressed in its material environment, customs, and traditions.

The letters given here are carefully adapted to a range of conditions among the recipients:[20] busy abbesses directing their communities are offered examples of mature courage and resolution, and are encouraged to see the life of chastity as an active life of almsgiving outside the convent and guidance for all under their charge within. Young women are offered versions of themselves as high-ranking brides at the court of heaven. Abelard's letters to Heloise argue for women as special and specially capable in God's purposes. And within the traditions of the virginity treatise and the heroic virgin or chaste biography, we can also glimpse something of the preoccupa-

---

[20] For further examples of the care with which virginity and chastity letters were adapted for particular recipients, see Elisabeth Bos, 'The Literature of Spiritual Formation for Women in France and England, 1080–1180', in *Listen, Daughter: The* Speculum Virginum *and the Formation of Religious Women in the Middle Ages*, ed. Constant J. Mews (New York: Palgrave, 2001), pp. 201–20 (204–8).

tions and interrelations of female communities, as in, for instance, Goscelin's unexpectedly moving account of the abbess of Barking, supported in a difficult and expensive rebuilding project by consolatory appearances and encouragement from her saintly female predecessor (VI, p. 154 below).

In various ways the life of virginity and chastity could both reconfirm and challenge many of the cultural stereotypes and the daily occupations of women's lives. These letters and lives give us images of women as churchmen felt they should see themselves. Read carefully, and sometimes against the grain of their overt intentions, they also allow us a sense of medieval women's own aspirations and achievements.

Note on Texts and Translations

Texts

The sources of the texts translated here are:

I. E. W. Williamson (ed.), *The Letters of Osbert of Clare* (London: Oxford University Press, 1929), Letter 42, pp. 153–79.

II. J. T. Muckle (ed.), 'The Letters of Heloise on Religious Life and Abelard's First Reply', *Mediaeval Studies* 17 (1955), pp. 253–81. (Although numbered as Letter 6 by Muckle and by Betty Radice in her translation of the correspondence between Heloise and Abelard, this Letter is number 7 in PL 178: 225–56, and will be referred to as Letter 7 in the present volume).

III. Giles Constable (ed.), *The Letters of Peter the Venerable*, 2 vols. (Cambridge, Mass.: Harvard University Press, 1967), Letter 185, 1: 427–34.

IV. E. W. Williamson (ed.), *The Letters of Osbert of Clare*, Letter 21 (to Margaret) pp. 89–91; Letter 22 (to Cecilia), pp. 92–6.

V. E. R. Smits (ed.), *Peter Abelard. Letters IX–XIV: An Edition with an Introduction* (Groningen, 1983), Letter IX, pp. 219–37 (= Letter 9, PL 178: 325–6).

VI. Marvin L. Colker, 'Texts of Jocelyn of Canterbury which Relate to the History of Barking Abbey', *Studia Monastica* 7 (1965), pp. 383–460:

(a) *Vita et virtutes sanctae Ethelburgae virginis*, iiii, Colker, pp. 404/8–405/47; ibid. viii, p. 409/1–3; ibid. xiii, pp. 412/32–413/29.

(b) *Vita et virtutes sanctae Ethelburgae virginis*, xi, Colker, pp. 410/41–411/22.

(c) *Lecciones de Sancta Hildelitha*, ii, Colker, pp. 455–6.

(d) *De translatione sanctae Wlfildae*, xi, Colker, p. 431/1–17 and ibid., xiii, pp. 432/7–433/19.

(e) *De translatione vel elevatione sanctarum virginum Ethelburgae, Hildelithae, ac Wlfildae*, ii–vi, pp. 437–41 and '*A Vision about the Translation*', i–iii, Colker, pp. 453–4.

The Translations
Translations are as close as possible to the original Latin, consistent with the demands of clear modern English. Manuscript titles and subtitles, whether authorial or scribal, are given in italics. Titles and subheadings supplied by the translator are given in italics in square brackets. Paragraphing and punctuation have been modernised. Most of the writers in this volume quote the Bible from Jerome's Vulgate, sometimes with variation due to differing texts or quotation from memory. The Authorised (King James) Version is used in translations of quotations where a biblical register is invoked, but where bible verses are cited only by number in the original the verse numbering given in the translation is that of the Jerusalem Bible.

I Osbert of Clare, Prior of Westminster, to Adelidis, Abbess of Barking: A Thank-You Letter on Holy Widows, Virgin Fecundity and Precedents for Female Authority (Letter 42)

A stranger to medieval letters beginning to read Osbert of Clare's letter to Adelidis will be struck first by the elaborate courtesy of his thanks to the abbess for her generous hospitality and by his encouragement to her to continue in the way of virtue; a picture of a way of life that is wealthy, formal, and devout begins to form itself. Barking was a prestigious abbey, rich and governed by noble or royal ladies. Its location gave it access to, but some detachment from, London; situated on Barking Creek a few miles down the Thames from London, it was a convenient staging post on the way to France or across the lowlands of Essex and the Fens to the flourishing monastic houses of East Anglia. There must have been many visitors like Osbert at Barking, though not many have left such eloquent traces of their stay. With its formal gratitude and expression of love and respect, Osbert's letter makes us ask what kind of man was this; what was his relationship with the abbess?

It is not easy to disentangle the events of his life, but it appears that Osbert was born some time towards the end of the eleventh century at Clare in Suffolk.[1] The name 'de Clare' need not imply that he was of noble family, but his name, Osbert, is probably Norman-French and we may surmise that he belonged to the minor gentry. He was a monk at Clare and (after that monastery was moved) at Stoke. It is difficult to be sure of the order of events in the next few years, but it seems that having been prior at Westminster Abbey for some years, Osbert was passed over for the abbacy in 1121. He then spent time away at Ely, and later at Bury and other monasteries: it is probable that his letter to Adelidis was written during some journey between Ely and Westminster. He returned to Westminster c. 1134 and was elected, or re-elected, prior, but subse-

---

[1] For Osbert's life, see J. Armitage Robinson, 'A Sketch of Osbert's Career', in E. W. Williamson, *The Letters of Osbert of Clare* (London: Oxford University Press, 1929), pp. 1–20.

quently failed again to gain the succession to the abbacy. In about 1139 on the orders of the new abbot, Gervase (the King's natural son), Osbert went to Rome to petition for the canonisation of Edward the Confessor, taking with him his own biography of the saint. A letter from the Lateran commends Osbert, but rejects the canonization on the grounds that the request had come only from Westminster, 'for since so great a festival ought to be for the honour and profit of the whole realm, it must needs be demanded by the whole realm'.[2]

If, as has been thought, the deposition of Abbot Gervase in 1146 was in any way due to Osbert's report to the pope, it reinforces the impression that Osbert's troubles were in part due to the unpopularity of a clever man quick to spot abuses and equally quick to make them public. Osbert again appears during the vacancy after Gervase's expulsion, although not as prior. He died about 1170.

In his letter to Adelidis (most probably written between January 1156 and April 1157 while King Henry II was in France), Osbert's purpose is not only to maintain Adelidis in a love of the celibate life and to commend chaste and virtuous living, but also to show how a capable, ambitious woman might fulfil herself as manager of a large household and business establishment such as Barking.[3] Nor is this all. Osbert lays great stress on the relationship between the abbess and her nuns. She is to be their mother and to regard them as the children born of the union between her and Christ. The love and care which any mistress might have for her dependants is to be intensified by this relationship. Osbert also makes great use of the Song of Songs with its concentration on the intensity of emotion in love. He refers often to Christ as the Bridegroom, the lover of whom the nun must be worthy. The Bridegroom promises his reward of sensuous pleasure, of dress, of food and drink, and of status, but above all, of love. The greatest earthly joy that a nun must forego is probably that of having children, but Osbert invokes the physical horrors of pregnancy and, by contrast, the joy of being in love with the Bridegroom and having spiritual children conceived by the love of God and brought up in his honour. He concludes by encouraging Adelidis in actions characteristic of the mistresses of great noble houses as well as of nunneries: acts of charity, such as entertaining guests as he

---

2 Williamson, *The Letters of Osbert of Clare*, p. 19. Lateran: Basilica and Palace of San Giovanni in Laterano, the official residence of the pope from the fourth to the fourteenth century.

3 Williamson, p. 225.

himself has been entertained, and giving alms, so that she may share in the joys of heaven with the holy virgins.

Osbert wrote to several other nuns in addition to his letters to Adelidis and his nieces at Barking, and he successfully founded a house for vowed women – Augustinian canonesses – at Kilburn. That Osbert himself was engaged by the ideals of virginity and chastity is suggested not only by the passion and ingenuity of his letter to Adelidis, but from his involvement in the contemporary cult of the Virgin and the move to promote the doctrine and feast of the Immaculate Conception. A doctrine of the sinlessness of Mary had to reconcile the Virgin's human status with the original sin inherited from Adam, but could lean on the theological cogency of acclaiming her as a new Eve, sinless as Eve was before the Fall, just as Christ represented the new Adam. Osbert was an eager advocate of recognition of the festival. While at Pershore Abbey in 1136/37, he wrote part at least of a set of new readings for the feast of St Anne, mother of the Virgin Mary.[4]

A notable feature of Osbert's style is his large vocabulary and habit of repetition of words and phrases imitating the parallelism of the psalms. Not surprisingly the Latin of the Vulgate Bible is a major influence on Osbert's style. Osbert also uses the *Ecclesiastical History (Historia Ecclesiastica Gentis Anglorum)* of the Venerable Bede (d. 735), and refers the reader to Bede rather than explaining him, as if expecting his readers to be familiar with the reference. The letter's two direct quotations from the classics (from Seneca and Virgil) also have the air of being commonplace rather than exceptional quotations.[5] Taken all in all, Osbert's letters to Adelidis, as also those to his nieces (IV below) allude to writings about which an ordinary educated person may have some knowledge rather than to the special learning of a scholar, such as Abelard displays (II below). Nevertheless, some learning in Osbert's audience there clearly was. His letter, addressed to Adelidis, is in some ways very personal, but

---

4   See A. Wilmart, 'Les compositions d'Osbert de Clare en l'honneur de Sainte Anne', in *Annales de Bretagne* 37 (1926), pp. 1–33.

5   Pseudo-Seneca, *De Moribus (Morals)* and Virgil, *Aeneid* 4.569. Williamson comments (p. 226 n. 6) that classical texts were used as school textbooks so that quotations from Virgil, and even more from Ovid, would be familiar to everyone who had any Latin.

in the letter to his niece Margaret (IV below) he asks that the letter should be imparted to the nuns gathered in their chapter.[6] We may conclude that these letters were read aloud as well as studied privately. Since Barking was an aristocratic house, the common language, at least of the choir nuns, was most likely Norman-French. It gives a very respectable idea of the learning of these nuns that they could be addressed in Osbert's Latin.

In the letter to Adelidis, Osbert invokes a number of virginal and chaste heroines to illustrate the theme of the beauty and blessing of chastity, a heroic virtue and a positive quality for him, as for other writers of the twelfth century. His exemplary and inspirational figures are carefully chosen with this in mind. They seem to have been specially tailored to the interests of a chaste abbess as compared with, for instance, those of young consecrated virgins (see further IV below). Osbert's first example, St Cecilia, is a married virgin martyr, a respectable Roman matron. According to her legend, Cecilia was a Roman patrician of the third century and Christian from the cradle. She was married against her will to Valerian but persuaded him to allow her to preserve her virginity in a chaste marriage. Under the persecutions of Almachius, Cecilia encouraged her husband and his brothers in the faith to which she had converted them and saw to their burial after their execution as martyrs. She herself preached to the pagan tyrant and his executioners, continuing to do so for three days after botched attempts to behead her, until she died. Her house subsequently became the site of a Christian church, dedicated by her admirer Pope Urban. Cecilia's heroism may seem remote from Barking, but it is worthwhile to remember that the Civil War between Stephen and Matilda, if it did no worse, set bands of soldiers marauding around the countryside. Memories of Danish raids were still alive in minds at Barking (see VI below), and courage in the face of violence might still be needed. Cecilia's steadfast retention of her virginity is a commonplace among the lives of female saints but, nevertheless, a fitting model for a nun. Osbert also presents in Cecilia a good model for an abbess, a woman of firm character who was a leader to her husband and brother-in-law, the friend of the pope, and a woman famed as a preacher.

Osbert's second figure, St Etheldreda of Ely, is a model still closer to home for Adelidis. Etheldreda (later known as Audrey) had

---

6   'Chapter' was the name given to the deliberative assembly of the members of the convent or to the place in which it met.

founded her monastery at Ely in seventh-century Anglo-Saxon England at about the same time as St Ethelburga founded Barking. According to Bede, Etheldreda preserved her virginity through two unwanted marriages, becoming first a widow and then formally separating from her second husband before retiring to the Isle of Ely (given to her as her dower at her first marriage). Here, in 673, she founded a double monastery under the patronage of St Wilfrid. She was renowned for her austerities in dress (she wore a hairshirt), in eating, in prayer, and even in bathing, for she is reputed to have bathed only three times a year. Hers was a highly successful foundation and her shrine at Ely attracted many pilgrims and great fame and wealth. Osbert had received hospitality at Ely Abbey when he was banished from Westminster and had good reason to be grateful. Etheldreda, virgin, wife, and spiritual mother to her minster, was in any case an excellent model for an English abbess.

Even the pagans might show God's love of devout virginity. Vestal virgins worshipped according to ancient rituals, washing consecrated vessels in the water of the river for the Roman temple of Vesta and tending its sacred fire; it is not difficult to see them as foreshadowing Christian nuns living apart from the world, preserving their virginity, engaging in sacred rites and venerating the pure Virgin. Osbert emphasises both the analogy and the imperfection of the pagans by including a grotesque version of virgin birth: he reworks Ovid's story of Silvia the vestal Virgin, who bears two sons, and becomes thereby God's instrument in the origin and subsequent glory of the Roman Empire. The story of the Virgin Mary differs from that of Silvia for she consciously and willingly accepts the message of God.[7] The story of Silvia's children as suckled by a she-wolf, though involving the intervention of the supernatural, is directed to explaining the name and origins of Rome and showing how Roman rustic gods and possibly tribal totems might be incorporated into the myth of Rome. (One may surmise that stories such as that of Silvia were known, at least in outline by Adelidis, since they are referred to rather than told in detail, and she is offered a fairly complex allegory of Christian meanings for these pagan events and signs).

From Silvia, Osbert turns to Judith's heroic action in saving the Jewish people from the Babylonians, while also preserving her chastity in the face of strong pressure. Judith was a popular figure in medieval writing: a widow, chaste but not virgin, rich, beautiful,

---

7 Luke 1.38.

pious and with heroic virtues, ingenious, confident and courageous – nothing heroic was wanting. Adelidis is urged to imitate her. Osbert writes of Adelidis' own widowhood, probably with reference to her actual status (it would be odd to write thus to a virginal abbess, though no record of Adelidis' husband has been found). Yet more than chastity is asked of Adelidis; Judith's encounter with Holofernes becomes an allegory on the avoidance of greed and avarice, sins in themselves and sins seen as particularly leading to fornication. Holofernes is presented as a type of temptation to lust, and Osbert begs Adelidis to consider the temptations of the flesh as being as powerful and destructive as was Holofernes, and to use all her powers of will and ingenuity to resist.

Osbert is at pains to show how the various details of the narrative each have their allegorical significance, and also tell a gripping story. It culminates in Holofernes' beheading, when Judith 'came near to the bed, seized the hair of his head, struck him twice on the neck and cut off Holofernes' head. . . . Do you not delay to strike twice in your own virtue', Osbert adds. An entertaining story, a powerful sermon; is it anything more?

If Osbert's letter was indeed written between January 1156 and April 1157 while King Henry II was in France it was written long after Adelidis' appointment. It was also written at a time when Adelidis was involved in some mysterious scandal. Of Adelidis herself we know very little. She was the daughter of John de Burgh and sister of Eustace and Pain FitzJohn, brothers who appear to have been members of the rising administrative class under Henry I. Under this king, Eustace FitzJohn acquired much power, especially in the north-east of England, and both brothers were generous in gifts of land to the Church. After King Stephen's accession, when a Scottish invasion took place in 1136, Eustace held out for about three months, then yielded to David, King of Scotland, and was obliged to take refuge in his court. Adelidis is said to have become abbess of Barking in 1136/38. The earlier date seems the more likely, for the appointment looks like an attempt by the king to attach the family (particularly Eustace) to his cause.[8]

At about the same time as Osbert wrote his letter to Adelidis, who

8   On the FitzJohn family, see Paul Dalton, 'Eustace Fitz-John and the Politics of Anglo-Norman England: the Rise and Survival of the Twelfth-Century Royal Servant', *Speculum* 71 (1996), pp. 358–83, like her brothers, Adelidis seems to have been enterprising and is thought to have founded St Mary's hospital at Ilford while abbess, see *VCH, Essex*, ii, p. 116.

had then been some twenty years in office, she received another from Archbishop Theobald very offensively telling her to give up her relationship with 'Hugh', her officer, warning her 'you should abstain from your notorious familiarity and cohabitation (or, perhaps, 'near presence').[9] Hugh was a senior official of the convent and continued administering the abbey's estates in the later years of the century after Adelidis' death in about 1166. At about the probable time of Osbert's letter, Adelidis was occupied in a long-running dispute with Roger, priest of Ingatestone, over some tithes, so that the 'near presence' of her senior administrator does not seem unwarranted. A similar situation had arisen earlier at the nunnery of Amesbury. There the king intended to oust the abbess and to introduce nuns from Fontevrault, a relatively inexpensive way of establishing a 'new' foundation in penance for the murder of Becket in 1170. His purpose was assisted by the circulation of a sensational scandal against the abbess. It seems at least possible that the archbishop's letter to Adelidis testifies less to her imprudent conduct than to the interests of the archbishop and his priest. If Osbert got wind of this he may have felt that Adelidis needed a private word of warning not to compromise herself inadvertently, nor to allow herself to be led into dangerous appearances. While it is unwise to allow the fancy of ascribing motives to people about whom one knows very little, it is a tribute to the liveliness, sympathy and piety of Osbert's letter that the reader wants to know more.

Osbert of Clare, Prior of Westminster, to Adelidis, Abbess of Barking

Here begins the letter of Osbert of Clare to the lady Adelidis, the reverend abbess of the convent of Barking, concerning the armour of chastity[10]
Giving thanks in gratitude for kindnesses received, Osbert of Clare greets, among the renowned and chaste ladies endowed with the glory of virginity, his most noble lady Adelidis; for it is truly to be believed that it is through the guidance of the Holy Spirit that she is superior of the holy virgins and, by the grace of God, distinguished virgin mother of the community of the convent at Barking: Osbert,

---

9 Letter 69, 'ut a famosa familiaritate et cohabitatione . . . abstinares', in *The Letters of John of Salisbury*, ed. W. J. Miller and H. E. Butler, vol. 1 (London: Nelson, 1955), p. 111.
10 See Eph. 6.11–17.

the lover in Christ of virgin modesty and zealous imitator of her holiness. May she be crowned with the laurel of celestial victory by Christ in the choir of virgins, and grow rich with the undying palm of white virginity.

Your recent generous entertainment must be recorded today with thanks and greetings to you, and, excellent woman, you must never be afraid to stretch out your hand in such generosity, since, in fortifying us with yesterday's repast, you restored not our stomach but our heart, and sent us away laden not with food but with divine services. On that account, my lady, you have bound to yourself a not unuseful soldier and an unwearying friend, bought not with coin but with love (although, indeed, my right hand is filled full with your gifts and reflects the worth of your bounty and generosity). And I consider this gift more valuable than any other because through it you demonstrate not your resources, but your generous habit of mind, not your abundance of provisions, but your good will. And for this reason, I am so bound to you that you will have my allegiance for ever and not for anybody's embraces will my jealousy accept the sundering of your love. For this is what has pierced my heart,[11] my sister and bride; you have pierced my heart with charity and love. 'Sister', I call you because we have one father in God and we are reborn by the same grace in baptism; you are moreover the bride of my Lord and friend of my king, and from the seed of his Word you will bear children to him in a chaste marriage and will continue mother and virgin. Oh how lovely, how chaste, how joyful, how spotless is this childbearing when the woman in labour does not bring forth in sorrow like the daughters of Eve,[12] and the offspring which she bears among the sons of Adam do not gain bread by sweat, nor does that mother plough or sow that cursed land which brings forth thorns and thistles, but Jesus tends the field of virginity with the mother and brings forth a hundredfold.[13]

For virginity, taking its heavenly origin among those above, has obtained the chief place among the first and most excellent citizens of the heavenly city, and has descended in perfect form in the coming of God to man, and of man in the Virgin mother, queen of purity. For she is the mistress of virtues, and jewel of all good works, for in her child-bearing God has become expressly united with man, and

---

[11] Song of Songs 4.9.
[12] Gen. 3.16–18.
[13] Matt. 13.8.

without the virtue of virginity his worthy and unstained mother would neither have conceived nor given birth. Other women give birth without the blessing of virginity; from corruptible flesh they give birth to mortal flesh; they give birth, I say, to what they conceive; sin from sin, and not seldom do they bring forth a happy issue at great cost to their own life. But indeed, virgins are in no way put in danger in childbirth of that kind when they bear spiritual offspring to God; when the creator of virginity, the virgin bridegroom, is he who begets and bears the virgin heart and as a father makes the flesh fruitful with that grace and heavenly seed.

These women are imitators of her who, unstained in flesh, bore the Son of God, the son who has consecrated you for himself as bride and Virgin. For you conceive offspring from him in such a way that you give birth but do not experience corruption of the flesh. For under the law the woman who did not procreate offspring in Israel was accursed; by the grace of God she will be blessed, and the mother bears daughters to the Lord of Judah and bears Emmanuel to the king.[14] Take fire then, lady, take fire, highness, with love for him, and proclaim with him what he has proclaimed, and strive for the everlasting rewards which he has promised, so that as beloved of the king you may fulfil the ardent desire of love, and as a mother you may gain outstanding reputation through the Word. For he whose grace you spread abroad with your lips is glorious in appearance beyond the sons of men[15] and sprinkles the garments of the inner man with 'myrrh and aloes and cassia'.[16] May you, then, shine brightly, adorned with every kind of virtue so that you may do good to your followers not so much by your word as by your example.

---

14 Childbearing was highly valued in the precepts of the Old Testament and though there could be no legal penalties condemning a woman because she was barren, there are several women who lament barrenness as a great misfortune – Sarah (Gen. 16), Hannah (I Sam. 1) and Elizabeth (Luke 1) among them. Moreover the law of Levirate marriage (Deut. 25.5–10) obliged a childless widow to be married to her deceased husband's brother. Accordingly it seems best to translate *maledicta* as 'accursed', i.e. 'desperately unfortunate', rather than 'cursed', with implication of sin and punishment. Similarly, *in lege* is translated not as 'written in the law' but as 'under the law' in the sense often implied in St Paul's use of it, i.e. in the harsh dispensation before Christ's grace was available to mankind.

15 Ps. 45.2.

16 See Ps. 45.8. Cassia = cinnamon. 'Aloes' in the AV and the Jerusalem Bible is an unexpected accompaniment of fragrant shrubs. Although 'aloe' has the modern association of a bitter purgative from a plant of the Liliacae family, the word was used in the Middle Ages to translate the Hebrew 'agalloch' – a tree producing fragrant wood and resin.

A mirror of virginity in Saint Cecilia[17]
The most renowned virgin and most noble of learned women, blessed
Cecilia, what fruit have you been allowed to bring forth to the Lord,
you for whom the white rose of virginity is graced by suffering![18]
Fair linen and purple are her habit[19] because the virgin has preserved
her flesh spotless and untouched and she has consecrated her purple
with her own blood to the king and Lord of angels. For because she
performed her office of preaching not like a woman, but like a
bishop, by the gift of the Lord she gained a tomb among the greatest
bishops of the Roman Church. No woman before her gained the
distinction of this privilege nor will any other after her. You have read
how she wore away her body with a hairshirt beneath the gilded vestments, how she used to sing to the Lord in her heart with musical
instruments, how she would have a guardian angel as companion,
how she supported Christ's poor with her alms on the Appian Way,
how she converted her husband Valerian with his brother Tiburcius
to the faith, how with the constancy of a noble spirit she proclaimed
the gospel truth. You have also read how she loved the blessed Pope
Urban with the zeal of heavenly love and how she showed his angelic
countenance to her brothers, and how, when she had won them for
Christ, they were baptised by him and committed to heaven. These
are the outstanding works of evangelising by this wonderful woman;
they do not express a woman's mind but in the privileged position of
her burial reflect masculine firmness. So not only was all she did
more than feminine, but, taught by her, the whole of the female sex is
able to escape ruin. Holy Scripture does not lack examples to instruct
you in this, woman of virtue, so that you may achieve close and religious friendship with holy men such as we read this glorious virgin
gained with the blessed Pope Urban.

*Concerning the glory of unstained virginity exemplified to holy
virgins through the blessed Etheldreda*[20]
We have very many examples near to hand which, if they were to be
repeated separately would make, not a letter that I hammered out, but

---

[17] For St Cecilia, see David Hugh Farmer, *Oxford Dictionary of Saints* (Oxford:
Oxford University Press, 1987), *s.v.* Cecilia.
[18] Suffering is perhaps too weak a word to translate *passio* with its association with
the Passion of Christ. The word could also be used for 'martyrdom' or 'suffering
of a martyr'.
[19] Prov. 31.22.
[20] For St Etheldreda, see pp. 18–19 above; Farmer, *s.v.* Etheldreda; and Bede,

lengthy volumes.[21] But I neither dare, nor ought to keep silent about how the most blessed Etheldreda, that matchless virgin, sprinkled with the dew of the Holy Spirit in the Babylonian furnace, did not feel the heat of the burning fire because she trembled at the burning flame of impious unchastity.[22] It has never been heard about any woman that she experienced what this woman did in her own person. For when she had first been married she remained untouched by man, and a virgin; when given in marriage to a mortal prince she married the king of the angels as an untouched virgin.[23] For this man was cut off by unexpected death and left her untouched and spotless as though the chaste love of Christ had joined her to himself in an unstained marriage. Then she was joined to a king by a most binding oath, but the ceremony of marriage was not performed in the flesh. She served him for twelve years, but she did not lose the enjoyment of her virginity. Her outward appearance bespoke the queen, but her inward devotion showed her to be the humble handmaid of God. Gaze then, daughter of God, on how many crosses she bore for so long; what disgust that husband of hers brought on her when he desired her as a wife and she rejected passion; and what conflicts this glorious virgin engaged in.

What greater witness can there be in the flesh than abstinence among the thorns of voluptuousness?[24] But she escaped unharmed by the world, and the offering of her virginity, though cloaked in a wedding veil, was manifest to God. When a great battle has taken place then a greater victory follows for the combatants. Assuredly

---

History of the English Church and People 4.19. Osbert was received at Ely when he was obliged to leave Westminster and for this reason he regards St Etheldreda as his patron and protectress.

21 *Cuderentur* is difficult to interpret. *Cudere* would normally mean 'to strike', 'beat', or 'knock', and so 'to stamp' or 'coin'. None of these seems appropriate to writing a letter, unless Osbert uses it in the sense of striking coins and wishes to imply the great value of his letter. He uses the word later (Williamson, *The Letters of Osbert of Clare*, p. 135, line 34) in connection with 'fashioning' jewellery.

22 See Dan. 3. During the Jews' exile in Babylon, three Jews, Shadrach, Meshach, and Abednigo, were thrown into a 'burning fiery furnace' because they would not worship king Nebuchadnezzar. They walked unscathed through the furnace and bystanders were convinced that they saw a fourth figure accompanying them. Virginity was commonly compared to gold refined in the furnace of trials and temptations.

23 A pun in the Latin. Ecgfrid was *Rex Anglorum*, i.e. King of the English. Christ is *Rex Angelorum*, i.e., king of the Angels.

24 *Martyrium* in modern usage may have the meaning of 'death' or 'great suffering', but its root meaning is 'witness' and is so translated here.

Christ shows such honour even today to her body which rests incorruptible as though asleep in a marble tomb.

A commemoration of the blessings of the holy virgin Etheldreda and why when he was going to King Henry he was obliged to cross the sea[25]
This is my lady, this is my queen who received me, a stranger and traveller, and with her hospitality restored the life of each of us with food and lavished us with garments. I shall cross the Jordan again with my pilgrim staff,[26] but with so many prayers interceding for us with God I hope to return with my company to the land of my birth. I have drawn devoutly near to her tomb, I have humbly observed her solemn vigil; I have often bent my knee before her; I have watered the floor where I was lying with my tears; weeping and lamenting I asked her leave when I departed. I believe that I shall be kept safe through the separating seas by her merits, and the grace of my princess will protect me in a foreign land. In this manner my hope rests in her and on her depends my trust; such is and will remain my confidence that she is my leader and my comfort. For she has never deserted those who call on her in faith for aid when they are in trouble.

Concerning the vision which, according to the fables of poets, was seen by Silvia, the vestal virgin, and how she was raped by Mars[27]
This warning story is designed of holy purpose not only for you, daughter of Syon among the daughters of Jerusalem, but it also concerns the daughters of the Chaldeans.[28] The daughters of the

---

25 The reason why Osbert was going to France to see the king is never stated. Although he speaks feelingly of his apprehensions about the voyage he then turns abruptly to the story of Silvia. The king was in France for long periods in the early part of his reign (Williamson, p. 225): it is possible to make an unsubstantiated guess that Osbert, whose embassy in 1139 to seek the canonization of Edward the Confessor had failed, hoped to be sent on a second embassy to Rome. This embassy was successful and Edward was canonized in 1161, but it is unlikely that Osbert, then in his seventies and in poor health, had any active part in it.

26 Gen. 32.10.

27 For Silvia and her children, see p. 19 above.

28 Daughter of Syon: Syon (Sion, Zion) the fortress of Jerusalem captured by David (II Sam. 5.7). Jerusalem, the capital of the Jewish kingdom, also stood for heaven, the new Jerusalem, to Christians. Any Christians might be called dwellers in Jerusalem, but it was particularly applicable to nuns who were thought of as especially close to heaven. Adelidis, whose duty it was to watch

heavenly city are not alone in showing the way but the daughters of Babylon among the gentiles surely do so too. We sometimes pick up gold from the mud and find a precious pearl in a dunghill. In the Roman histories we read that Silvia, whom we also call Ilia, was a sacred virgin in the temple of Vesta. Begotten by her father Numitor, she was distinguished by the nobility of her famous ancestry. When she was going to perform her duties as faithful handmaiden to her goddess and mistress she went, as custom directed, to the bank of the river for water to wash the sacred objects. As the poets have written, a strange murmur rose gently from the sounding water and, weighed upon by sleep she sank down, faint and weary.[29] When Mars, who had long desired her, saw this sight then at last the virgin was defiled by deceiving sleep. She conceived twin sons from the divine seed and, waking, she realised that she had had a dream which, she did not doubt, was a good omen and would be of significance to her. For she had seen herself in the temple of Venus keeping watch before the sacred fire which (by a device contrived out of juniper wood by skill of the Albans) appeared to be undying.[30] In that very place she saw her vestal fillet slipping off and she perceived two palm trees rising in swift growth. One of them was the taller and, spreading round the whole surface of the world, had covered it with its leaves and branches; its foliage was so tall that in height it reached right up to the heavens. Observing her uncle Amulius taking an axe to it so as to cut it down, she marvelled at the depiction of such a sight, astonished that while it was being felled in this way it was defended by a woodpecker and a she-wolf.[31] So the virgin (but now no more a virgin) carried the waters back to the holy temple and did not fear to report what she had seen in her dreams.

In the fullness of time the burden of her belly grew. When the day

over her nuns, might appropriately be described as an inhabitant of the fortress keeping watch over Jerusalem. 'Chaldeans', inhabitants of Babylon.

[29] Ovid, *Fasti* 3.11.

[30] Rome was believed to have been founded from Alba Longa; an essential part of planting a colony was to take the sacred fire, which symbolized the life of the mother city, to the new foundation. Wood dried in the air or over a slow fire after having been soaked in water or oil was called 'acapna' or 'coctilia' according to the method used, and would burn without smoke. It might easily give the impression of being everlasting for it would not blaze and flare and then die down like an ordinary fire.

[31] A woodpecker and a she-wolf were creatures sacred to Mars, the war god and, as this story of Silvia illustrates, the reputed father of the Romans. *Silva* is the Latin word for 'a wood'.

marked out for Silvia's delivery arrived, she was in labour and gave birth to twin babies. As she travailed, the altar of the goddess shook and the statue of the goddess covered its virginal eyes with its hands, for it trembled at the shameful deed and was filled with horror when the ravished virgin gave birth. At such an obscene deed, the perpetual fire itself retreated under the ashes and no longer sent forth a glimmer of flame.

Amulius had stolen the realm from his brother Numitor so when he learned that Romulus and Remus were born to his niece, he gave orders that the babies should be drowned in the river. But, as we read, the very waves shrank back from that sin. The boys were set down naked on dry land and in that very place a wolf nourished them with her own milk and the woodpecker, the bird of Mars, brought them food.

An explanation of the vision according to an understanding of the truth

But let us go back to the story again and let us turn our thoughts to the truth of the matter so that we can clear our mind of the false fictions of the poets. In the temple of Vesta, there were virgins devoted to her service, so we may learn from such an example that even the gentiles have high regard for purity of life and chastity. So the philosophers understand nothing by 'Vesta' but the flame, since the flame is virgin, and no substance is produced from it, and therefore in obedience to the rule no substance was placed there that was not distinguished by virginity. So the virgin was ravished by Mars, not in a dream, but in truth: then, having conceived, she saw a dream which foreshadowed great eminence for her offspring. The bridal veil which fell from her head proclaimed that her maidenhood was lost. The palm trees which she had seen were Romulus and Remus or those two famous Caesars descended from the stock of Romulus, Julius and Augustus.[32] That one palm seemed greater and the other smaller was brought about, not without reason, but for the creation of the mystery (for the Holy Spirit not infrequently shows his mystery to his enemies). The palm, therefore, which reached the heavens in height signifies Romulus: from his name the city of Rome is said to

[32] Julius (Caesar) and Augustus claimed descent from Iulus, son of Aeneas, the Trojan hero, who sailed westwards after the destruction of Troy and, after many adventures, settled in Italy, possibly founding Alba Longa. See also Virgil, *Aeneid* Book II. Augustus was the son of Gaius Octavius Caesar and adopted by his great-uncle Gaius Julius Caesar. Augustus was a title bestowed on him later.

have acquired its name. For Rome is the mistress of the whole earth, imperial ruler of all the cities in the world. It embraces the whole world with its leaves and branches (that is, with the apostles and martyrs) and is borne aloft by the greatness of its miracles. But Remus is signified by the name of the smaller palm, for, transgressing the laws established by Romulus, he was adjudged to die and was condemned by his brother's authority on the Aventine hill. Again, we call the smaller palm Julius Caesar for he, though outstanding through his military glory, his reputation and his prowess, was nevertheless a minor figure in comparison with Augustus. For Augustus grew into a huge tree which encompassed the whole face of the earth with its leaves, since it filled the breadth of the whole world with such peace that in his days every man beat sword and lance into ploughshare and mattock.[33]

While Augustus was emperor, the world was taxed and a census of the whole world was made,[34] and in the forty-second year of his reign in Bethlehem, the city of David, Christ was born of a virgin mother: he who was true God in the Father and the Holy Spirit, before the beginning of time, and who also appeared as man, having put on our mortality within the bounds of time. And not without some truth is Augustus so-called, since his peace received such great and priceless increase from the peace of heaven, when the seed of holy virginity which had never before had power upon earth received incorruptible access of power in the body which was God and man. The name of Caesar Augustus is said to be Octavian from Octave, nor is this meaning judged to be without divine significance, for wherever the heading of the psalm is written PRO OCTAVA this refers to the sure repose and glory of our resurrection.[35] Under the reign, therefore, of Octavius Caesar, who was also called Augustus, was Christ blessedly born; by his birth we are born again to life and with him we shall rise again on the eighth day to the immortality and glory of new bodies. For on six days we labour and on the seventh we rest, but on the

---

[33] A reminiscence of Isaiah 2.4, and Micah 4.

[34] Luke 2.1

[35] The 'repose and glory of our resurrection' may be said to be derived from Ps. 6.5. and Ps. 11.1–5. The Octave (eighth day) is the day one week after a festival when there is a concluding commemoration of the festival. The Christian observance began with the Octaves of Easter and Pentecost and gradually extended to the major saints. By the twelfth century, the days between the festival and the octave were beginning to be celebrated as well. The custom may have arisen from the Jewish celebration of the Octave of the Feast of the Tabernacles and of the Dedication of the Temple.

eighth we shall flourish again in the new brightness of our glorified flesh.[36]

According to what I have been able to understand of the vision of Silvia I have made out the significance of the two palm trees, even as one is seen to grow luxuriant with leaves and branches, the other to remain in its fading weakness. Whores are rightly called she-wolves on account of the seething greed of their loathsome avarice and because of their flaming excess in the habits of lust, yet Acca, who is also called Laurentia, though she formerly appeared a shameless whore, faithfully nourished the babies she found in the wood with her own milk. On the other hand, the bird of Mars, the husband of Laurentia, was Faustulus who brought the means of life from the mother to the first-born children. These, therefore, are the woodpecker and the she-wolf. Because of their protection the tree stands in no danger of felling: since Faustulus and Acca were its defence lest Romulus should be at risk of danger of death through Amulius.

Proof through examples from among the Gentiles that purity of body is to be prized
So you see, o most excellent spouse of the prince of heaven, how precious stones are made from hail just as flowers of gold and silver are produced from the mire.[37] Among the gods of those heathen races, as the stories of the poets adduce, even among those who had no concept of a Lord and creator, we read that virginity was regarded as of great worth. For when the goddess Vesta was moved to anger at the defilement of her servant it is clear that in her eyes chastity was highly honoured and the statue of the goddess did not put her hands before her eyes when Silvia was giving birth unless the union of this illicit love offended her. And although she was said to have conceived by the god Mars and to have given birth to Romulus, the founder of the city of Rome, yet it horrified Vesta that in that union Cupid had brandished his torch and destroyed the chastity of Silvia's virgin body. Cupid, then, is the evil spirit of fornication and is

---

[36] The eighth day was popularly thought of as the day of resurrection because God had made the world in six days and rested on the seventh.

[37] Lapidaries, a genre of text describing the appearance, qualities and symbolism of precious stones, were much read: see John M. Riddle, ed., *Marbode of Rennes (1035–1123); De Lapidibus considered as a Medical Treatise* (Wiesbaden: Franz Steiner, 1977); J. Evans and M. S. Serjeantson, *English Mediaeval Lapidaries* EETS os 190 (London: Oxford University Press, 1933). Osbert writes here as though he is referring to something well known to both Adelidis and himself.

portrayed as flying from both directions, since nothing is lighter than lovers; nothing is proven more inconstant. He is formed as a naked boy because love is shown to be irrational and stupid; he holds an arrow because he wounds, and he lights a torch because he sets lovers on fire.[38] Thus, whoever is struck by his dart is consumed by his fires. Let the lover imagine for himself in his heart the lovely face of the Virgin's son who preferred death on the cross for the restoration of mankind and who presents his virgin mother to his virgin disciple.[39] Let him imagine how this same Lord, most beautiful to look upon, teaches chastity: chastity which he offers to everyone and does not exact from anyone. Let him imagine also how human nature, which had grown old through sin in our first parent, is trans-formed to the vigour of youth in his passion. You may read, besides, how the strong son entered on a victorious encounter with the tyrant for the sake of that father, decrepit through the enfeeblement of age. Thus our old father Adam through the offspring of his body in Christ, and we with him, have all been led back to the freedom which is our nature. Anyone who has applied his mind to meditation on this will be able to heal his mind of the wounds of perverse love: and while he savours the delight of so much sweetness he will empty himself of the relish of illicit love.

For what reason the figure of Judith is to be spiritually understood and how the victory against the old enemy is to be gained
You must, then, go secretly into the chamber of your soul and take on the nature of Judith, so that you may seize the sword and, with Holofernes lying dead, you may free the Jewish town from danger. For in the days of her widowhood Judith was in the habit of praying to the Lord;[40] Valerian found Cecilia too, praying in her chamber, in the presence of an angel.[41] In this way the Hebrews are 'transients' since they sought no abiding city in this world.[42] Thus indeed those sanctified souls whom you lead cross over every day to the feast of

---

38 *Et ex utroque latere alatus depinguitur:* literally 'is presented as flying from both directions (either direction)', an almost meaningless expression. The most convincing interpretation appears to refer to the inconstancy of love and perhaps to the suddenness and unexpectedness of falling in love, and the translation would be 'is winged on both shoulders.'
39 John 19.25–27.
40 Judith 8.5.
41 On St Cecilia, see pp. 18, 24.
42 Heb. 13.14: A reference to the Jews' journey in the Wilderness from Egypt to the Promised Land, but also to the Christian theme of life as a pilgrimage.

the eternal king so that they may enjoy the repast of the heavenly banquet. They have turned away from pleasure in the victuals of the Assyrians and the pollution of their voluptuous sauces. And what says Scripture? It says that Holofernes was lying on his bed under a canopy made of gold and purple and emerald and precious stones when they announced Judith to him.[43] When he heard them, he went out in front of his tent with very many silver lamps preceding him. Now the canopy is said to be a kind of mosquito net, a device made like a net in regular lines in which the rich are in the habit of escaping plagues of flies. Holofernes believed that he had settled himself at rest in it, but though he was exhausted by lust the urgency of sin excited him. For it was not enough for him to keep his face untouched by insect stings and to have an evil conscience. Holofernes' canopy was made of gold and purple and emerald and precious stones. But Holofernes was an image of that fallen angel who always lies in ambush for comeliness and chastity. For expensive trappings and ornamented dress became the cause of downfall and ruin, for by them the lust of the eyes is nourished. And you know that the apostle bears witness that Satan transforms himself into an angel of light.[44] This was the transfiguration of Holofernes by which he determined to unsettle a woman of virtue from her resolution of mind and her habit of holy widowhood and to mould her will to accept illicit embraces.

By these desirable trappings of worldly allurement we admit within ourselves enticement to different forms of pleasure. The burning lamps which went before the tyrant are perverse desires which are daily striving to attract the holy soul to love of the world. The miser burns with longing for possession. He toils and wears himself out so that his piles of possessions may grow. He spreads usury abroad when he reckons up his outlay; he seeks for quantities of gold and silver and cannot satisfy his unlimited wants. He thirsts and drinks, he feels cold and is in need, but his thirst is not allayed, nor the cold driven off, and the poverty of his mind is not mitigated by the abundance of his possessions. The more debauchery, which is the mother of lust, is employed for sexual purposes the more powerfully does it enkindle the desires and deeds of Venus; after a full

---

43 Judith 10.21. Osbert's story of Judith is taken from the *Vetus Latina* version sometimes included in early medieval copies of the Vulgate. See Williamson, *The Letters of Osbert of Clare*, p. 226.
44 II Cor. 11.14.

measure which is not seldom served up to him, to his disgust he is set alight with vicious longings even when he is destitute of desire.

Concerning the two daughters of the leech who tear to pieces the souls of the faithful
'The horse leech has two daughters, crying "Give, give".'[45] They are greed and lust who, pursuing their lawless disposition in every way, have no power to keep their appetite in check. These are they who have assailed every realm on earth and subjugated them to their dominion. Almost the whole globe labours beneath them and is wounded by the bloodstained teeth of these reptiles. There is scarcely found in any nook of the land in any direction a congregation of the faithful whose leaders are not stained with one disease or the other. These creatures, insatiably sucking blood among the voluptuous pleasures of Holofernes, could not supply the emptiness of their penury. So flee the deadly venom of this poisonous brood with Judith, and with her destroy the proud untameable neck of Holofernes. Thus may the heads of this twofold hydra be destroyed, lest you should suffer new damage from the darts of either of them.[46] But first you must start on the path where this famous woman preceded you and carry out with constancy what she, with greater constancy, has already performed.

Concerning Judith's three-day tarrying
Judith, Scripture says, remained in the camp for three days and went out by night to the valley of Bethulia and washed, and as it were, baptized herself in the waters of the spring.[47] We understand these three days as the death and burial and resurrection of the Lord. Supported by this belief, we undergo confrontation and conflict with the enemy in the encampments of our pilgrimage. We know also that by this word of 'three days' are represented faith, hope, and charity by which this virtuous woman was victorious and for which she deserves to be held in public honour. For she conquered by faith since she trusted without hesitation that the power of God would maintain the strength of the right hand of a woman. By hope she roused her

---

45 Prov. 30.15.
46 A monster from Greek mythology. When one head was cut off, two more grew in its place. Hercules defeated it by dipping his arrows in the Hydra's blood to make them poisonous. The two heads refer here to greed and lust, the daughters of the horse-leech (Williamson p. 163 line 1; Proverbs 30.15).
47 Judith 12.6.

spirit, victorious over the neck of Holofernes, for she sought no visible champion in the world but hoped for invisible aid from heaven. Her whole body was filled with love when she took her courage into her hand and did not fear to face death for the safety of the people.

So, like Judith, you must remain for three days in your encampment, so that as victor in the spiritual conflict and adorned with the palm of victory you may have your power to stand as a heroic woman. For indeed a noble woman is honour and glory to a noble man. Take pains, therefore, and strive with the whole feeling of your heart so that in the time of your widowhood you may daily recall faithfully to your memory the greatness and the nature of the man whose wife you are.[48] A great man, you say, of noble blood, abundant in wealth, abounding in charm. Who is he? Christ, indeed. Who is Christ? God and man, God from God, the son of the Father before time, virgin born of a virgin mother in time; he is your bridegroom, his beauty is indescribable, his engendering is not to be narrated. When you were rough and hideous he washed you in his blood[49] so that you should be graceful and beautiful without spot or wrinkle, and he delighted in your beauty. The cruel despot rushed in to seize you for himself and violate your untouched skin by baptism of death in adultery.[50] And your splendid bridegroom loves the sight of you so much that he has contended in war even to the death with this same despot and has set you up as victor in everlasting liberty.

For it is certain that your bridegroom died for you. For you are a widow and in the days of your widowhood you ought to reflect with anxious care on the blessing of such a man and not divorce him so as to love another man and turn away cruelly from his love. But you say, 'My man is dead, my husband has been carried off. It is not a divorce if when one is dead I marry another,[51] for when he was alive I was indeed bound to him by law, but when he is dead I am now freed from that fetter; I have the power to marry whomever I wish only "in the Lord".' You say well, 'in the Lord'. What is 'in the Lord'? It is that it should be pleasing to the Lord and there should be no marriage union which does wrong to him. This is how we understand 'in the Lord'. In this way you too must understand it, because your spouse has died

---

48   There is no record of Adelidis' husband, but almost certainly she was widowed.
49   Eph. 5.27.
50   It is difficult to know whether this is to be taken literally, but see above, p. 21, n. 9.
51   Rom. 7.2.

for you, but he has been restored to life: He has risen again, but he has gone to a far country to receive his kingdom.[52] At length he will come again with glory to place an everlasting diadem on your head. Then your longing will be satisfied when he crowns you in his glory. So preserve your untainted faith in him and you will be able to look for an uncorrupted reward.

In the same way you must faithfully imitate Judith and you must imprint her appearance on your eyes in a spiritual manner so that at night you may go out and baptize yourself in the waters of the fountain. For however long we are in the body and wander about away from the Lord, at night we turn away from mist and uncertainty, for at night in the secret performance of holy duties, you must seek that fountain, that is the fountain of Bethulia, the fountain of life. Your conscience must be baptized in tears and confession. Nicodemus, too, came to the Lord by night so that he could learn of the sacred mystery of baptism for salvation.[53] Assuredly, the angels' manner of life cannot be reached in the daily life of men. For this reason holy tears must be hidden and offered to the sight of God's eyes alone. For we say 'Bethulia' in Hebrew; interpreted in Latin, we say 'Virgin'. So 'going down into the valley of Bethulia' is passing into virgin humility. She who baptized herself daily in the pure clear spring of that valley said, 'For he has regarded the lowliness of his hand-maiden, for behold from henceforth all generations shall call me blessed.'[54] Oh, what humility does the lowly handmaid, who was the sovereign lady of heaven and queen of angels, prophesy for herself![55]

You too baptize yourself in this fountain and whoever knows her will know you. You too will be able to become the mother of Christ if you conceive the seed of the word of God in your heart and carry it to the fullness of time. If you are a virgin do not be proud of your virginity. He who chose a humble mother seeks for a humble hand-maid. If you are humble you will be blessed. What says that virgin who was made mother with the untouched womb of a virgin; what says she in the virgin's hymn: 'Henceforth all generations shall call me blessed'. Why? Because, as she says, 'He perceived that I am humble; he sealed my virginity to himself for this reason: that he delighted in purity of heart in me, he sprinkled the mother's womb in

---

52 Luke 19.12.
53 John 3.1–2.
54 Luke 1.46–55.
55 From the hymn of the Virgin Mary, 'My soul doth magnify the Lord', commonly known by its first word in Latin: *Magnificat*.

me with the dew of the Holy Spirit.' Take heed, wise virgin; if he had found you proud, virginity of the body would not have been sufficient for him. What the mother achieved by giving praise to God, humility has given to a virgin.

Act then, my beloved, in such a way that you retain your chastity and do not fall away from humility; wash your conscience clean with tears and confession; go down to the valley of Bethulia and be baptized in the spring.

Next in that very story it is reported, 'And, when she came out she besought the Lord God of Israel to direct her way to raise up the children of her people. So she came in clean and remained in the tent, until she ate her meal in the evening.'[56] A fitting order and a fair procedure, so that whatever degrees you descended in humility you mount again by good deeds. But the etymology of her name will show you true learning, for 'Judith' means praising and confessing. So let confession be so honest and faultless in your mouth that the whole of your life may be praise to the bridegroom of virgins. Then you will be able to pray confidently to the Lord and effectively seek forgiveness for your sins, for he will hear your voice and provide an answer to your prayers. If your life is adorned with holy deeds your way through it will be taken with rightly-directed steps: but if, God forbid, you are given up to corrupt desires you will be a deadly snare and destruction to those who behold you. For that reason the pattern of goodness is set out for you in Judith, that virtuous woman, so that first you go down to the valley and baptize yourself in the spring, and from this you may ascend purified, and make your prayer to the Lord if you follow his way.

He will direct your life as is pleasing to him. And through you he will set free his people if you enter your tent pure and clean. Clean you will enter in; clean you will remain. But the tent is the earthen vessel of your body, in which God has set a precious treasure: that is, a holy soul which he has arrayed in the dress of innocence and milk-white purity. See that you do not pollute it, nor let it appear stained before the eye of the Creator; let it remain intact and spotless in that tabernacle. Judith was clean in her tent, so too she was beautiful in the tabernacle of her mortal body.

But how long did she remain in her beauty? How long did she remain in her chastity? Right to the evening; and vespers marks the last hour of the day. Vespers signifies the end of life's activities when

---

[56] Judith 12.8–9.

in death there comes a spiritual refreshment for souls. Until the evening, until the last day, until the end of life, until the parting of soul and body, let the splendour of chastity be attended by humility and then you will be satisfied from love's dish at the heavenly banquet, 'For me the reward of virtue is to see your face.'[57] For this is the satisfaction which does not satiate, this abundance of heavenly things does not grow less by being used. For each one possesses it individually, so that it is sufficient for each, and each receives different rewards according to the diversity of merit. Jesus, he who is splendid in glory, is seen by all, desired by all, and loved by all, but whoever has desired him most in this life will be satisfied most fruitfully in the heavenly life. The prophet said: 'They feast on the bounty of your house, you give them drink from your river of pleasure.'[58] That intoxication is the immeasurable longing which is not diminished by abundance, the abundance which is not restricted by any shortages. This pleasure is gained by purity of heart and chastity of body, where holy humility defeats the raised sword of the proud and wise virtue restrains the shameless appetite of lust.

In what clothing glorious virginity should be arrayed in the victorious conflict

If, therefore, you undertake to ascend to the realm of the living God with the tokens of triumph, ornamented like Judith with precious garments, proceed in such a way that when Holofernes breaks in on you he will find you on the coverlet which your maid received from a eunuch and spread out for you.[59] Now Holofernes presents a typical example of the devil, but Bagoas, the eunuch, bears the form of a churchman. The cover then, since it is spread with varied colours in the weave, symbolizes the diversity of holy virtues; the handmaid who performs this service for you is your body which subjects itself to the spirit like a beast of burden. You must take up, accordingly, the protection of this cover so that on it you may eat and rest. It is written in the Apocalypse concerning this clothing, 'Happy is the man who has stayed awake and has not taken off his clothes so that he does not

57 This quotation (Ps. 17.15) is not an exact quotation from the Vulgate, nor apparently from the sources of the AV. Similar minor variations can be found in the passage; they may be derived from an Old Latin version, now lost, or from Osbert's imperfect recollection.
58 Ps. 36.8.
59 Judith 12.15.

go out naked and expose his shame.'[60] Faith and innocence of life and notable works of charity are the precious garments of the soul; it ought to appear with these adornments. But whoever is not dressed in these glories, the shame of his sins will be apparent. For the rest, ecclesiastics make themselves eunuchs for the sake of the kingdom of God and they courageously endeavour to demonstrate in their own flesh that charity which they preach to others. Their hands are full of purity so that they may be outstanding in caring for the wounds of others, for their minds overflow with heavenly showers striving to stream into the aridity of human hearts so that they may seek to bring forth to good purpose the rich fruits of holy virtues. Through their hands your maid's bedcover is taken up; when they preach they stir us to embrace chastity of the body. And indeed the cover does not appear to be woven of one plain colour, for modesty does not shine in beauty without the other virtues.

So if you do not lack the desire to reign as queen for ever, and you determine to stand at the right hand of the prince dressed in golden garments, you may claim from your handmaid, the body, a coverlet woven in the colours which the diversity of your virtues reveals. If any enemy of human kind looks longingly at you as Holofernes did Judith, his soul will be in great dread and be disturbed, longing indeed to lie with you and from the very day when he has first gazed on you in your splendour will seek an opportunity when he can meet you. But indeed it is your task not to turn back, not to look round nor to shut out an honourable resolution from your mind. It is his custom when he has seduced someone by his allurements to entice them and straightway to drive them into the depths of evil. We read that this was done to Dina, the daughter of Jacob;[61] we grieve greatly that this is done every day to many souls.

Beware therefore; reject his craftiness and his cunning. He will make a banquet for his friends on purpose to entrap you: that is with a multitude of vices with which he strives to entangle you to sin, and he will not summon anyone to bring the necessities of life which supply the citadel of chastity. For it is written that Holofernes made a banquet for his household alone and gave no one orders about the necessary provisions,[62] yet our necessities are the angelic spirits sent from God to guard our virtues. The devil does not call them when he

[60] Rev. 16.15.
[61] Gen. 34.1–31.
[62] Judith 12.10.

strives to tempt anyone; when he corrupts holy souls with deadly desires he does not delay. Indeed he prepares a dinner for his household alone when he incites a mood of depraved desire in perverted spirits so that he may make, as it were, a last meal for the soul for which he intends cursed damnation.

If the evil spirit of fornication has not been able to rule you, the spirit of avarice may, God forbid, rule over you. Of that sin the apostle writes 'avarice which is the servant of idols'.[63] Reflect then, my dearest one, what a hateful thing and how vicious is greed which, in the apostle's opinion, is no different from enslavement to idols, and consider how it is embodied and entwined with lechery. For many women prostituting their bodies to open shame are violated by a stranger not for love, but for money. So where lust does not pollute the mind, often unyielding greed will enkindle lust.

These two inseparable things existing in one body attempted to allure holy Judith, but they were unable to take possession of any part of her. Concerning this kind of feasting, Jude the apostle wrote in his epistle, 'These people are a dangerous object to your community meals, coming for the food and quite shamelessly only looking after themselves.'[64] When they ought to be consulting their own honour and advantage they are unreasonably eager to please the palate of self-indulgent flesh. They feed themselves and not Christ's poor; nor do they seek the bread of life with which he feeds his sheep, and for his sheep he lays down his life.[65] But concerning those who are ruled by this kind of sin, the apostle said, 'They are mischief-makers, governed only by their own desires ready with flattery for other people when they see some advantage in it.'[66] Whoever neglects to suppress the base desires of the flesh murmurs and complains because he must continue the works of holy Church in his ordeal. This holy Daniel, and other men who longed for holy things, did not do, for the more they sighed for the joys of the angels, so much the more did they despise all transitory things and counted as little all the things heaped up against them.[67] For those who walk according to their own desires fall wretchedly from sin to sin; their mouth speaks great swelling words, boasting that they do not care about any fears and that they take no notice of the crimes to which they have become

---

63 Col. 3.5.
64 Jude 12.
65 John 10.15.
66 Jude 16.
67 Possibly a reference to Dan. 10.1–5.

habituated. These are they who admire men's looks on account of their wealth, not through Christian love; they despise the poor but give honour to the rich in all things. Of them it is written in the prophet Zacharias, 'Open your doors, O Lebanon, that the fire may devour your cedars.'[68] For indeed Lebanon is to be understood as 'whiteness', Lebanon is properly called a Christian soul which in evil manner opens its doors and consumes and burns its cedars when it thus subjects the five senses of the body to depraved desires so that the fire of lust and greed consumes its good spiritual parts.

So let your spirit be manly, even though your gender is womanly. Ecclesiastes says, 'One man among a thousand have I found, but a woman among all these have I not found.'[69] The clear-sighted meditation of humans is mystically described under the name of 'man', but feeble thinking is designated under the title of 'womanish'. Indeed, we call good works masculine, but we present evil deeds under the image of the inferior gender; whence the poet said, 'Whatever is inconstant and changeable is always woman.'[70] When every human heart is subject to evil and difficulty from youth, in this downfall of the human race the woman more easily sinks to ruin.

So, from among a thousand rational minds that have no semblance of woman's weakness, you must seek out that man, you must find that man whose flesh has not been polluted in the world by any human stain, whose soul has not been invaded by any spot of sin in the body. Make your most urgent desire therefore that which the bride spoke of in the Canticle: when she was faint with love for this man she constantly sought out his paths.[71]

Concerning thanks for hospitality: models of the holy fathers to be imitated
'By night upon my bed I sought him whom my soul loves.'[72] That bed of yours, O Daughter of Sion, is that in which you must seek the man whom your soul loves; you must be wise and understand the quiet of contemplation although it appears 'in a glass and darkly', for in the night of this mortal life the eye is clouded and cannot see the perfect vision of God. This is what the prophet spoke about, 'Behold the man

---

68 Zach. 11.1.
69 Eccles. 7.28.
70 Virgil, *Aeneid* 4.569.
71 Song of Songs 2.5.
72 Song of Songs 3.1.

whose name is Dayspring.'[73] This very man has risen for you, if you will seek him, pure and comely, that he might make you pure and beautiful and establish his perfect peace in you for ever. Place his brothers in an inn, and his poor in a guest chamber.

We have frequently heard that those who have devoted themselves to giving charity have often, in performing this act of charity, received the Lord himself or the holy angels. So the apostle Peter in his epistle says, 'Use hospitality one to another without grudging',[74] and Paul, the chosen vessel and teacher of the Gentiles writing in the Epistle to the Hebrews, said, 'Let brotherly love continue among you and do not be forgetful to entertain strangers',[75] for thereby some have entertained angels unawares.[76] Abraham, the father of the faith, offered the acts of hospitality and knew by undoubted signs that God spoke to him in the three angels when with his human eyes he saw them going to heaven after the meal. Lot also, thinking they were human, invited those men to a meal and in Sodom knew them for angels and, led by them, escaped the destruction by fire of the wicked citizens.[77] Indeed Christ's two disciples thought that it was a man from distant parts whom they met on the way and they pressed him to stay at night. They were worthy to recognize the Lord in the breaking of bread, but they could not[78] recognise the one who had gone with them through the whole day. Yet they knew him in the act of hospitality and in the meal.[79] This is what you have often heard, what we very often read, about the woman of authority, 'She stretches out her hand to the poor, yes, she reaches forth her hands to the needy.'[80] And certainly, we understand that this refers to holy Church who opens the mysteries of faith and who has spread preachers far and wide to teach the foolish races of man, and plainly reaches out, according to the word of Scripture, to all those who are performing acts of charity. Whence Ecclesiastes also, the Son of David, the king of Jerusalem, summons your soul to deeds of piety and gives practical instruction on what ought to be done.[81] 'Cast',

73 Zach. 6.12.
74 1 Pet. 4.9.
75 Heb. 13.2.
76 Gen. 18.1–33.
77 Gen. 19.1–29.
78 Eccles. 11.1.
79 Luke 24.13.
80 Prov. 31.20.
81 'Ecclesiastes' is a Greek translation of a Hebrew word meaning approximately 'the Preacher'; it is one of a number of books of moral advice and practical

says he, 'your bread upon the waters, for you shall find it after many days.'[82]

Ecclesiastes is the preacher, and his sermon teaches and exhorts everyone: he is the son of David, son of the longed-for father, the son of the stalwart, son of the king of Jerusalem who cries out this universal truth to all. The son of David says, 'Cast your bread upon the passing waters': the Son of God, our teacher says, 'Give alms, and behold, all beautiful things are yours',[83] so that whoever disburses what is needful to the poor, let him first perform a deed of charity toward himself, so that his works shall find favour in the presence of God. For whoever is pressed down by luxury, or maimed by greed, to whom possessions are dear and whose conscience is defiled, let him not assert that all his possessions are his; granted that he doles out earthly bread to the poor; unless his life was rich before, the fruits of charity will not be pleasing in him. This is what Solomon says, 'Cast your bread on the passing waters', for as we see waters going past with violent flow, just so we do not doubt that all temporal things crumble and fall away. They rise and increase, they pass and fade away. So the bread must be put on the passing waters to lay out for Christ the good deeds that are needful, and their assembly will shine bright in the heavens although they are laid out in the body. For as John bears witness,[84] 'the many waters' are the people who go beyond ordinary life with their virtues and do not desire the perishable joys of the world. They are those who raise themselves like winged beings above the waters, that is, above transitory things, by contemplation. Rise, therefore, above yourself, and strive to fly from the depths to the heights and redeem your soul by precious deeds. Cast your bread upon the passing waters; it is enough that you share your bodily supplies with the brothers of Christ, because you will find him after a long time, that is after the passage of this world you will receive, for earthly bread, the bread of angels. 'Give alms', says the Lord.

wisdom known as the Wisdom Books. Since Solomon was reputed to have been the wisest of men this book has been ascribed to a [fictitious] son of his, though probably written some centuries later.

82 Eccles. 11.1.
83 Luke 11.41.
84 Rev. 17.15.

Concerning the acts of mercy
First, then, perform deeds of mercy towards yourself, and after a while turn your mercy to others. Whoever fornicates practises adultery; whoever commits sacrilege, whoever performs murder, whoever engages in incest, whoever gives time to lies and perjury, whoever first turns his heart and then his body to illicit deeds of perversion, however much he gives alms in accordance with the precepts of the Lord, yet all these sins are not freed from guilt for him. He that has clean hands and a pure heart, who has not lifted up his soul to worthless things, nor sworn deceitfully, shall receive blessing and mercy from the Lord.[85]

Concerning the spiritual vestments of the soul
Listen to what the apostle John says, 'I advise you, buy from me gold tested in the fire to make you really rich; and white raiment to clothe you and cover your shameful nakedness, and eye-salve so that you may see.'[86] If you wish to be rich and to gather for yourself lasting riches, buy for yourself gold tried in the fire. From whom? From Christ. What is gold tried in the fire? The gift of perfect love. Then whoever is refined by that love shall be found worthy to become gold. When it burns white-hot that violent heat consumes all dross by the grace of that perfection. And that the robes are white with innocence and righteousness signifies that you should live innocently and not fall away from righteous deeds; for where the root has been planted the tree will not lack leaves and fruit. For a good deed is increased by other virtues in the person in whom burning spiritual love is firmly rooted, for those who are of this nature, like a fruitful tree, spread abroad their priceless deeds like fruit and do not, like barren and unfruitful trees, give words for leaves. For whoever makes use of such garments while he remains in the body will not have the shame of his nakedness displayed in the future. For whoever has appeared misshapen like Adam will appear beautiful like Christ on the day of judgement. So anoint your eyes with eye-salve, that is occupy yourself perpetually in meditation on Holy Scripture, and so permeate yourself with it, that it is to be seen that God pours himself into you. For 'blessed are the pure in heart for they shall see God.'[87]

[85] Ps. 24.4.
[86] Rev. 3.18.
[87] Matt. 5.8.

Concerning spiritual banquets, and the sword of the spirit with which to destroy the enemy

Having run through all these things, let us return to our subject and with unfettered foot follow the path we have begun. Beware then, my dearest, lest the Holofernes of the spirit turn you to self-indulgence since he has been accustomed to provide pleasures in abundance for you. If he hands you anything to drink from a Babylonian cup, guard the lips of the inner being lest it be drowned in the wine of evil delight. If he places the food of sin before you to eat, do not touch the enticing delicacy but do what that honourable and steadfast woman did.[88] At the feast this holy woman ate only the dishes that her maid had prepared. And you too, do not fail to do this, but let your soul habituate herself the more frequently to those spiritual virtues in which your body has been employed from your childhood. For if it should ever happen to you to make use at some place or time of bodily delicacies, use them not for themselves, but for yourself; use them I say not for enjoyment, but for need. Not for excitement but for humbling; not for the palate but to sustain the body in God's service; not for illicit pleasure but to support the Lord's beast of burden, 'I am as a beast of burden before you', the psalmist says.[89] Do not let the beast of burden become haughty; let it be made strong again on humble rations, and made subject to carrying heavy loads.

Thus too our flesh, on whatever rations it is fed, will always be subject to the rules of sagacity. If Holofernes contemplates doing this he will be deceived by the heavenly trick with which he has been served and completely destroyed by his abounding drunkenness. His aim is that he may violate your modesty, but you will ensnare him to his ruin in his evil thoughts. And when other moral weaknesses have power, because the desire of the flesh has overcome him and subdued his masculine powers to the softness of a woman, do not delay to seize the sword of the holy spirit and cut off the head of the venomous Holofernes. 'This kind', says the Lord, 'can come forth by nothing but by prayer and fasting.'[90] What is this kind? Plainly demonic, since just as it miserably afflicts the bodies of many people, it is accustomed in the same way to torture most cruelly the souls that it invades.

For that reason, it befits you to abstain and also to pray in that hour

---

88 Judith 12.19.
89 Ps. 73.22.
90 Mark 9.29.

when some evil temptation assaults you: when any titillation of the flesh comes upon you, call upon your bridegroom; pray to your Lord that he will exalt his city of Jerusalem, your soul. In what way did the holy Judith pray? 'Lord God of all power' she said 'look favourably at this present time on the works of my hands for the exaltation of Jerusalem. For now is the time to help your inheritance, and to execute my enterprises to the destruction of the enemies that are risen against us.'[91] Therefore do you also pray that he who is the God of all power should bring it about that all the holy virtues should be united in your inner being so that you march on, always fortified with this glorious defence: and in that hour when some evil temptation assaults you, when any titillation of the flesh comes upon you, call upon your bridegroom, pray to your Lord that he will exalt his city of Jerusalem, your soul. It is she, your soul, who ought to stand continually upon a watchtower of internal peace and to shun the strife which has its origin in sin, to consider king Solomon in his diadem, to gaze with longing on the assembly of all its citizens; to wonder at the brightness that shines as roses in the martyrs, in confessors as violets and as lilies in the virgins.

Then the time will come for taking up his inheritance, the welcome inheritance, the delightful inheritance: your body and soul. So long as any seed of the devil comes forth in original sin between these two, the soul and the body, this is not the inheritance of Christ. For many are the people and dense and innumerable the throng of sins which seek to overthrow this inheritance and subject it miserably to themselves. 'Without me', says the Lord, 'You can do nothing.'[92] The strength of the Lord was assuredly with Judith for she could not gain victory over the tyrant without the support of his strength. So she drew the sword, came near to the bed, seized the hair of his head, struck him twice on the neck and cut off Holofernes' head.[93] Just as this holy woman struck twice through the power of her virtue, so do not delay to strike twice in your own virtue. Thus your goodness may be supported by the goodness of God so that by a twofold blow the chief means of invasion of the ancient enemy may be cut off. For what else is this twofold blow but the love of God and of your neighbour? By them the enemy is ground to dust; with the sword of the word of God the heart of the faithful is pierced to the pricking of

---

[91] Judith 13.4.
[92] John 15.5.
[93] Judith 13.9.

conscience. In this way, being armed with the defence of chastity, you will be able to please the Lord of Glory and enter the gates of the city of heaven.

Concerning the chariot by which the blessed Ethelburga was raised to the heavens[94]
You have all you need in your convent before your eyes every day: may you heartily imitate the deeds of her sanctity. Ethelburga, glorious, renowned and dearest bride of the highest king, has provided you with a mirror of holy virginity. She does not cease to fashion ornaments of holy chastity for you; she herself prints a pattern of carefulness for you, showing with what earnestness you ought to keep watch over the safety of the flock committed to you by God. Keep these souls in such a way that you do not deprive their spirits of the bread of life. That happy mother of yours, the blessed and renowned Ethelburga, acted thus, providing an example of heavenly wisdom and remaining emaciated by divine influence through discipline of the holy spirit. This was accompanied in word and deed by temperance, which is a way of life. The holy virgin, whom humility has watched over everywhere like a guardian, is not puffed up above herself. Humility was joined to holy modesty as inseparable companion and by this peace of mind has continued steadfast and unshaken. Chastity was garlanded by virginal abstemiousness and from it, like twin shoots, proceed glory and honour. This virtue restrained anger, and did not pay back affronts to anyone.

The wise virgin has been furnished with these qualities by the knowledge of a true faith and is not a little adorned by knowledge of the Scriptures. She read the stories of the Old Testament so that she took to heart the image of spiritual virtues; the sweet Song of Songs echoed in her ears so that they created spiritually a symbolic conception in the secret places of her heart; thus among these songs, she meditated upon the holy sacraments so that no inducements of

---

[94] Elijah was carried off to heaven in a fiery chariot (II Kings 3.11). It seems that Osbert wishes to say that Ethelburga too has been carried to heaven in a chariot drawn by four horses which symbolize four virtues: true faith; a knowledge of the Scriptures, and righteousness and steadfastness. This would symbolically express Ethelburga's way of reaching heaven, and adding two more horses (i.e. righteousness and steadfastness) to the original two would then be reasonable, but Osbert's subsequent reference to Aminadab (Williamson p. 176 line 20 and see n. 96 below) remains confusing. The Authorized Version reads: 'Or ever I was aware, my soul made me like the chariots of Amminadib [*sic*] (Song of Songs 6.12). The Jerusalem Bible omits the name entirely.

bodily lust titillated her. To this Aminadab added a third wheel, that of righteousness, to his chariot,[95] and the first of its qualities is to love God with fear and to exercise true religion with reverence, for its spokes are of gold; they are of use to everyone, they hurt no one by stirring up envy, they hasten to the aid of the household with the greater devotion.[96]

We read that all these things were perfected in the blessed Ethelburga who, embracing the bonds of sisterly love, took upon herself the dangers of others. She reverently cherished the holy virgins by the rule of religious order; the glorious mother did not delay in taking succour to the unfortunate; she repaid the interchange of benefits that she had received; she maintained fairness in judgement. Hence it is that the fourth wheel, steadfastness, is added to her chariot, and this greatness of spirit is rightly remembered. She rose above wealth and despised and spat out entangling possessions and advancement. She resisted misfortunes bravely and yielded patiently to adversity; she was not made soft by allurements, nor high and mighty by prosperity, not broken down nor wearied by adverse circumstances. She is strong in danger and found to be undefeated by toil; she fled from greed, despised wealth. She resolutely equips her mind against danger from evil-doers, she yields to no misfortunes and escapes greed for fame. For Seneca writes thus on this subject, 'He is a stronger man who overcomes greed than the one who defeats an enemy.'[97] In this chariot, the holy virgin is carried aloft; the manifold glories of immortal life are prepared for her by the Lord, and she, the sister of the holy bishop Erkenwald, gained the triumphal reward of her service in the army of heaven, while rivalling her brother's zeal in the labours of earthly life.[98] For, to her celestial renown, she gave a sign to show what should be the burial place of their holy bodies. For truly the form of her glory was expressed beforehand in her human body, for her own disciple saw her taken

---

95 Song of Songs 6.12.

96 The chariot of Aminadab, was variously treated in contemporary exegesis and iconography: Abbot Suger had a window made on the theme at St Denis in Paris; the biography of St Gilbert of Sempringham, England's major monastic founder in the twelfth century, uses it as an image of his double order of nuns served by laybrothers (see R. Foreville and G. Keir, *The Book of St Gilbert* [Oxford: Clarendon Press, 1987]), pp. 50–3, 336–7.

97 See Pseudo-Seneca, *De Moribus* 81.

98 Erkenwald (d. c. 693) founded Barking Abbey (c. 666) where his sister Ethelburga became abbess.

heavenwards from the dormitory and raised by ropes of virtues to the joys above.

So, dear mother Adelidis, resolve to imitate the famous deeds of this woman and determine that they should be imitated by your daughters to whom you have given birth by the gospel of Christ. Whoever wishes to learn more fully of her life should read what Bede has recounted about her with his brilliant pen in his *History of the English Church and People* and will without doubt succeed in knowing how great is her worth in God's sight.[99] According to the etymology of her name her deeds shine in the world, for in English Ethelburga means a 'noble city or kingdom', because she is distinguished both by her nobility of mind and her royal splendour. She will bring further blessings from the Lord to you and the rest of the holy virgins who have gained a famous burial in the convent where you alone share authority with her.

The Epilogue of the whole work and the recommendation of the author

Because, most distinguished lady, I have been zealous to beat out a necklace of virtues in a series of letters and to make a new mirror in golden lustre and precious stones, give heed attentively to the fine apparel of heavenly wisdom. Consider in what and how much you please the heavenly bridegroom with these virtues and hasten to the long-sought glory of the beatific vision. There you will find the sabbath of all most solemn sabbaths, for there you will reach the longed-for triumph of eternal happiness with the angelic spirits. A new song will be sung by the holy virgins there,[100] and every single one following the Lamb will be dressed in everlasting robes of state. Would that I may see with you the wages of my life as precious in that light, which will, for me, always be beyond price forever.

The sharers in my flesh and blood, Cecilia and Margaret, I call my co-heirs in maiden sanctity; born of my sister; through the purity of their innocent life they grace your children in every circumstance so that they always return praise and honour to the heavenly bridegroom of holy virgins. I exult to see their splendour, wearing the diadem of the eternal king, and, drawn by the odour of virginity, I pant, running breathless after them to the blessed vision of God. I have never

---

[99]   Both Osbert and Goscelin (see VI below) took their material on Ethelburga from Bede 4.7 and 9.

[100]   Rev. 14.3–4.

possessed any honour for myself for long without their sharing it, there will never be any glorification in the spirit without their glorification. Therefore in truth I love them specially before all relations and friends and unhesitatingly place them before all my kindred from my feelings of love; and because I find them worthy in every way I commend them, holy mother, as deserving the love of one of your eminent rank. I pray that you will receive them in my place as deserving praise and will share your good fortune with them with your wonderful generosity.[101]

If anything in what I have already said in this work has been able to inflame you to a love of the heavenly bridegroom, let it not be attributed to me but to the Holy Spirit who, on many occasions, is not unwilling to speak through the mouth even of his enemy. If, indeed, I have offered you some not inappropriate words concerning the armour of holy chastity, it ought not to be ascribed undeservedly to the poverty of my exiguous thought. But whatever it is that has been drawn for you by the grace of God from the fountain of my heart, it has flowed from the richness and the overflowing fullness of love. I therefore wish for you a nature such as I have described, that you should be strong to perform everything which Christ has thought you worthy to undertake in the rule of chastity. Commend me therefore to your religious community, so that in the presence of David the memory of me shall be thought fit to be recorded in vigils and fasts and holy prayers and I have no doubt that I shall have them as co-heirs in the inheritance of the saints.[102] May it come to pass that in this inheritance I may gaze upon your face in the new glory of the resurrection when the bodies of the saints, defeated by death, rise transformed and are crowned with unwithering laurels by the author of life. May he who rules the realm above lead us to that kingdom of everlasting life and may unceasing praise sound with the voices of holy angels in unwearied concert to him whose majesty neither begins nor ends through all ages. Amen.

---

101 For letters from Osbert to his nieces in Barking, see IV below.
102 Osbert writes as though David is well known to both parties. He may be the messenger who carried the letter to Barking. There was a David at Westminster to whom Osbert is known to have written a letter (Williamson, no. 4, pp. 58–62, and n. 34).

II From Abelard to Heloise: The History of Women's Roles in Christianity (Letter 7)

The tragic story of the love of Heloise (d. 1164) and Abelard (1079–1142) is well known, especially for the episode when, following their marriage, Heloise's uncle and guardian, Fulbert, had Abelard castrated. Less well recognized is the fact that after they had both entered the religious life in 1118, Heloise had a career for some thirty years as a successful and respected abbess. Their correspondence, in which both Abelard's replies and the letters from Heloise which occasioned them have been preserved, is the most famous of the Middle Ages. Once celebrated as the letters of two unfortunate lovers, the correspondence is now seen to embrace further dimensions. It is now generally accepted that it is a mutual correspondence, in which Heloise did actually compose the letters attributed to her and actively shaped the nature of the exchange. It is as an exchange between an unusually gifted cleric and abbess regarding the theory and practice of the religious life for women that it features here. The letter translated here (Letter 6 in the numbering of Muckle and Radice, although traditionally numbered as Letter 7 in the correspondence) was written while Heloise was abbess of the Paraclete (as also Letter 9, no V below, which was written as a sermon on learning for Heloise's nuns). Radice offers only an abbreviated version of this letter in her translation of the letters of Abelard and Heloise.

In 1129 Abbot Suger of St Denis, Paris, laid claim to the abbey of Argenteuil where Heloise was prioress, and ejected the nuns. Abelard gave shelter to Heloise and some of her nuns at the Paraclete, an oratory or house of prayer, which he had founded near Troyes. Heloise's letters to Abelard witness not only to her scholarship but to her strength of character in managing this disruption in the life of the community: they also make it plain that in the nine or so years between her entry to the religious life and her opening letter to Abelard, she had been racked by thwarted desire and by memories of her lost love and so by the feeling of hypocrisy in her position. When Abelard's account of their affair, the *Historia Calamitatum* (The Story of My Misfortunes), came into her hands, Heloise wrote to him with pity for his sufferings but also with reproach because he had not visited the convent at the Paraclete with any personal help or support for her in the spiritual and practical difficulties of her new life. They embarked on a correspondence in which both provision for her community and new understandings of their personal relations were negotiated. Heloise begins by asking several practical questions about the adaptation of the Benedictine Rule to women. Her questions and the reasons for asking them show her thorough understanding of her position and her spiritual and administrative duties in her convent. They also suggest that what she longed for, and felt entitled to, was some personal support and comfort from the former lover and husband at whose wish she had originally entered the religious life.

Both personal and professional comfort was, in a sense, supplied by Letter 7. Heloise had asked for information on the origin of the order of nuns. Abelard replies with an account not only of medieval nuns, but of their predecessors, the women of the Bible and the deaconesses of the early Christian centuries, who had served God and his servants by devoting themselves to them and supplying their needs. He also includes some account of the pagan classical equivalent of nuns, the vestal virgins. The letter starts with the women who served Christ in the Gospel and who were the first witnesses of the resurrection and who thus demonstrated their spiritual perceptiveness. The women of the Old Testament are then reviewed as prophetesses and heroic leaders. Their gifts, it is suggested, witness to special grace from God: Miriam and Deborah did not merely serve men, they led them. Together with his contemporaries Abelard believed women to be physically weaker than men, but he was prepared to argue that this made their achievement all the greater. Women, Abelard implies, are capable of greater feeling, greater love and greater self-sacrifice than men, and he goes on to find a number of ways in which nuns are given greater honour than monks: more is expected of them, he says, just as more was expected of the early Christian widows who became deaconesses. He is concerned to show that these forerunners in the female religious life were honoured by men because they received a special grace of God. For women who could fulfill the role of pious widowhood, who could live in chastity and devotion, there was a special reward waiting in heaven.

The end of Letter 7 is concerned with the ordering of Christian society and particularly with the place of widows. Abelard may well have regarded Heloise as in some ways a widow: she had lost him as a husband and he commends her to the life of chaste widowhood with its emotional focus on Christ as husband, in what can be seen as, in part, an indirect response to Heloise's requests for support.

Abelard's style in Letter 7 makes his reply seem at first sight impersonal and lacking in sympathy: the sentence construction is complex and difficult to translate because of the number of subordinate clauses to each main clause. The style is not different, however, from Abelard's other writings: he seems to have adopted a shorthand and impersonal pedagogic style (almost as in extempore lecturing), in which one can hear the teacher's voice making a brief statement then qualifying it by one, two, or three relative clauses. This style can create an impression of perfunctoriness, sometimes strengthened by Abelard's handling of argument, but it may also testify to his confidence in Heloise's ability to take the material of his letter and use and develop it.

Abelard to Heloise: The History of Women's Roles in Christianity (Letter 7)

[A reply to Heloise concerning the authority and dignity of the order of nuns][1]
Dearest sister, I will reply concisely and in a few words if I can, in love both to you and to your spiritual daughters, when you enquire about the origin of the religious life of nuns. Indeed the order of monks as also that of nuns clearly took the pattern of its observance from our Lord Jesus Christ, though not a few of these orders had their beginnings before his incarnation. Hence also Jerome, writing to Eustochium said, 'the sons of the prophets whom we take to be the monks of the Old Testament etc.'[2] The evangelist tells of Anna also, a widow who zealously attended the temple at divine service, and who was found worthy equally with Simeon to take up our Lord in the Temple and to be filled with prophecy.[3] Christ then is the object of righteousness and the perfection of all good things; coming in the fullness of time so that he may bring to their consummation the good things that are incomplete, or may make known what is secret. As he

---

1   The subheadings given in this translation are not part of the original text. They are included here to assist comprehension of the range and structure of Abelard's argument.
2   The passage is in fact from Jerome's Letter 125 to Rusticus, a monk who later became Bishop of Narbonne (CSEL 56: 125). There is a similar discussion about the sons of the prophets in Letter 22 to Eustochium (CSEL 54: 156).
3   Luke 2.25.

came to call and to redeem each gender, so he did not disdain to inscribe each gender in the true monastic order of his flock, so that authority for this calling should be given to women as to men, and the perfection of life should be set equally before all to imitate.

[Women in the Gospels: the anointing of Christ]
Assuredly we have read there of associations of holy women with apostles and other disciples and with his own mother, renouncing, as it were, and giving up every possession so as to possess Christ alone; as it is written of them, 'The Lord is the share of my inheritance.'[4] They faithfully make up the number by which they are all converted from the world to the community of this life, according to the rule handed down from Christ: 'If a man will not give up all that he possesses he cannot be my disciple.'[5] Holy stories carefully record how these blessed women and true nuns were faithful followers of Christ, and tell what grace and honour Christ himself, and afterwards the apostles, showed to their devotion. We read in the Gospel of the grumbling of the Pharisee who received the Lord as his guest and was rebuked by him, and how the devotion of the sinful woman was valued far beyond the Pharisee's hospitality.[6] We read also that when Lazarus had been raised to life and was reclining at table, his sister Martha alone waited at the tables while Mary poured a pound of precious balm on the feet of the Lord and wiped them with her own hair, and the house was filled with the odour of the balm.[7] Judas was led into greed because it seemed to have been used up wastefully, and the disciples were indignant. So Martha was busy in offering the food, but Mary offered the balm; one restored the inner man, the other cherished the outer man in his weariness.

[Women ministered to the Lord]
The writings of the Gospels record that no one but women ministered to the Lord, and devoted their goods in daily alms to him; they chiefly provided the necessities of life for him.[8] He showed himself the lowliest of servants to his disciples at table and in washing their feet.[9] But we know that he did not receive this service from any of the

---

4 Luke 8.2; Ps. 16.5.
5 Luke 14.33.
6 Luke 7.36–50.
7 See Matt. 26.6–11; Mark 14.3–9; John 12.1–8.
8 Cf. Luke 8.3.
9 Cf. John 13.5.

disciples or even from the men, but, as we have said, the women alone devoted their service in these and other offices of loving kindness. As we recognize Martha's service, we also recognize Mary's that was so much the more devoted as she had formerly been more culpable.[10] Our Lord put water in a basin and carried out the duty of washing, but she showed her devotion with tears of inward penitence and not by water on the outside.

[Women's part in the sacrament of anointing]
When he had washed the disciples' feet he wiped them with a linen cloth, but she used her hair as a cloth. Moreover, she added balm as unguent which we never read of the Lord using. For who does not know that the woman had already received so much of his grace that she anointed his head as well by pouring out the balm? It is recorded that this balm was poured out not when it was taken out of an alabaster jar but when the jar was broken; thus she forcibly expressed her ardent longing and extreme devotion, for she thought that what she had used in so great a service should not be kept for any other purpose. By these deeds this act of anointing clearly fulfils what Daniel prophesied should take place when the holy of holies was anointed.[11] For note the woman anoints the holy of holies and indeed he is what she believes him to be, and she proclaimed what the prophet proclaimed in those words. What, I ask, is that blessing of God, or what the glory of the women, but that he offers his head as well as his feet only to the woman for anointing? What, I beg you, is the privilege of the weaker gender but that a woman should also anoint, as it were with a bodily sacrament, Christ who was anointed with all the balms of the Holy Spirit from his conception; consecrating him Priest and king; that is she created in the flesh the anointed Christ? We know that the Patriarch Jacob first anointed a stone with oil as a symbol of the Lord and afterwards the anointing of kings or priests took place, and any rites of anointing were allowed to be performed only by men, even though women have sometimes taken it on themselves to baptize.[12] Once the patriarch hallowed the

---

10 Following Gregory the Great, *Homilies on the Gospels* 2.25 and 2.33 (PL 76: 1189BC, 1242A), Abelard conflates Mary of Bethany, sister of Martha and Lazarus, who washes the feet of Jesus (John 11.2) with both Mary of Magdala (Luke 8.2) and the female sinner who wipes Christ's feet with her hair (Luke 7.36–50).

11 Daniel 9.24.

12 Women were forbidden to baptize, except in cases of necessity, according to the

stone with oil;[13] now the pontiff hallows the temple and the altar. Thus men give form to the sacraments. But the woman has performed in reality as Truth itself bears witness, saying, 'She has performed a good deed in me.'[14] Christ was anointed by a woman; Christians by men. That is to say: the head by a woman, the limbs by men. This woman is said to have acted well when she poured the balm on his head, not trickled it drop by drop; according to what the bride in the Canticle sings of him, 'Your name is as a balm poured out.'[15] The psalmist also prefigures mystically the abundance of this balm in which it flowed down from the head to the hem of the garment, saying, 'Like the precious balm on the head that ran down upon the beard, even Aaron's beard: that it ran down to the skirts of his garments.'[16]

We read that David received three anointings, as Jerome notes.[17] Christ too received three, and Christians also. Assuredly the feet of the Lord or his head received the woman's anointing; after his death Joseph of Arimathea and Nicodemus, as John records,[18] prepared him with spices for burial. Christians too are sanctified with three anointings; of which one is performed in baptism, the second in confirmation, and the third is for the sick. Consider, therefore, the high honour of woman, for Christ was anointed by her twice in his life, that is on his feet and on his head, and received the sacrament of king and priest. The balm of myrrh and aloes which is used to preserve the bodies of the dead signified the future incorruptibility of the Lord's body which all the elect will attain in the resurrection.[19] For the previous anointing by a woman shows his matchless glory as king and priest; the anointing indeed of his head as the higher, of his feet the lower. See how he received from a woman the consecration as a king; he who scorned to accept the kingdom for himself when it

---

Fifth Council of Carthage, *Collectio canonum V* 3.48 (CCCM 6: 334); Peter Lombard, *Sententiae* 4.6.1 (Paris: Vives, 1892), p. 565.

13 Gen. 28.18.
14 Mark 14.6.
15 Song of Songs 1.3.
16 Ps. 133.2.
17 Jerome, *Short Commentary on Psalm 26* (CCSL 72: 201).
18 John 19.39.
19 See Ambrose, *Exposition on Luke* 2.44 (CCSL 14: 51) where he names the gifts of the Magi as gold, frankincense, and myrrh, and states that myrrh will preserve a dead body.

was offered by men, 'and when they would come and take him by force to make him a king, he departed'.[20]

The woman performs the sacraments of the heavenly king, not of an earthly one; of him, I say, who later said of himself, 'My kingdom is not of this world.'[21] Bishops pride themselves when, to the applause of the people, they anoint earthly kings, when they anoint mortal priests adorned with splendid golden vestments. And often they bless also those whom God curses. The humble woman, not changing her garments, not preparing what she would say, when the apostles, too, were offended at her, carried out these rites, not as a duty of office, but as a service of self-sacrificing love. O great constancy of faith! O immeasurable zeal of love, which believes all things, hopes all things, endures all things.[22] The Pharisee grumbled when the Lord's feet were washed by a sinful woman. The apostles complained openly because the woman had also taken a liberty as regards his head.[23] The faith of the woman remained unmoving, trusting in God's goodness, and she did not lack God's approval on either account. For the Lord himself showed how dear and how welcome this balm was to him, desiring that it should be reserved for him. He said to the indignant Judas, 'Leave her alone; she had to keep this scent for the day of my burial.'[24] As if he were to say, 'Do not reject this service of hers done to a living person, lest in doing so you take away the expression of devotion given to the dead.' For it is sure that holy women also prepared spices for the Lord's burial; if she had been restrained by bashfulness now, she would assuredly have been less prepared for the Lord's burial. When the disciples were indignant at the woman's presumption and, as Mark reminds us, complained loudly against her, he overcame them with the mildest of replies and she did him such service that Mark thought that it should be introduced into the Gospel and with these words too, 'Wherever the good news is proclaimed, what she has done will be told also in remembrance of her', ascribing not a little importance to her.[25] By this we read that there are no services done by any people whatever

---

[20] John 6.15.
[21] John 18.36.
[22] I Cor. 13.7.
[23] Luke 7.39. The Pharisee grumbled because the woman poured balm on the Lord; but there is no indication in the Gospel that the anointing of his head caused particular offence. See Matt. 26.7; Mark 14.3.
[24] John 12.7.
[25] Mark 14.9.

that are so commended and sanctioned by the Lord's authority. For he preferred the alms of a poor widow before all the temple offerings:[26] this shows clearly how welcome to him is the devotion of women.

[Women's faith surpasses that of men]
Peter, indeed, dared to declare publicly that he and his fellow apostles had left all for Christ, and Zacchaeus, seized with longing for the coming of the Lord generously gave half of his goods to the poor and if he had defrauded anyone restored it fourfold.[27] And many others made great gifts in Christ or for Christ and offered much more valuable things in holy obedience to Christ, or left them for Christ, but did not gain such praise for the Lord's approval, as the women did for their excellence. For their devotion to him was always outstanding. The ending of the Lord's life clearly shows this. When the leader of the apostles himself denied the Lord, the beloved of the Lord fled, and the rest of the disciples scattered, these women endured fearlessly and no error or despair could separate them from Christ, neither in suffering nor in death: so that the saying of the apostle seems to be particularly appropriate, 'Who will separate us from the love of God; tribulation or distress? etc.'[28] Whence Matthew, when he reported both of himself and the others, 'Then all the disciples forsook him and fled', added a little later the steadfastness of the women.[29] For even when he was crucified they helped him as much as they were allowed. 'And', he says, 'Many women were there watching from a distance; and they had followed Jesus from Galilee, ministering to him, etc.'[30] When they finally stayed unmoved by the sepulchre, the evangelist faithfully records it, saying, 'And there was Mary Magdalene and the other Mary, sitting by the sepulchre.'[31] And about these women Mark relates, 'There were also women watching from a distance among whom was Mary Magdalene, and Mary the mother of James the Less and of Joseph and Salome.'[32] They also followed him when he was in Galilee, and ministered to him, and there were many other women who came up with him to Jerusalem. John tells us that he stood near the cross and even stood by the cruci-

26 Mark 14.41–44.
27 Luke 19.2–9.
28 Rom. 8.35.
29 Matt. 26.56.
30 Matt. 27.55.
31 Matt. 27.61.
32 Mark 15.40–41.

fied Lord, he who had first fled; but he put first the women's constancy as if he was stirred by it and so called to return. 'Now there stood by the cross of Jesus', he says, 'his mother and his mother's sister, Mary Cleopas, and Mary Magdalene. When Jesus therefore saw his Mother and the disciple standing, etc.'[33]

The blessed Job long before foretold this constancy of the holy women and the desertion of the disciples, referring to the person of the Lord, he said, 'My flesh is consumed away and my bones stick to my skin, and my lips only remain about my teeth.'[34] For indeed the strength of the body is in the bone which supports and bears flesh and skin. In the body of Christ, therefore, which is the Church, the bone itself is said to be the firm foundation of the Christian faith, or the zeal of that love of which it is sung, 'Many waters cannot quench love, etc.'[35] And about it the apostle said, '[Love] bears all things, believes all things, hopes all things, endures all things.'[36] But in the body the flesh is the inner part and the skin the outer. Therefore, the apostles, reaching out with food for the inner spirit by preaching, and the women looking after the bodily necessities, are compared to flesh and skin. So, when the flesh is consumed, the bone of Christ adheres to the skin; for when the apostles found cause of shame in the passion of the Lord and were without hope because of his death, the devotion of the holy women remained unshaken and did not withdraw at all from the bone of Christ, because their devotion retained its constancy in hope and faith and love, so that they were not separated in mind or body from him when he was dead. Men, by nature, are stronger in body as in mind than women. From this, masculine nature is with reason defined as the flesh, which is nearer to the bones, and womanly weakness as the skin. Moreover, those apostles whose function is to bite at the lapses of others in censure are called 'the teeth of God'.[37] For them the lips, that is words, have remained more powerful than deeds, since those who despair now speak more about Christ than they perform for Christ. Certainly such were the disciples to whom he appeared when they were going to the fortress

---

33 John 19.25.
34 See Job 19.20. A difficult sentence to translate literally: AV: 'My bone cleaveth to my skin and to my flesh, and I am escaped with the skin of my teeth.' Jerusalem Bible: 'Beneath my skin, my flesh begins to rot and my bones stick out like teeth.'
35 Song of Songs 8.7.
36 I Cor. 13.7.
37 Gregory, *Moralia in Job* 14.50 (CCSL 143A: 733).

of Emmaus and speaking to one another about all the things that had happened, and he corrected their despair.[38]

[Women's devotion at the crucifixion and the resurrection]
Finally, what did Peter and the rest of the disciples have then to offer besides words when the time of the Lord's passion came and the Lord himself prophesied the shame that they would feel, 'And if all men shall be offended because of you yet will I never lose faith' said Peter, and again, 'Though I should die with you yet will I never be offended.'[39] All the disciples said the same. They spoke, I say, rather than acted. He, the first and greatest of the apostles who showed such constancy in words that he said to the Lord, 'I am prepared to go to prison and death with you', and to whom the Lord, in committing the Church to him, had said, 'And when you have recovered, strengthen your brothers',[40] even he did not fear to deny him at the single word of a maidservant, and not once but three times did he deny him while he was still alive, and likewise all the disciples fled from him in one fleeting moment of time.[41] Yet the women were not separated from him in death, neither in mind nor body. One of them, that blessed sinner seeking him even in death and confessing her Lord, said 'They have taken away the Lord out of the tomb', and again, 'If you have taken him away tell me where you have put him and I will go and remove him.'[42] The rams fled and, indeed, the shepherds of the Lord's flock, but the sheep remained undaunted. The Lord shows us how feeble is our flesh, in that even in the moment of his passion they could not watch even one hour with him.[43] The women who passed a sleepless night at his tomb deserved to be the first to see the glory of his resurrection. They had loved him as faithfully in death as in life, and they showed this not in words but in deeds. And just as they had such concern about his suffering and death, they were the first to be made glad of his risen life. For when, according to John, Joseph of Arimathea and Nicodemus were binding the body of the Lord with aromatic bandages and burying him, Mark reports about the zeal of Mary Magdalene and of Mary mother of Joseph that they

38 Luke 24.13–32.
39 Matt. 26.33–35.
40 Luke 22.32–33.
41 Matt. 26.69–75; 14.50.
42 John 20.2, 15.
43 Matt. 26.40.

watched where he was placed.[44] And concerning them Luke also bears record saying, 'The women also who had come with Jesus from Galilee saw the tomb and how his body was laid, and prepared balm';[45] clearly because Nicodemus would not have had sufficient balm if they had not added their own. And on the sabbath they rested according to the law. Indeed, according to Mark, when the sabbath was passed, there came to the sepulchre very early on the day of resurrection – Mary Magdalene, Salome and Mary the mother of James.[46]

Now, since we are demonstrating their devotion, we will continue with the honours of which they were worthy. First, they were consoled by the angelic vision about the resurrection of the Lord, now fulfilled; then they were first to see and hold the Lord. First, indeed, was Mary Magdalene who was more eager than the others; afterwards she and the others, as has been written of them, 'left the sepulchre . . . running to announce to the disciples the resurrection of the Lord.[47] And behold, Jesus met them saying "Hail", but the woman came near and held his feet and worshipped him. Then Jesus said to them, "Go, tell my brothers to go into Galilee, they will see me there." '[48] About this, Luke continues, 'There were Mary Magdalene, and Joanna, and Mary the Mother of James and others who were with them, who told these things to the apostles.'[49] Mark does not fail to tell us that they were sent first by the angel to bring news to the apostles, where it is written, 'He is risen. He is not here . . . but go your way, tell his disciples and Peter that he goes before you into Galilee.'[50] And the Lord appearing first to Mary Magdalene said to her, 'Go to my brothers and say to them, "I am ascending to my Father, etc." '[51] From these words we gather that these holy women were placed as apostles, yet above the apostles, and were sent either by the Lord or by the angels. They proclaimed the supreme joy of his resurrection which everyone was looking for; so that the apostles first learned through them what they afterwards proclaimed throughout the world.

44   John 19.38–39; Mark 15.47.
45   Luke 23.55–56.
46   Mark 16.1–2.
47   Matt. 28.8ff.
48   Mark 16.6–7.
49   Luke 24.10.
50   Mark 16.6–7.
51   John 20.17.

The evangelist records that, meeting the Lord after the resurrection, these women were greeted by him, showing by the meeting and salutation how much concern and favour he had for them. For we read that he did not offer a personal word of greeting, that is 'Hail', to others, but rather previously restrained the disciples from greetings when he said to them, 'Greet no one on the way,'[52] as if he now reserved this privilege for faithful women and he showed it to them alone, when he had acquired the glory of immortality. When the Acts of the Apostles reports that immediately after the Ascension the apostles returned from the Mount of Olives to Jerusalem, it carefully describes the worship of that holy assembly and does not omit the constancy of devotion of these holy women when it says, 'All these joined in continuous prayer with several women and Mary the Mother of Jesus.'[53]

[Women's part in the growth of the new Church]
Leaving aside the Hebrew women who first turned to the faith while the Lord was still living in the flesh and preaching, and who first began the liturgy of the faith, let us consider the widows of the Greeks who were afterwards received by the apostles. With what zeal, with what care they too were drawn in by the apostles when Stephen the protomartyr and most glorious standard bearer was commissioned into the Christian army with certain other men full of faith. For it is written in the same Acts of the Apostles that when the number of the disciples was multiplied, there arose a murmuring of the Greeks against the Hebrews, because their widows were neglected in the daily administration. 'Then the twelve called a full meeting of the disciples to them, and said, "It is not reasonable that we should leave the word of God and serve at tables. Therefore, brothers select from among you seven men of good reputation, full of the Holy Spirit and wisdom, whom we may appoint over this business. But we will give ourselves continually to prayer, and to the ministry of the Word". And the saying pleased the whole assembly and they chose Stephen, a man full of faith and of the Holy Spirit, and Philip, and Prochorus, and Nicanor, and Timothy and Parmenas and Nicholas, a proselyte of Antioch, whom they set before the apostles; and when they had prayed, they laid their hands on them.'[54] The

---

52 Luke 10.4.
53 Acts 1.14.
54 Acts 6.1–6.

continence of Stephen was so much respected that he was entrusted with the provision and service of the holy women. That the administration of his service was so excellent and as pleasing to God as to the apostles themselves, they showed by their own words and by the laying-on of hands; as though they who had appointed them to do this were adjuring them to act faithfully and were helping them to do so as much by blessing as by prayers. Even Paul claimed full rights for himself in the conduct of his apostolate, 'Have we not power to take a woman as a sister, like the apostles?'[55] As if he said openly, 'And are we not allowed to have a convent of dedicated women, and to lead them in preaching as other apostles do, that they should furnish the apostles' necessities from their own possessions?' Hence, Augustine in the book *The Work of Monks* says: 'Moreover, faithful women who had earthly possessions went with them and supplied them from their own possessions, so that none of them lacked whatever was necessary for his life.' Again 'Whoever does not think it was arranged by the apostles that women of a holy way of life went about with them and with those who preached the Gospel, let them hear the Gospel and know how they made this on the model of the Lord himself. For it is written in the Gospel, "He went throughout every city and village . . . preaching the kingdom, and the twelve were with him, and certain women who had been healed of evil spirits and infirmities, Mary called Magdalene . . . And Joanna the wife of Chuza, Herod's steward, and Suzanna, and many others who supported him from their own resources." '[56] So that, from this too, it is clear that the Lord was supported physically by the care of women as he went around preaching and that they were joined to him as inseparable companions equally with the apostles.

Eventually, indeed, the religion of this hard way of life flourished among women as much as it had among men at the start of the growth of the Church. But then at length the observances of this faith were increased as much in women as in men, in that in the beginning of the growing Church women possessed monastic dwellings of their own just as much as men. So the *Ecclesiastical History* spoke magnificently in praise not only of Philo, most learned of Jews, but also wrote about the Alexandrian church under Mark. It commemorates it among other things in the second book, chapter XVII: 'In

---

[55] I Corinth. 9.5.
[56] Augustine, *The Work of Monks* 4.1, 5.6 (CSEL 41: 538, 540), quoting Luke 8.1–3.

many parts of the world', he says, 'there are men of this kind.' And
after other matters, 'In separate places there is a house dedicated to
prayer which is called *semneion* or "monastery".' Again, later, 'So
they not only understand the simple hymns of old, but they make new
hymns to God singing them in every metre, with exceedingly fine
and smooth-flowing notes.' [57]

[The austere life of men and women in the desert]
Again, having said much about their abstinence and the offices of
divine worship, he adds: 'But alongside the men whom we speak of,
there are also women, among whom many are virgins of great age
guarding the integrity and chastity of the body, not for any necessity
but through devotion. While they are eager to consecrate not only the
soul, but also the body, to intercourse with the divine word, they
bring the unworthy vessel freed from lust and prepared for receiving
wisdom. Giving up their mortal childbearing they sought a sacred
and immortal offspring through which succeeding generations
should not be subject to corrupting mortality.' [58]
    Again, in the same place following Philo, he also writes
concerning their convents that the men indeed assemble separately
from the women in these places; and that while they commit themselves to the study of wisdom, they create for themselves not only a
soul but also a body, considering it unworthy for them to hand over a
vessel, prepared for receiving wisdom, to lust, and to waste it on
mortal children; and he writes that they perform the vigils as is
customary with us. This is consequently in praise of Christian philosophy, namely of the special claim of the monastic life, which, the
Tripartite History records, has been taken up by women no less than
by men. For it says thus in Book I, chapter XI: 'The leader of this
finest of philosophies was indeed, as certain people say, Elijah the
prophet, also John the Baptist. Philo the Pythagorean refers to wise
men of the Hebrews from all around in his days, in a certain estate
placed round the pool of Mary set on a hill. John instituted that poor
dwelling of theirs and their food and manner of living such as we
now see among Egyptian monks. Philo wrote that they did not taste
food before sunset; they always abstained from wine and from creatures with blood; their food was bread and salt and hyssop and their

[57] Eusebius, *Ecclesiastical History* 2.17, trans. Rufinus, Corpus Berolinense 9.1: 145, 149.
[58] Ibid. 2.17, Corpus Berolinense 9.1: 151.

drink was water. Older women lived with them as virgins from a natural love of wisdom, abstaining out of free will from marriage.[59] Again, Jerome also says in *The Book of Famous Men*, chapter VII, writing thus in praise of Mark and the Church: 'He, the first to proclaim Christ at Alexandria, established the Church with such learning and abstemiousness of life, that he moved all followers of Christ to follow his example. Finally, Philo, most fluent of Jews, seeing the first church at Alexandria, and still acting as a Jew, wrote a book as though in praise of his own people about their way of life; and that Luke tells how all the believers lived life in common in Jerusalem; thus he handed on to remembrance what he learnt was done at Alexandria under the teacher Mark.'[60] Again, in chapter XI: 'Philo of Alexandria, Jew by birth, priest by descent, is placed by us on that account among religious writers since, writing a book about the first church of Mark the Evangelist at Alexandria, he turned it into praise of our people. He not only spoke of those people there, but also reported that there were others in many provinces, and he called their huts monasteries.'[61]

From this it appears that the church of believers in Christ in the beginning was such as monks now seek to imitate; they hold that nothing should be personal to anyone, none should be rich among them, no one poor; their patrimony should be shared with the poor. There was to be time for prayer and psalms, for instruction, for discussion. Such were the people whom Luke reports to have been the original believers in Jerusalem.

[Music and prophecy among women]
Now if we go back to the old histories, we shall find there that women were not segregated from men in those things which belong to God or in the particularity of any religious practice, no matter in what unique religious way they lived. The sacred histories tell that they not only sang the holy canticles like men, but also composed them. For not only men, but women too, sang to the Lord the first song of the liberation of the people of Israel, and hence they gain authority for celebrating divine office in church. For thus it is written: 'And Mary the prophetess, the sister of Aaron, took a timbrel in her hand; and all the women went out after her with

---

[59] Cassiodorus, *The Tripartite History* 1.11.7 (CSEL 71: 35).
[60] Jerome, *Book of Famous Men* 7, Texte und Untersuchungen 14.1a: 12.
[61] Ibid. 11, Texte und Untersuchungen 14.1a: 14.

timbrels and with dancing. And Mary answered them, "Let us sing to the Lord for he has triumphed gloriously etc." '[62] And certainly it is not Moses the prophet who is remembered there, nor is he said to have sung as Mary did, nor are the men said to have the timbrels and song like the women. Therefore when Mary the prophetess is reported as singing, it appears that she proclaimed this song, not chanting or reciting, but prophesying. For when she is described as singing with the others it is clear that they sing harmoniously and in concord. For they sang not only with the voice but with timbrel and in the dance; it not only made known their own great devotion but also, in truth, it faithfully expresses in a mystical way the form of holy singing in monastic communities. The psalmist, too, exhorts us to this, saying, 'Praise him with timbrel and dance',[63] that is, in the mortification of the flesh and that concord of love about which it is written: 'And the multitude of them that believed were of one heart and of one soul.'[64] Nor is there anything lacking to the mystery since it is reported that they went out to sing songs in which are figured the joys of the contemplative soul, which dedicates itself to heavenly things as though it deserts the castle of its earthly habitation and from the intimate joys of its contemplation releases a spiritual hymn of the highest exaltation to the Lord. We have there the songs of Deborah and Anna[65] too, not least those of Judith the widow,[66] likewise in the gospel, of Mary, the Mother of God.[67] And, of course, Hannah offering her little son Samuel at the tabernacle of the Lord[68] gave authority for receiving children in the monasteries. From this Isidore, writing to the brothers forming the hermitage of Honorian, chapter V: 'Whoever', he says, 'shall have been sent away by his natural parents to a monastery shall know that he is to stay there for ever. For Hannah offered the boy Samuel to God and he remained in the service of the temple to which he had been engaged by his mother and where he was appointed there he served.'[69]

[62] Exod. 15.21.
[63] Ps. 150.4.
[64] Acts 4.32.
[65] I Sam. 2.1–10.
[66] Judith 16.2–21.
[67] Luke 1.46–55.
[68] I Sam. 1.24–28
[69] I Sam. 2.11. Quoted by Smaragdus, *Commentary on the Rule of St Benedict* 59 (PL 102: 905AB) and Gratian, *Decretum* 2.20.1.4.

[Women sharing in religious observance]

And it is agreed that the daughters of Aaron equally with their brothers held to the holy places and the hereditary lot of Levi so that here too God had established their means of maintenance. Thus it is written in the book of Numbers speaking to Aaron: 'All that the children of Israel set aside for the Lord from the holy things I give to you and to your sons and daughters by perpetual right.'[70] From this the religious observance of women does not appear to be made separate from the rule of clerics. It is clear that the women are joined to the men by name since in fact we call them as much deaconesses as deacons as though we see the tribe of Levi in each of them and recognize them as Levites.[71] In the very same book we have that great vow and consecration of the Nazarenes to the Lord established as well for women as for men, when the Lord himself speaks to Moses: 'Speak to the children of Israel and say to them: "When either man or woman shall make a vow to be sanctified and they wish to consecrate themselves to the Lord, they shall separate themselves from wine and strong drink, neither shall they drink any liquor of grapes, nor eat moist grapes, or dried. All the days of their separation shall they eat nothing that is made of the vine, from the kernels even to the husk. . . ." '[72]

Indeed I am certain that the women were sharers in this religious observance when they were keeping watch at the door of the tabernacle, and from their mirrors Moses made a bronze basin from which Aaron and his sons were washed; as it is written: 'And he made a basin of brass, and the foot of it of brass, of the looking-glasses of the women assembling, who served at the door of the tabernacle of the congregation.'[73] The fervour of their great devotion is carefully depicted; even when the tabernacle was closed, they kept close to its doors, observing the watch of the holy vigils, even passing that night in prayer and not ceasing to be occupied in the divine service when the men were silent. It is recorded that the tabernacle was closed to

---

[70] I Sam. 1.24–28

[71] Levites were descendants of the tribe of Levi who had remained faithful to God when other tribes worshipped the Golden Calf (Ex. 32.1–29). They were supported by tithes, and it was their duty to carry the Ark of the Covenant and to assist the priests. Deacons were the Christian equivalent of the Levites, assisting the priest but not themselves celebrating the Eucharist.

[72] Numbers 6.1–5.

[73] Ex. 30.18–19, 38.8; cf. Gregory, *Homilies on the Gospels* 17.10 (PL 76: 1143 C).

them; it is a life suited to penitents who separate themselves from others so that they may afflict themselves the more harshly with penitential laments. Certainly this is asserted to be a life of monastic calling, for that order is said to be nothing other than a form of self-denying penitence. In truth the tabernacle at whose entrance they kept watch is to be understood mystically; the apostle wrote of it to the Hebrews: 'We have an altar from which those who serve the tabernacle have no right to eat',[74] that is: those who devote themselves to voluptuous indulgence in their body, yet serve in it as in a travelling camp, are not worthy to share in the service of the altar.[75]

For indeed, the entrance of the tabernacle is the end of the present life when the soul goes hence from the body and enters on its future life. At this entrance those who are full of apprehension about the departure from this life and the entrance to the future are waiting, and they set their departure in order by penitence, so that they may be worthy to enter. And concerning this, the prayer of the psalmist at the daily entering and leaving of the holy church is: 'The Lord preserve thy coming in and thy going out.'[76] For then at the same time he preserves our coming in and our going out. When we are going hence, now purged through penitence, he straightway leads us in there. But it is well that he named 'entrance' before 'exit', paying attention not only to due order but to deserts, since the departure of this mortal life is in sorrow, but the entrance to eternal life is the greatest delight. Their mirrors are indeed those corporeal acts from which the shame and the comeliness of the soul is discerned just as the character of a human face is from a mirror. From these mirrors of theirs is formed the basin in which Aaron and his sons wash themselves. By the deeds of saintly women and such constancy towards God shown by the weaker gender, they forcefully rebuke the negligence of bishops and priests and in particular stir them to tears of conscience. And if they show concern as they ought, the deeds of these women prepare the pardon by which the men are cleansed. Certainly the blessed Gregory prepared the basin of pity from these

---

[74] Hebrews 13.10.

[75] 'As in a travelling camp' obviously refers to the journey in the wilderness, and the concept of human life as a journey is a commonplace of religious imagery, but there may also be the idea that those who use their body for voluptuous pleasure are like someone without a sense of responsibility for the place where he lives. The relationship with Heb. 13.10 is obscure since that implies that to receive the grace of Christ is better than to observe strict dietary laws.

[76] Ps. 121.8.

mirrors when, marvelling at the virtue of holy women and the victory in martyrdom of the weaker gender, he uttered a groan and asked, 'What are bearded men to be called when tender girls endure so much for Christ, and the weaker gender rejoices exceedingly in such bodily contest that we shall so often know by the twin crowns of virginity and martyrdom that their gender prevails.'[77]

[Anna and Simeon]
Then I do not doubt that the blessed Anna belongs with these women watching, as I have said, at the entrance to the tabernacle, and who now, like Nazarites, have consecrated their widowhood to their Lord.[78] Anna, unmarried for the sake of the Lord of the Nazarites, was worthy, like holy Simeon, to take up the Lord Jesus Christ in the temple and, as many a prophet did, to recognize him in the same hour as Simeon, to show him in person and to proclaim him publicly. The evangelist continued the more carefully in her praise and said: 'And there was one Anna, a prophetess, the daughter of Phanuel of the tribe of Aser: she was of a great age and had lived with her husband for seven years from the days of her virginity. And she was a widow of about eighty-four years who never left the temple but served God with fasting and prayers night and day. And, coming in at that moment, she also gave thanks to the Lord and spoke of him to all those that looked forward to the deliverance of Jerusalem.'[79] Take note of the several things that are said and consider carefully how keen the evangelist was in praise of this widow and with what commendation he lauded her excellence. For she was accustomed to feel gratitude for this gift of prophecy, and her father and tribe, and the seven years she had passed with a husband, the long lasting time of holy widowhood in which she bound herself to the Lord, and her assiduous attendance in the temple, her urgency in fasting and prayer, and her declaration of praise which she offered to the Lord, and her public prophesying concerning the promise and birth of the Saviour; all these the evangelist had already zealously expressed. Simeon indeed, the evangelist had already commended as superior according to righteousness not according to prophecy; neither did he

---

[77] Gregory, *Homilies on the Gospels* 11.3 (PL 76: 1116A).

[78] Nazarite: a Jew who took a vow for life or for any shorter time to abstain from the grape and its products, from touching a dead body, and from cutting his/her hair. At the end of the period of the vow the hair was cut and presented with very generous offerings in the temple.

[79] Luke 2.36–38.

record so great a power of continence and abstinence in Simeon, nor that he had submitted to holy obedience, nor did he add anything about his preaching to others.[80]

[The place of widows in the Church]
Those true widows about whom the apostle wrote in his letter to Timothy shared this undertaking, and purpose: 'Honour widows that are widows indeed', he said.[81] And again, 'Now she that is a widow indeed, and desolate, trusts in God and continues in supplication and prayer night and day';[82] 'Remind them of all this, too, so that their lives may be blameless',[83] and again, 'If any of the faithful have widows, let them help them, and not let the church be charged so that it may support those that are widows indeed.'[84] He speaks of true widows who have not dishonoured their widowhood with second marriages and who consecrate themselves, persevering in the Lord more by devotion than by necessity. He calls those desolate who renounce everything so that they retain no help of worldly comfort and have no one to take responsibility for them. He counsels that they should be treated with respect and considers that they should be supported as though by their own gifts to Christ, their spouse. From these he carefully describes those who are fit to be chosen for the office of deacon saying: 'Let not a widow be taken into the number under sixty years old, having been the wife of one man, well reported for good works; if she has brought up children, if she has lodged strangers, if she has washed the saints' feet, if she has relieved the afflicted, if she has diligently followed every good work. But avoid the younger widows.'[85]

[Deaconesses]
The blessed Jerome expounds this; 'Avoid', he says, 'setting them in the office of deacon lest they give a bad example instead of a good.' For if, for example, younger women are chosen for this, those who are more inclined to temptation and lighter by nature, not prudent through the experience of a long life, offer a bad example to those to

[80] Luke 2.25–35.
[81] I Tim. 5.3.
[82] I Tim. 5.5.
[83] 1 Tim. 5.7.
[84] 1 Tim. 5.16.
[85] I Tim. 5.9–11.

whom, above all, they ought to give a good one.[86] This bad example in younger widows is openly discussed since the apostle has already stated it with sure proofs and moreover offered further advice when he began: 'But avoid young widows.'[87] He straightway sets down the reason for this matter and the remedy he advises, saying, 'If their natural desires get stronger than their dedication to Christ they want to marry; earning damnation because they have cast off their first faith. And besides they learn to be idle, wandering about from house to house; and not only idle but tattlers also and busybodies, speaking things which they ought not to. I will therefore that the younger women marry, bear children, guide the house, give no occasion to the Adversary to speak reproachfully.'[88]

The blessed Gregory also followed the precaution of the apostle, that is about selecting deaconesses. He writes in these words to Maximus, the bishop of Syracuse: 'We strongly forbid young abbesses. Do not let your brotherhood permit any bishop to veil any but virgins of sixty years whose life and conduct justify it.'[89] For those we now call 'abbesses' were in former times called 'deaconesses', as though they were servants rather than mothers.[90] For 'deacon' means 'servant', because they were thought of as doing service rather than preaching, just as the Lord himself instituted by example and words, saying: 'But he that is greatest among you shall be your Servant',[91] and again: 'For who is greater, he that reclines or he that serves? But I am among you as one that serves',[92] and elsewhere, 'Even as the Son of Man came not to be served but to serve.'[93] For this reason, Jerome dared, in no small degree, to find fault with this name of abbot, in which he knew many then took pride, on the authority of the Lord himself. Indeed when expounding the very place where it is written in the Epistle to the Galatians, 'Crying, Abba, Father':[94] 'Abba (he says) is Hebrew with the same meaning as

[86] In fact Pelagius, *Expositions of The Thirteen Epistles of St Paul II*, ed. A. Souter (Cambridge: Cambridge University Press 1926), p. 495 (PL 30: 926C).
[87] I Tim. 5.11.
[88] I Tim. 5.11–14.
[89] Gregory, *Letters* 4.11 (CCSL 140: 229).
[90] Abelard makes a similar remark in his Commentary on Romans 4 (16.2): 'What antiquity called diaconesses, namely servants, we now call abbesses, namely mothers.' (CCCM 11: 327).
[91] Matt. 23.11.
[92] Luke 22.27.
[93] Matt. 20.28.
[94] Gal. 4.6.

father . . . but since abba means father in Hebrew and Syrian, and the Lord instructs in the Gospel[95] that no one should be called Father but God, I do not know by what licence we call some men in monasteries by this name, or are willing to be called by this name ourselves. And certainly he teaches them that we are not to swear at all; if we do not swear all, neither ought we to call anyone Father. If we conclude otherwise about the Father, we are compelled to feel otherwise about swearing.'[96]

[Phoebe, a deaconess from Cenchrea]
It is certainly clear that Phoebe, whom the apostle earnestly commended, was one of the deaconesses. Praying for her, he said: 'I commend to you our sister Phoebe who is a servant of the church which is at Cenchrea that you receive her for the Lord's sake as befits saints, and that you help her with anything she needs; for she has looked after many.'[97] In expounding this passage, Cassiodorus, as well as Claudius, states that she was a deaconess of that church. Cassiodorus: 'It indicates (he says) that she was a deaconess of the Mother Church which to this day is conducted in Greek regions on military lines.' Claudius: 'In this passage he teaches that even women were established in the service of the Church with apostolic authority. Phoebe was placed in this position in the church at Cenchrea. The apostle honoured her with great praise and commendation.'[98]

[The qualifications of a deaconess]
When he was writing such things to Timothy, he gathered together the deacons and ordered their life with instructions of the same kind. Since he was ordering the ranks of ministers of the church, when he came down from the bishop to the deacons, he said, 'Likewise the deacons must be grave, not double-tongued, not given to much wine, or squalid greed for money: holding the mystery of the faith in a pure conscience. And let them also first be tested; then let them perform the office of a deacon (when they are found blameless). Even so,

[95] Matt. 23.9.
[96] Jerome, *Commentary on Galatians* 2 (PL 26: 400AB).
[97] Rom. 16.1–2.
[98] Cassiodorus, probably from a lost commentary on Romans, also quoted by Abelard in his *Commentary on Romans* 4 (16.2) (CCCM 11: 327) and in his Sermon 31 (PL 178: 572B). In the same passage Abelard quotes from an unpublished commentary on Romans by Claudius of Turin.

their wives must be grave, not slanderers, sober, faithful in all things. Let the deacons be the husband of one wife, ruling their children and their own houses well. For they that have used the office of a deacon will earn a high standing for themselves and be rewarded with great assurance in the faith which is in Christ Jesus.'[99] And so what he says there about deacons, 'not double-tongued', in the same manner he says about deaconesses: 'not slanderers'. What he said there – 'not given to much wine' – he says in the same way about deaconesses: 'sober'. Indeed he expresses briefly all the other things that follow, saying, 'faithful in all things'. And he forbids both bishops and deacons to have two wives; in the same way he decrees that deaconesses should be the wife of one husband, as we recall above. 'Let not a widow be taken into the number under sixty years old, having been the wife of one man. Well reported of for good works; if she brought up children, if she lodged strangers, if she washed the saints' feet, if she relieved the afflicted, if she diligently followed every good work. But avoid the younger widows.'[100]

It is easy to recognize, from the previously mentioned arrangement for both bishops and deacons, how the apostle was even more scrupulous in the description and instruction of deaconesses. For certainly, when he says, 'well reported for good works' and 'if she lodged strangers', he does not mention this with regard to deacons. But when he adds, 'if she washed the saints' feet, if she relieved the afflicted etc.', he is silent as regards the bishops as well as the priests. And he says of both the bishops and the deacons too: 'being found blameless', but also says that: 'they must be known for their good works'.[101] For he is prudently careful about the maturity of their years so that they should have authority in all matters saying, 'not less than sixty years', and they are reverenced not only for their way of life, but also for the length of life demonstrated in them. Thus it is admitted that the Lord loved John most, but he put Peter, being the elder, in charge of both John and the others.[102] Naturally, they were all less offended that the eldest had been placed at their head than the youngest and we submit more freely to one who has been put first not only by his life but by nature and the passage of time.

Hence Jerome too, in the beginning of *Against Jovinian* when he reminds us of Peter's preaching: 'One (he says) was chosen so that

---

99   I Tim. 3.8–13.
100   I Tim. 5.9–11.
101   I Tim. 5.10.
102   Matt. 16.16–19.

when the leader had been put in authority, the opportunity for schism would be removed. But why was John not chosen? It was put down to his age, because Peter was the elder; one still an adolescent and almost a boy should not be preferred to men of full age, and the good master who was bound to keep his disciples from any opportunity for quarrels should not be seen to offer a cause for envy of the youth whom he loved.'[103] As is written in the *Lives of the Fathers*, the abbot carefully considered this when he took the primacy from a younger brother who had come first to a religious way of life but passed it to an elder because he took precedence over the former by age.[104] He feared lest even the blood brother should be offended if the younger were to be put ahead of himself. He recorded that the apostles were offended about two of their number when their mother intervened before Christ and they appeared to try to obtain a particular advantage, particularly when one of these two was younger than the other apostles; he was indeed the very John of whom we were lately speaking.

The apostle's care was not only most watchful in regulating deaconesses but it is clear that in general he proceeded zealously towards the widows of holy calling so that he removed every possibility of temptation. For when he previously said: 'Honour widows that are widows indeed, but if any widow have children or grandchildren let them learn first to show piety at home and to requite their parents';[105] he afterwards added: 'But if any does not provide for his own and especially for those of his own house, he has denied the faith, and is worse than an infidel.'[106] Now in these words he provides at the same time for the obligations of humanity and the purposes of religion, lest under cover of religion the young should be left unprovided for and human compassion towards the needy should disturb the holy intentions of the widow and compel her to look back and, not infrequently, lead her to sacrilege and to giving something to her family by which she defrauds the community. Thus the necessary counsel presents itself: before entering on true widowhood and transferring themselves to complete holy obedience, those women who are involved in household cares should requite their parents' care of them so that, as they were brought up by them, so they may provide for their own descendants by the same law.

[103] Jerome, *Against Jovinian* 1.26 (PL 23: 258).
[104] *Lives of the Fathers* 10.113 (PL 73: 932D).
[105] I Tim. 5.3–4.
[106] I Tim. 5.16.

[The honour given to widows]
Even increasing the religious duties of widows he advises them to be immediate in prayers and supplications day and night. Yet even he is greatly concerned by their needs. 'If any of the faithful have widows', he says, 'let them relieve them, and let not the Church be charged; that it may relieve those that are widows indeed.'[107] As if he said plainly: 'If anyone who is a widow has servants such as are able to provide necessities to her from their own resources, let them provide for this, so that the public expense of the Church may be sufficient to maintain the others.' Indeed he makes his opinion plain; if anyone is unyielding towards his own widow in this way, he should be compelled to this duty by the authority of the apostle.

He was not only providing for their needs, but also for their honour: 'Honour', he says, 'widows that are widows indeed.'[108] Such indeed we believe them to have been; one of them he (Paul) calls 'mother' and the other John the Evangelist calls 'lady' out of respect for her holy vows. 'Salute Rufus', said Paul, writing to the Romans, 'chosen in the Lord, and his mother and mine.'[109] John too, in the second epistle that he wrote: 'The Elder unto the elect lady and her children etc.'[110] From her he even asked that she would love him; he added below, 'And now I beseech thee, lady, that we love one another.'[111] Relying also on his authority, the blessed Jerome, writing to the virgin Eustochium of your profession, did not blush to call her 'lady'. He immediately added, as indeed he ought: 'On this account I call you my lady Eustochium. For I ought to call the bride of my Lord, lady, etc.' And a little later, in the same epistle, placing the special claim of this holy intention above all earthly happiness in glory, he said: 'I do not wish you to keep company with married women; I do not wish you to visit the nobles' houses; I do not wish you to see frequently what you despised when you chose to remain a virgin. If desire for public greeting hastens you to the emperor's wife, why do you do injustice to your own husband? Why do you hurry to marriage to a man when you are the bride of God? Learn heavenly pride in this matter; know that you are better than they.'[112]

Writing to the virgin dedicated to God about virgins consecrated

---

[107] I Tim. 5.16.
[108] I Tim. 5.3.
[109] Rom. 16.13.
[110] II John 1.1.
[111] II John 1.5.
[112] Jerome, Letter 22.2 (CSEL 54: 145).

to God, what blessedness they have in heaven and what honour on earth, he began thus, saying: 'We are taught by the custom of the Church, apart from the evidence of Holy Scripture, what blessedness holy virginity will possess in heaven. By this we learn particularly that merit belongs to those whose dedication is spiritual, for when each one of the multitude of believers receives equal gifts of grace and all rejoice in the blessings of the sacraments, these women possess something of their own beyond others, when from that holy and immaculate flock of the Church some are chosen by the Holy Spirit as holier and purer sacrifices on account of the merit of their desires and are offered to the altar of God by the high priest.' Again: 'virginity therefore possesses . . . what others have not . . . and also gains special grace and rejoices, as I have said, in its own special privilege of consecration.'[113]

Certainly, the consecration of virgins is not allowed to be celebrated (except in case of urgent danger of death) at any other time than at Epiphany and white Easter and on the nativities of the apostles: only by the chief priest, that is the bishop, are nuns themselves consecrated and the veils to be placed on their holy heads. Monks, however, although they are of the same profession and order and a more worthy gender, are allowed, even if they are virgins, to receive benediction and to receive from the abbot what is their proper garment, that is the cowl, on any day. Priests also, and the other lower ranks of clerics are always to be ordained during the fasts of the Four Seasons, and bishops on every Sunday.[114] But how much more precious is the consecration of virgins, so much the rarer that it claims for itself the joyful celebration of special ceremonies. The universal Church, to be sure, rejoices more at their miraculous virtue, as the psalmist too foretold in these words: 'The virgin and her companions that follow her shall be brought to you', and again, 'With gladness and rejoicing they shall be brought: they shall enter the king's palace.'[115] Matthew, both apostle and evangelist, is said to have composed and written a form of consecration for women, as it is read in his passion where it is recorded that he lay dead, a martyr for their consecration and the defence of their virgin resolution.[116]

---

[113] A treatise often attributed to Jerome, but in fact by Pelagius, *In Praise of Virgins* (PL 30: 168).

[114] Fasts of the Four Seasons: four groups of three-day fasts through the year, commonly known as Ember Days.

[115] Ps. 44.15–16.

[116] *Acts of St Matthew* 2.19, *Acta Sanctorum*, Sept. VI: 224.

But the apostles have left us no written form of consecration either for priests or monks.

[The weakness and strength of women]
Moreover, the religious life of women alone is marked out with the name of sanctity when they are called *sanctimoniales* from *sanctimonia*, that is, 'sanctity'. Because the female gender is the weaker, their strength is more pleasing to God and is more perfect according to the word of God himself by which he encouraged the weakness of the apostle to the crown of victory, saying: 'My grace is enough for you, for my strength is at its best in weakness.'[117] And speaking to the members of his body, that is the Church, through the same apostle, he especially commended the honour of the weaker members and he added in the same epistle (that is the first to the Corinthians): 'What is more, it is precisely those parts of the body that seem to be the weakest which are the indispensable ones and it is the least honourable parts of the body that we clothe with the greatest care. So our more improper parts get decorated in a way that our more proper parts do not need. God has arranged the body so that more dignity is given to the parts which are without it, and so that there may not be disagreements inside the body, but that each part may be equally concerned for all the others.'[118]

But who could honestly have said anywhere that it was by divine grace that woman was filled with these qualities, as if he had made her in addition to the weakness of her woman's gender as guilty as she was feebler? Look round at the different ranks in this gender, not only virgins and widows, but even those abominations of harlots, and you will see the grace of Christ more generous in them as in the word of the Lord and the apostle: 'So the last shall be first and the first last',[119] and 'However great the number of sins committed, grace was even greater.'[120] Indeed if we trace the benefits of this divine grace and the honour shown to women from the creation of the world, we at once find that the creation of woman excelled by a certain dignity, since it was clearly in paradise. Man was created outside paradise, so that, by this, women are particularly reminded that paradise was their natural homeland and so it is more fitting for them to lead the chaste life of paradise. Whence Ambrose in his book *About Paradise*: 'And

<hr>

117 II Cor. 12.9.
118 I Cor. 12.22–25.
119 Matt. 20.16.
120 Rom. 5.20.

God saw (he says) the man whom he had made and placed him in paradise. You see how he who existed was taken . . . and he placed him in paradise. . . . Notice that because man was made outside paradise and woman inside . . . the man who was better was found in a lower place and she who was made in a better place is perceived to be inferior.'[121]

[Heroic women]
Before the Lord restored Eve, the source of all evil, in Mary he renewed Adam in Christ and since sin began in a woman, so grace began in a woman and the special claim of virginity grew again. But already the pattern for widows and virgins of holy obligation is shown in Anna and Mary, before examples of monastic living are set before men in John and the apostles. But if, after Eve, we look at the virtue of Deborah, Judith, Esther, we bring no small sense of shame to the strength of the manly gender. Deborah, because she was a judge of the Lord's people, gave battle when the strength of the people was lacking and triumphed powerfully when the enemy was defeated and the people of the Lord were set free.[122] Judith, unarmed, attacked a terrible army with her handmaid; alone and single-handed cut off Holofernes' head with his own sword and scattered the whole army and liberated her desperate people.[123] Esther, taking courage in secret, against the very decree of the law married a Gentile king, prevailed against the plot of the wicked Haman and the cruel ordinance of the king, and changed the settled decision of the royal deliberations to the opposite in a moment of time. It is ascribed to David's valour that he attacked Goliath with sling and stone and defeated him. Judith the widow went to the hostile army without sling or stone; she was to fight without any help of weapons. Esther freed her people with one word alone, and when judgement was turned against her enemies they ran into the snare which they themselves had laid. Indeed the memory of her famous deed deserves to be held by the Jews with solemn rejoicing every year, because never was anything done by any man soever which gained such glory.[124]

Who does not marvel at the incomparable courage of the mother of seven sons, captured with their mother, as the history of the

---

121   Ambrose, *About Paradise* 4.24 (CSEL 32.1: 280).
122   Judges 4.4.
123   Judith 13.5; see also Osbert of Clare's letter to Adelidis (I, pp. 31–9 above).
124   See Esther 8. The Jewish Festival of Purim, held in the spring, commemorates the deliverance brought about by Esther from massacre by the Persians.

Maccabees tells, when the impious king Antiochus tried in vain to force them to eat the flesh of pigs against the law.[125] And she, forgetful of her natural maternal love and untouched by human affections and having nothing before her eyes but the Lord, sent her children with so many exhortations to their crown and herself triumphed in so many martyrdoms, and finally ended in her own martyrdom. If we consider the whole sequence of the Old Testament, what shall we be able to compare with the constancy of this woman? He who tempted the blessed Job to the limits so violently, when he considered the weakness of human nature in the face of death, said, 'Skin for skin, a man will give all that he has for his life.'[126] We all naturally feel such horror of the grip of death that often for the protection of one member we expose another and to save this life we fear no injury.[127] In truth, this woman endured the loss not only of her possessions but her own life and those of her sons, lest she should incur the violation of a single law. What, I ask, is that sin to which she was driven? Was she compelled to renounce God or give incense to idols? Nothing, I say, was demanded of them except to eat the meat which the law forbade them.

O brothers and fellow monks who every day shamelessly gaze with longing at meat, against the instruction of the Rule and your profession, what can you say to the constancy of this woman? Surely you are not so shameless that you are not covered with blushes when you hear this? You must know, brothers, what the Lord said about the Queen of the South when he reproached the unbelievers, 'The Queen of the South shall rise up in judgement with this generation and condemn it.'[128] How much more do you deserve to be reproached in respect of the endurance of this woman who did far more than you, though you are more strictly bound by the vows of your religious profession. For her virtue, tested by such suffering, deserves to gain such privilege in the Church that her martyrdom should have solemn readings and a mass. This was not allowed to any of the ancient saints who died before the coming of the Lord, though in that story of the Maccabees, Eliazar, that venerable old man, is now said, alone of the first of the scribes, to have been crowned by martyrdom for the same cause.[129]

125 II Macc. 7.
126 Job 2.4.
127 See Gregory, *Moralia In Job* 3.4 (CCSL 143: 117).
128 Matt. 12.42; Luke 11.31.
129 II Macc. 6.18–31.

But since, as we have said, the feminine gender is weaker, its courage is so much the more acceptable to God and more worthy of honour. A martyrdom which did not differ from the woman's was not in any way worthy to be handed down to posterity in a feast day, as if it should not be considered any great thing; if the gender was stronger, it endured more strongly. Because of this Scripture breaks out in praise of that woman and says, 'But above all was the mother marvellous and worthy of honourable memory, for when she looked on seven sons perishing within the space of one day, she bore the sight with a good courage for the hopes that she had set in the Lord.'[130]

[Jephtha's daughter]
Who does not think that the only daughter of Jephtha should be included in the praise of virgins?[131] Lest her father should be held guilty about what might be called a foolish vow, and the gift of God's grace be defrauded of the promised sacrifice, she guided her father's hand to her own throat. What, I ask, would she have done in the suffering of martyrdom if she had, by chance, been compelled by infidels to apostatize by denying God? If she was questioned about Christ, would she have said with him who was already the first of the apostles, 'I do not know him?'[132]

She was sent away free for two months by her father; when they had passed, she returned to be killed by her father. Of her own will she threw herself on death and invited it rather than feared it. She was punished for her father's foolish vow and, a great lover of faithfulness, she redeemed her father's falsehood. How much more would she abhor in herself the fault which she did not condemn in her father! How great is the devotion of this virgin for her earthly as for her heavenly father, since she determined by her death to free the one from falsehood and to keep her promise to the other. It was deservedly that the great courage of this maiden was found worthy to have a special claim to bring it about that, year by year, the daughters of Israel came together with solemn hymns, performing her virgin funeral rites and grieving over the virgin's sufferings, to mourn together with pious lamentations.[133]

130 II Macc. 7.20.
131 Judges 11.30.
132 Luke 22.57.
133 Judges 11.39–40.

[The perfect woman: the mother of the incarnate Lord]
But so that we may leave aside all the other matters, what would be so needful for our redemption and the salvation of the whole world as the female gender which bore the Saviour himself for us? And that woman was the first to claim that signal honour when she dared to burst in and amazed the blessed Hilarion saying to him, 'Why do you turn your eyes away? What questions do you try to escape? Do not see me as a wretch but as a woman. This gender bore the Saviour.'[134] What glory can be compared to this; that one of that gender should attain to be the mother of God? No doubt our Redeemer could, if he wished, have taken on a body from a man, just as it was his will to make the first woman from the body of a man.[135] But the unique grace of his humility brought honour to the weaker gender. He might have been born from another more honoured part of a woman's body than are the rest of men who are born from the vilest part, the same part through which they were conceived.[136] But to the incomparable honour of the weaker body he consecrated the female genitals far more highly by his birth than he had done the male's by circumcision. But as I now pass over this matchless honour of virgins, it is pleasant to turn our pen, as intended, to the rest of women too. Notice, then, that the coming of Christ brought to Elisabeth, the married woman, as much grace as it gave to the widow Anna. Mistrust through lack of faith kept Zachariah, Elizabeth's husband and the great priest of God, unable to speak; while at the invitation and salutation of Mary, Elizabeth was herself straightway filled with the Holy Spirit and felt her infant rejoicing in her womb, and being the first to proclaim a prophecy concerning that perfect conception of Mary's, she stood forth as more than a prophet.[137] For she proclaimed a virgin's conception in that place and she stirred the Mother of God herself to praise the Lord for this.[138] For the gift of prophecy is fully seen in Elisabeth: to recognize without hesitation in the conception of the Son of God a more excellent gift than through John to proclaim him once born. So as we call Mary Magdalene the prophet, the apostle of the apostles, we do not hesitate to call the

---

134 Jerome, *Life of St Hilarion* 13 (PL 23: 34C).
135 See Augustine, *Sermon* 51.2 (PL 38: 34).
136 See Augustine, *On the Literal Interpretation of Genesis* 9.16.30 (CSEL 28.3.2: 290).
137 Luke 1.5–45.
138 See Luke 1.20 for Zachariah's dumbness and Luke 1.46 for Mary's hymn of praise at her conception, the *Magnificat*.

blessed widow Anna, about whom we have written above at greater
length the prophet of the prophets.[139]

[Women prophets]
But if we extend this gift of prophecy as far as the Gentiles, the
prophetess Sybilla comes in the midst and presents those things that
were revealed to her about Christ.[140] With her, if we speak of
prophets of the whole world (even including Isaiah himself who, as
Jerome declares, ought to be called evangelist as much as prophet),
we shall see that in this gift too, women far surpass men.[141]
Concerning them, Augustine, presenting his testimony against five
heresies, says: 'Let us hear what the true prophet Sybilla says of them
concerning this: "God", she says, "has given another to faithful men
to worship. . . ." Again . . . "Know that your Lord is the Son of God."
In another place she calls the Son of God an adviser, that is counsellor or counsel. And the prophet says, "They shall call his name
wonderful counsellor." '[142] Again, Father Augustine says the same in
the eighteenth book of *The City of God*: 'At that time (he says) some
claimed that the Erythraean Sibyl (whom indeed some claimed rather
to be of Cumae) had prophesied . . . and there are twenty-seven lines
of hers . . . which . . . as someone interpreted them in Latin verses,
contain this:

> As a sign of judgement, the earth is damp with sweat
> The king who will be through the ages, comes from heaven.
> It is plain to see that he is present in the flesh
> So that he may judge the world etc.

In fact, the first letters of these lines in Greek when joined together
form: Jesus Christ, Son of God, Saviour. Lactantius, indeed, adduces
the prophecies of the Sibyl concerning Christ: "Afterwards he will
come", he says, "into the hands of infidels, they will give . . . blows to

139 Jerome describes the women who witnessed the resurrection as apostles of the
apostles, *Commentary on the Lesser Prophets*, In Sophoniam Prol. (CCSL 76A:
655). For Anna, see p. 68 above.
140 The Sibylline books contained prophecies and oracles made in a state of ecstasy
by priestesses (Sibyls) under the influence of a god (generally Apollo) at
various places in the world, amongst them Erythrae and Cumae. Jewish imita-
tions arose from the second century BC, and Christian in the second to fourth
centuries AD. They were much consulted by Lactantius and Augustine; for their
twelfth-century reputation, see Peter Dronke, *Hermes and the Sybils* (Cambridge: Cambridge University Press, 1990).
141 Jerome, *Commentary on the Prophet Isaiah*, Prologue (CCSL 73: 465–6).
142 Isa. 9.6.

God with unclean hands, and will spit out poisonous spittle from an unclean mouth, but he will give his sacred back to the blows in silence lest any should discover the word and whence it comes; so that he may speak to the dead and be crowned with the crown of thorns. But they gave him gall for food and vinegar for his thirst, they will offer this [inhospitable] repast. For, foolish race that you are, you have not comprehended your God; you made fools of the minds of men, but you have plaited a crown of thorns; you have mixed the gall. The veil of the temple shall be torn and in the middle of the day it will be night for three hours, and he will submit to sleep and will be dead for three days, and then, returning from the dead, he will be the first to return to the light, shown forth as the beginning of the resurrection." '[143]

If I am not mistaken, the greatest of our poets, Virgil, had certainly heard and marked this prophecy of the Sibyl when in the fourth Eclogue he foretold a marvellous birth under Augustus Caesar in the time when Pollio was consul, when a child would be sent from heaven to earth who would bear the sins of the world and would, as it were, marvellously ordain a new age; he was inspired, as he says himself, by the prophesy of the Cumaean song, that is of the Sibyl who is called Cumaean. For he spoke thus as if he was exhorting everyone to rejoice and to sing about this boy who was to be born, in comparison with which he considers all other subjects base and worthless, saying:

> Sicilian Muse, let us sing a little of greater things
> Not everyone delights in vineyards and common tamarisk.
> The last age of Cumaean song approaches
> Now too the virgin returns and the kingdom of Saturn
> Now a new lineage is sent down from heaven above, etc.[144]

Consider the words of the Sibyl one by one and how completely they sum up the essentials of Christian faith concerning Christ. She has omitted neither the divinity nor the humanity; nor the coming of each, nor the judgement by prophesying or by writing, the one as well as the other; the first judgement by which he was unjustly judged in his passion, and the second in which he will justly judge the world in majesty. And omitting neither his descent to Hell nor the

---

[143] Augustine, *City of God* 18.23 (CCSL 48: 613–14), quoting from Lactantius, *Divine Institutes* 4.18 (CSEL 19.1: 299); cf. Isaiah 53.2; Matt. 27.51; Mark 15.37; Luke 23.45. This passage, and that following, had originally been quoted by Abelard in his *Christian Theology* 1.127–8 (CCCM 12: 126–7).

[144] Virgil, *Eclogue* 4.1.11–14 and 17.

glory of his resurrection, the Sibyl surpassed not only the prophets but even the evangelists themselves who have written very little about his descent.

[The Samaritan woman in the Gospels]
For who would not marvel at his intimate and free conversation in which he condescended so willingly to instruct that solitary woman, a Gentile and a Samaritan, about which the apostles themselves were completely dumbstruck.[145] He was willing to ask a drink from her who was an infidel, despised even by the crowds of men of her own race, yet we know that he never asked any food of anyone. Then the apostles came and offered the food that they had bought, saying, 'Eat, Master.' We do not observe that he took what was offered but, as it were, excusing himself, he made this reply, 'I have food to eat that you do not know of.'[146] He asks a drink from the woman and she, deprecating this favour, said, 'How is it that you, being a Jew, ask drink of me, who am a woman of Samaria, for the Jews have no dealings with the Samaritans?'[147] And again, 'You have nothing to draw with, and the well is deep.'[148] He asked, therefore, from an infidel woman who refused to give it, and he took no care for the food offered by the apostles.

What grace is this, I ask you, which he shows to the weaker gender from whom, as you can see, he asked for the water that gives life to all. What, I ask, unless to suggest clearly that the virtue of women was so much the more welcome to him as their nature is always the weaker. And as she thirsted with longing for salvation so her virtue is agreed to be the more wonderful. Whence, when he asks for a drink from a woman, he wishes to imply that he longs especially to satisfy his great thirst for the salvation of women. Calling this salvation drink and food, he said, 'I have food to eat that you do not know of.'[149] Afterwards, speaking of this food, he added, 'My food is to do the will of my Father'; thus giving a sign that it was particularly the will of the Father in what concerned the salvation of the feebler sex.

We read that the Lord had a private conversation with Nicodemus, the leader of the Jews who came to him secretly, and instructed him

---

145 See John 4.7.
146 John 4.32.
147 John 4.9.
148 John 4.11.
149 John 4.32, 34.

about his salvation, but this conversation had little fruit.[150] But you may see that the Samaritan woman too was filled with the spirit of prophecy; then it is clear that she knew that Christ had already come to the Jews and she prophesied that he would come to the Gentiles when she said, 'I know that Messiah is coming, who is called Christ; when he comes he will tell us all things.'[151] And many hastened out of that city because of what the woman said and they believed in him[152] and kept him there two days, but later he said to his disciples in another place, 'Do not go into the way of the Gentiles and do not enter into any city of the Samaritans.'[153] John himself reports elsewhere that those of the Gentiles who went up to Jerusalem to worship on the feast day said to Christ through Philip and Andrew that they wished to see him.[154] But he records that they were not admitted, nor was so great a fullness of Christ allowed to them when they sought him, as to this Samaritan who was not seeking it; it seems that, through her, his preaching to the Gentiles began, for he not only converted her, but through her, as it is reported, he added many more.[155]

The Magi who were instantaneously illuminated by the star and converted to Christ are not said to have drawn anyone to him by preaching or teaching, but came alone.[156] It is told that the Magi were drawn to Christ, not by his preaching, but only by their presence. From this you see how much grace this woman received from Christ among the Gentiles running before and announcing to the townspeople and proclaiming what she had heard; by this means many of her people were saved.

[Women and Christ in the Gospels]
But if we turn the pages of the Old Testament, or the evangelical Scriptures, we see the greatest blessing refers to those brought back from the dead; and this the divine grace devoted especially to women; no miracle was done except by or for them. First we read that, through Elijah and Elisha, children were brought to life and

---

150   John 4.32, 34.
151   John 4.25.
152   John 4.41.
153   Matt. 10.5.
154   John 12.20–22.
155   John 4.42.
156   Matt. 2.1–12.

given back to their mothers who interceded for them.[157] And the Lord himself restored to life the sons of widows and the daughter of the leader of the synagogue,[158] and Lazarus at the prayers of his sisters;[159] he pours out the blessing of this great miracle chiefly for women. Whence come these words of the apostle to the Hebrews, 'Women received their dead raised to life again',[160] for the girl brought back to life regained her mortal life and the other women who lamented in mourning for their own received their bodies restored to life. From this it is clear how much grace he always showed to women, and gladdened them both in their own return to life and the restoration of their dear ones.

Later, by his own resurrection, he offered most to those to whom, as is said, he first appeared,[161] since even in the crowd following him this gender was seen to be moved by a natural feeling of pity towards the Lord. So Luke remembers that, when men were leading him to crucifixion, women of the people followed him mourning and lamenting. He turned to them and, as though thinking pitifully of them because of their steady devotion to him in the time of his passion, he prophesied their future fate so that they could be aware of it, 'Daughters of Jerusalem, weep not for me, but weep for yourselves, and for your children. For the days are coming, when they shall say, "blessed are the barren, and the wombs that have never borne, etc." '[162] Matthew records that the wife of the unjust judge had previously struggled honestly for his release saying, 'When he was set down on the judgement seat, his wife sent to him saying, Have nothing to do with that just man: for I have been upset all this day because of a dream I had about him.'[163] We read that when he was preaching, only a woman out of the whole crowd raised her voice in such praise of him that she exclaimed that the womb that had borne him was blessed and the breasts that suckled him.[164] She deserved to hear the correction, quick and certain, of her holy recognition,

[157] See I Kings 17.22; II Kings 4.22–37.
[158] Mark 5.42.
[159] John 11.44.
[160] Hebrews 11.35.
[161] Matt. 28.9.
[162] Luke 23.28–29.
[163] Matt. 27.19.
[164] Cf. Luke 11.27.

though it was very true, when he replied to her forthwith, 'Blessed are they that hear the word of God and keep it.'[165]

John alone, among the apostles of Christ, gained the privilege of love that he was called the beloved of the Lord. But John himself wrote of Martha and Mary, 'Now Jesus loved Martha, and her sister, and Lazarus.'[166] That same apostle who, as has been said, through this special privilege of love recorded that he alone was loved by the Lord, gave pre-eminence to women by this honour which he ascribed to no other apostle. For in this honour, when he included even their brother with them, he set them before him, believing that they surpassed him in love.

Finally, to return to faithful or Christian women, it is pleasing to preach with amazement about and to be amazed while preaching about divine pity for the abject condition of common whores. For what was lower than Mary Magdalene or Mary of Egypt in their former status? Yet truly, a little time later heavenly grace raised them to honour and to divine favour. As we have commemorated above, one, indeed, remained in the society of the apostles, the other, as it is written, strove in the suffering of anchorites beyond human courage, so that, in the pattern of life of either kind of cenobite, the virtue of holy women surpasses all. What the Lord said to unbelievers, 'prostitutes will go before you into the kingdom'[167] seems unacceptable to people of good repute, and yet, according to the differences of gender and way of life, the last shall be first and the first last. Finally, who does not know that women seized upon the teaching of Christ and the counsel of the apostles with such fervour for chastity that, in order to preserve their purity of body as well as of mind, they offered themselves as a total sacrifice to God through martyrdom, and, triumphing with a twofold crown, were zealous to follow the Lamb, Bridegroom of virgins, wherever he went.

[The virginity and chastity of women, Gentile and Christian]
We know indeed that the perfection of virtue was rare among men, abundant among women. For we read that not a few of them have had such a zeal for this distinction of the flesh that they did not hesitate to turn their hand against themselves lest they should lose what they had vowed to God, their integrity, and should not come as virgins to

---

[165] Luke 11.28.
[166] John 11.5.
[167] Matt. 21.31.

their virgin Spouse.[168] And he showed that the devotion of holy virgins was so welcome to him that when a crowd of Gentile people were hurrying to the protection of the blessed Agatha her veil was placed before the terrible fire of burning and freed them from burning, of body as much as of soul. We know that no monk's hood was fit for the gift of such a blessing. We have read in fact that the Jordan was divided at the touch of Elijah's cloak,[169] and likewise a path by dry land was given to Elisha, but by the veil of a virgin an immense number of hitherto infidel people were saved in mind and body and thus the way to heaven lay open to these converts. In no small measure this presents favourably the honour of holy women, since they are hallowed in their own words: 'He has espoused me with his ring etc; I am wedded to him etc.'[170] For these are the words of the blessed Agnes in which virgins making their profession are wedded to Christ.

If anyone is eager to know the manner and reputation among the Gentiles of your religious observance and so to draw many examples for your preaching, he may easily understand that not a few institutions of this rule appeared first in the Gentiles, excepting what relates to the substance of your faith. Many things appeared first in them and similarly in the Jews, which the assembled Church preserved from each, but has changed to better things. For who does not know that the Church took from the synagogue the universal orders of clerics from the porter to the bishop, and the very custom of ecclesiastic tonsure by which they are made clerics, and the facts of the four seasons, and the sanctification of unleavened bread, not least the ornaments of priestly vestments, and not a few other sacraments of dedication. Who is ignorant that, by the most useful ordinance, not only the secular rank of high position in kings and other princes, and many decrees of the laws and philosophic teaching have been retained among converted races, but even those ranks of ecclesiastic dignitaries and the pattern of continence and the religious observance of bodily purity was acquired from them. For it is decreed that now bishops and archbishops preside where once the flamens and arch-flamens were found; then temples were set up for demons,

---

[168] See Augustine, *City of God* 1.19 (CCSL 47: 21–2).
[169] II Kings 2.8.
[170] On the consecration ceremony for virgins and other women in religion see René Metz, *La Femme et l'enfant dans le droit canonique mediéval* (London: Variorum Reprints, 1985), Essay VII, 'La Couronne et l'anneau dans la consécration des vierges'.

afterwards they were consecrated to God and distinguished as memorials of the saints.[171]

We know also that, even among the Gentiles, the special prestige of virginity shone forth: when the foul injunction of the law drove the Jews to marriage, this virtue or purity of the flesh was manifest as being so pleasing to the Gentiles that a great assembly of women dedicated themselves to a celibate life.[172] Whence Jerome in the third book of *On the Epistle to the Galatians* says, 'What ought we to do?[173] We are condemned because Juno has men worshippers with one wife and Vesta, too, has virgins, and other idols have chaste followers,' and he says that men with one wife and virgins are, as it were, nuns who had known men and nuns who were virgin. For *monos* whence *monachus* (monk) is said to be *solitarius*, which means one. And he has brought in many examples of chastity and continence of Gentile women in the first book of *Against Jovinian*.[174] 'I know', he says, 'that I have said many things in my catalogue of women, so that those who despise the faithfulness of Christian modesty may at least learn chastity from the heathen.' And he has also, in the same place above, commended this virtue of continence to such an extent that the Lord appears to have approved this outstanding cleanliness of the flesh in every race, and to have spread it abroad to many heathen by numbers of good deeds and the performance of miracles. 'Shall I not adduce (he says) the Erythraean Sibyl and the Cumaean and the eight others?' For Varro asserts that there were ten: and their virginity was their distinguishing quality, and divination the reward of virginity. Again: Claudia, the vestal Virgin, when she came under suspicion of defilement was able by her girdle to draw a boat which a thousand men could not move.[175] And Bishop Sidonius of Claremont in his *Propenticon* says thus:

> Such was neither Tanaquil nor she
> Whom you, Trecipitinus, begat

---

171 The ancient gods of Rome (not later, foreign introductions) were served by fifteen flamens whose principal duty was to perform the daily sacrifices. They received fees for certain duties and were maintained from the property of the temple but they were precluded from taking part in political or military activities. The resemblance to Christian priests is obvious.
172 See Deut. 25.5–10.
173 Jerome, *Letter to the Galatians* 3.6 (PL 26: 462B).
174 Jerome, *Against Jovinian* 1.47 (PL 23: 288–9).
175 Jerome, *Against Jovinian* 1.41 (PL 23: 283); cf. Ovid, *Fasti* 4.305.

Who against the swelling Albula
Drew the boat with her virgin hair.[176]

Augustine, *The City of God*, book XXII: 'Now if we come to their miracles which were performed by their gods and are compared with those of our martyrs, will they not be performed for us and be entirely useful? For among the great miracles of their gods, certainly great is that which Varro records, that a vestal virgin, when she was put on trial on a false suspicion of impurity, filled a sieve with water from the Tiber and carried it to her judges without spilling any drop of it. Who held . . . the weight of water . . . with so many open holes? . . . Would not Almighty God . . . be able to support the heavy weight of an earthly body, so that a body brought to life should live in the same element in which the life-giving spirit wished it to be?'[177]

Nor is it remarkable if God has displayed chastity to the heathen too by these and other miracles, and has allowed a demon to be extolled in worship so that the faithful are now the more incited to chastity because they have learnt that it is greatly valued among the heathen. We know also that the grace of prophecy was conferred on Caiphas [*sic*] as a priest, not as an individual.[178] Also false apostles not infrequently became celebrated for miracles and these were not granted to them personally but because of their office.[179] Nor is it remarkable if the Lord should have granted this, not to the individual heathen women but to their virtue of continence, in order to free the innocent virgin immediately and to destroy the shame of a false accusation. It is plain that the love of chastity is good, even in the heathen, so that observance of a conjugal vow is a gift of God for everyone. Thus, it does not seem marvellous if God is doing honour to his own gifts and not to the errors of the heathen. Such signs of honour are performed by heathen, not by the faithful, particularly when through them, as has been said, the innocent are set free; the evil deeds of wicked men are curbed.

In addition, it was much to the good that good men were greatly encouraged, and so the heathen commit sin so much less the more they withdraw from pleasure of the flesh. And this the blessed Jerome, with many others, not unfittingly advanced against the fornication of the heretics, about which I have spoken, so that what is not

---

176 Sidonius Apollinaris, *Carmina* 24, MGH AA 8: 262–63.
177 Augustine, *City of God* 22.11 (CCSL 48: 830); Pliny, *Natural History* 28.2; Valerius Maximus, *Memorable Deeds and Sayings* 8.1.5.
178 John 11.49–51.
179 See Matt. 24.24; Augustine, *On Various Questions* 79.3 (CCSL 44A: 228).

wondered at in Christians brings a blush of shame in pagans. For who would deny that these things are good because they are mixed with evil; particularly when, as the blessed Augustine adds, and clear reason bears witness, there cannot be evil things unless there are things that are by nature good?[180] Who does not approve the sentiment which poetic expressions adduce: 'good men hate to sin through love of virtue'?[181] Who does not approve the miracle which Suetonius reports was done by Vespasian when he was not yet emperor, that is of the blind man and the lame cured by him, rather than deny that princes wish to imitate his excellence?[182] Or who would disapprove what the blessed Gregory says was done for the soul of Trajan?[183] Men knew how to pick out a pearl from the mud and to separate the grain from the chaff. And God cannot be ignorant of his gifts linked to lack of faith, nor can he hate what he has made. For the brighter they shine with miracles, so much the more they show themselves to be his. His gifts are not polluted by the depravity of men and now he who reveals himself in such a way to the heathen should be desired by the faithful. But the redress of rape shows how much honour the heathen give to holy modesty in their temples. That redress Juvenal commemorates in the fourth satire *Against Crispinus* and says this about him: 'For whom there lay a priestess, about to be buried, bound with a fillet, with blood still warm.'[184]

In *The City of God*, book III, Augustine also said: 'For the Romans themselves buried alive vestal virgins found in unchastity, but adulterous wives, though they punished them with some other penalty, they never subjected to death unless they thought the sin more serious, so that they felt they were avenging the sanctuaries of the gods rather than the bedchambers of humans.'[185] Among us the concern of Christian princes cares for your chastity for they do not doubt that your chastity is the more sacrosanct. So Justinian Augustus: 'If anyone (he says), I will not say "rapes", but has dared to tamper with the holy virgins for the purpose of matrimony let him be executed by capital punishment.'[186] The rule of ecclesiastical

---

180   Augustine, *City of God* 12.6 (CCSL 48: 361).
181   Horace, *Letters* 1.16.52.
182   Suetonius, *Lives of the Caesars*, Vespasian 7.
183   John the Deacon, *Life of Pope Gregory* 44 (PL 75: 105AB).
184   Juvenal, *Satires* 1.4.8–9.
185   Augustine, *City of God* 3.5 (CCSL 48: 68).
186   Cf. Justinian, Codex 1.3.5, *Corpus Iuris Civilis* 2, ed. P. Kreuger (Berlin, 1915), p. 19.

discipline, which seeks the remedy of penitence, not the pains of death, is in no doubt that it should forestall your sins by severe punishments. Pope Innocent says the same to bishop Victricius of Rouen in chapter 13: 'If those who marry Christ spiritually and are veiled by a priest afterwards either marry openly or are corrupted in secret, they must not be admitted to perform penance unless the man with whom they were associated has left this life.'[187] Certainly the women who have not yet been covered by the sacred veil but represent themselves as intending to remain forever in their virginal resolution may remain unveiled, but they must perform their penance in some degree because they take their solemn engagement from God. For if it is customary among men that a bridal engagement made in good faith cannot be dissolved for any reason, how much more can that promise which they made with God not be dissolved without a punishment. For the apostle Paul said that those who departed from the intention of widowhood were to be condemned, because they made their first faith of no effect, and by how much more those virgins who do not in the least preserve their earlier resolution of faithfulness. Hence the famous Pelagius to the daughter of Mauritius: 'It is more reprehensible (he says) to commit adultery against Christ than against a husband.'[188] So, recently, the Roman Church has appropriately made such a severe decree of this kind that it judges that they who violate with lascivious foulness the body sanctified by God are scarcely worthy of penance.

[Devout women and the doctors of the Church]
But if we wish to examine how much care, how much diligence and love the holy doctors, stirred by the examples of the Lord and the apostles, always showed to devout women, we shall find that they loved and cherished the devotion of these women with the greatest warmth of affection, and encouraged them and perpetually taught and assisted their progress in religion with the greatest zeal of teaching and exhortation. And in order that I may leave out the others, let the principal doctors of the Church be brought out into our midst, that is Origen, Ambrose and Jerome. Of them the first is he who is the greatest philosopher of Christians, who embraced the religious life of women with such zeal that he turned his hand upon

---

187 Pope Innocent I to Victricius, bishop of Rouen (PL 20: 478–9).
188 Pelagius, *The Praise of Virginity* (PL 20: 478; 30: 181A); although often ascribed to Jerome, it was attributed to Pelagius by Guigo I of La Chartreuse (PL 153: 593).

himself, as the *Ecclesiastical History* says, lest any blame should lead him away from teaching and exhorting women.[189]

And who is ignorant about what a harvest of holy books of the church the blessed Jerome left behind at the request of Paula and Eustochium. Writing, among other things, a sermon on the assumption of the Mother of the Lord for them at their request he set forth the very same point saying, 'But because I am not able to refuse anything that you request, I am overcome by your very great affection, and I attempt what you ask me.'[190] But we know that not a few of the greatest doctors, exalted by position as well as by distinction of life, writing to him from a distance, looked in vain for letters from him and did not receive them. Whence comes this of the blessed Augustine in the second book of his *Retractions*: 'I have also written two books to the priest Jerome living in Bethlehem, one about the origin of souls, the other about the opinions of the apostle James where he says, "Whosoever shall keep the whole law and yet offend in one point, he is guilty of all",[191] consulting him on each point. But in the first question I have not solved the problem which I put to you. But in the second one, which seems to me capable of solution, I have not kept silent. He replied praising that debate of mine, but answered that he had not the leisure for replying. Indeed, as long as he was in the body, I did not wish to publish those books in case he might reply some time and they would be better published with that reply. Now that he is dead I have published them.'[192]

Behold then, how such a man neither looked for nor received in such a long time so few and such brief replies from the man of whom I spoke. Yet we know that, at the request of the aforesaid women, he sweated at conveying and dictating so many and such huge volumes, showing far greater respect for them than for the bishop in doing this. It may be that he embraced their virtue with so much greater enthusiasm and forbore to grieve them to such an extent as he considered their nature to be the weaker. Indeed, not infrequently the ardour of his love towards women of this kind is found to be so great that he seems to go rather beyond the way of truth as he seems to have been aware of in himself, for somewhere he records, 'Love', he says, 'has no limit', and in his praise of the life of St Paul he straightaway says,

189 Eusebius, *Ecclesiastical History* 6.8.1–2.
190 Paschasius Radbertus, *On the Assumption* (CCCM 56C: 109), a treatise always circulated under the name of Jerome.
191 James 2.10.
192 Augustine, *Retractions* 2.45 (CCSL 57: 127).

as though wishing to prepare the reader, 'If all the members of my body were turned into tongues, and all the joints resounded with a human voice, I should say nothing worthy of the virtues of the blessed and honoured Paula.'[193]

He has also delineated several venerable lives of the holy fathers which shine with miracles in which things far more wonderful are referred to. But no subject he wrote about received such praise as this widow. Even writing to the virgin Demetriades he marked the front of the letter with so much praise that he seems to have slipped into immoderate eulogy, saying: 'Among all the matters which I have written from childhood to this age, both by my own hand and that of secretaries, nothing is more difficult than the present work. For I am about to write to Demetriades, the virgin of Christ who by noble rank and by wealth is the first in Rome; if I were to tell everything related to her virtues I should be thought to flatter.'[194]

For it was very sweet to a holy man to encourage frail nature to the hard pursuit of virtue by whatever art of words. But to the end that deeds should stand out as more convincing arguments for us than words, he ennobled women with so great love of this kind, so that his immense sanctity should stamp them for his own with the mark of his reputation. And writing to Asella about his false friends and those who disparaged him, among other things he records this saying: 'And it is conceivable that some think that I am outrageous and weighed down with my evil deeds . . . but you do well because from your heart you think that even the evil are good. For it is dangerous to judge another's slave and not easy to speak with improper kindness about the good. For they kissed my hands and disparaged me with a viper's mouth. They gave pain with their lips and rejoiced with their heart. Let them say what they have ever seen in me which was not fitting for a Christian. With nothing have I been charged except my gender, and this has never been charged against me except when Paula set out for Jerusalem.' Again: 'Before I knew the house of Paula, the goodwill of the whole city centred on me. I was considered in the estimation of almost everyone to be worthy of the supreme priesthood. But after I began to reverence her for the worth of her holiness, to cherish her and to take her into my spiritual care, all my virtues left me in that

193 Jerome, Letter 46.1 (CSEL 54.1.1: 329) and Letter 108.1 (CSEL 55.2: 306).
194 Jerome, Letter 108.2 (CSEL 55.2: 306) and 130.1 (CSEL 56.1.3: 175).

respect.' And after other things, he says 'Greet Paula and Eustochium; whether they wish it or not, they are mine in Christ.'[195]

We read that the Lord himself showed such familiarity with the blessed harlot that when the Pharisee had invited him he mistrusted him in his own mind because of this, saying to himself, 'This man is a prophet; he should know who and of what kind she is who touches him, etc.'[196] What then is remarkable if through desire for such souls these members of Christ, spurred on by his example, do not flee damage to their own reputation? Origen indeed, as has been said, bore the infliction of infamy in his own body to avoid a graver harm.[197]

And the marvellous chastity of the holy fathers was seen not only in teaching and exhorting women, but also in comforting them; sometimes they appeared so ardent that, in order to lighten their sorrow, pity seemed to promise not a few miracles that are contrary to the faith. Indeed such consolation did the blessed Ambrose give, that on the death of the emperor Valentinian he dared to write to his sisters and promise salvation to him who died a catechumen, appearing to differ far from the catholic faith and the truth of the gospel.[198] For these doctors were not ignorant that the virtue of the weaker gender had always been acceptable to God. So when we see innumerable virgins following the mother of the Lord, this model of excellence, we acknowledge that few men reach the gift of this virtue through which they are worthy to follow the Lamb himself wherever he goes.[199] For by the fervour of virtue when many die by their own hand in order to keep their purity of flesh which they have vowed to God, not only is this not blameworthy but in many cases they have deserved the title of martyrs of the church. Betrothed virgins too, if they have decided to choose the nunnery before they have consorted carnally with their husbands and, rejecting men, to make God their husband, have unrestricted freedom to choose in this matter. We never read that this was allowed to men. Indeed many of these women have been so roused to zeal for chastity that they have not only taken masculine dress against the law to preserve their chastity, but have even been so prominent among the monks for their virtues that they were worthy to be abbots. Thus we read of the blessed

[195] Jerome, Letter 45.1.2 (CSEL 54.1.3: 175).
[196] Luke 7.39.
[197] Eusebius, *Ecclesiastical History* 6.8.
[198] See Ambrose, *Consolation for the Death of Valentinian* 51 (CSEL 73: 355).
[199] Rev. 14.4.

Eugenia who, with the knowledge of the blessed bishop Helenus, or even, in truth, his commanding it, took masculine dress and once baptized by him, she joined the college of monks.[200]

I judge that I have replied sufficiently, my dearest sister in Christ, to the first part of your latest request, that is about the origin of your order and in addition about the worth of its own particular character, so that you should embrace the vocation of your profession the more zealously, since you have learnt more fully its excellence. Now, so that I may, if the Lord wills it, succeed in the second request, may I gain it by your merits and prayers.

Farewell.

---

[200] See *Lives of the Fathers* 1 (PL 73: 610).

III Peter the Venerable to his Nieces Margaret and Pontia: Of Nieces and Grandmothers and the Virgin Life at Marcigny (Letter 185)[1]

Peter the Venerable was Abbot of Cluny near Macon-sur-Saône in France from 1122–1157 at a period when the Cluniac order was at the height of its influence.[1] The monastery had been founded in AD 910 by William the Pious, Duke of Aquitaine, with the purpose of returning to the strict observance of the Benedictine Rule. Its influence spread rapidly through France and Western Europe, and Cluniac monasteries became celebrated for the efficiency of their organisation as well as for their emphasis on the development of personal spiritual life. Great emphasis was placed on music and the service of the altar. The splendour of Cluniac worship led to the diminution of manual labour, but this only served to attract men of high rank, ability and austerity. Cluny had the confidence of kings and popes.

In 1056 Hugh of Semur persuaded his brother, Count Geoffrey of Semur, to provide a retreat for the women of his own family and for the wives of men who were temporarily or permanently at Cluny. There were to be ninety-nine nuns under a prioress who was also responsible for twelve monks living nearby in order to serve Marcigny's chapel. Contact was forbidden between the monks and the nuns, who were strictly enclosed. There was no human abbess; the blessed virgin was to be regarded as abbess and a stall in the choir was reserved for her.

Cluny attracted men of high social rank, and the ladies of Marcigny were equally distinguished. They were usually noble and, in some cases, royal; among them was Adela of Blois, the mother of King Stephen of England. Margaret and Pontia, daughters of Peter's brother Hugh, had been placed in the convent by their grandmother, Raingard.

The women of Marcigny appear to have lived a life of aristocratic austerity tempered by consideration for their 'weaknesses': 'Being

---

[1] On Peter the Venerable, see Giles Constable, ed., *The Letters of Peter the Venerable* (Cambridge, Mass.: Harvard University Press, 1967), Introduction.

noble and delicate, fragile and infirm', said Peter, 'they required many things on account of their gender, location and habit.'[2] Life for the young women of Marcigny must have been rather like life in a strict and well-run, but rather snobbish, lifelong boarding school. Indeed, Peter shows some sympathy by referring to Marcigny as 'prison' (p. 99) and feels the need to encourage his nieces by showing the heavenly rewards of their obedience and endurance. Peter's family seems not to have been of the highest rank, and he also takes care to show his nieces they might have an influence on others, even in a community where most inhabitants outrank them. Peter's father was Maurice of Montboissier, and one of his brothers was Hugh, the father of these nieces. Maurice died in 1116/17, and, not long after, his widow Raingard entered the convent of Marcigny. There she was celebrated for her piety and charity. Peter says that she lived there almost twenty years and was known as the 'mother of the monastery'. She seems to have been a woman of character and influence, well-suited to be a model for her granddaughters.

Despite his praise of his mother and his rebuke to his nieces for dabbling in medicine, Peter's letter appears less personal than Osbert of Clare's letter to Adelidis (I above). He is offering his nieces a *florilegium*, an anthology, of thoughts about virginity taken from the fathers of the Church, so that the attractiveness of the images is reinforced by their authority. As Peter's modern editor, Giles Constable, has said, the formal air of this letter reflects the fashion of the times.[3] Osbert's style had been much more free and flowery than became common in the letters of the later twelfth century. Nevertheless certain emphases and particularities are readily detectable in Peter's letter. In addition to praise of their grandmother, the young women were to be encouraged by images of the heavenly rewards of virginity, but, in contrast to Osbert of Clare's emphasis on the joys of love for Christ, Peter makes great use of the images of glory – the virgins will take precedence of everyone in heaven. There is no doubt that Peter wishes his nieces to be encouraged in piety, but there is always a suggestion of heaven as a compensation for what was lacking on earth: honour and glory to match that of the other ladies of Marcigny.

---

2   Constable, 2: 133.
3   Constable, 2: 29–44.

Peter the Venerable to his Nieces Margaret and Pontia at Marcigny: Of Nieces and Grandmothers and the Virgin Life at Marcigny

To his dearest nieces and sweetest girls, Peter, humble abbot of Cluny, sends all greetings and thanks

I have read the letter written from you to me in which you sympathized with my trouble[4] and in which you attempted to treat me with medical art as well as with spiritual prayers. I thank you for your dutiful care and I embrace your daughterly affection which befits a sweet and blessed heart. But I marvel from where the pupils of Jesus Christ imbibe the lessons of Hippocrates, why the daughters of Jerusalem should be trafficking in the merchandise of Babylon.[5] Certainly, I do not despise medical assistance which is often of benefit to corrupt nature, especially since the physician was created by the Most High,[6] and I have heard Christ say: 'Those that are whole need not a physician, but those that are sick.'[7]

Nevertheless I charge you, mortal enemies of nature which is innate in the flesh, you who are crucified with the Crucified, to think again and again of the ills and the significance of the body. Has the solemn word of Agatha, 'I have never employed carnal medicine for my body', slipped from your mind?[8] Was she not indeed a handmaid to Christ; was she not a bride of Christ? Are you not handmaids, are you not brides? And indeed is not that virgin martyr more renowned

---

4   Peter the Venerable suffered from constant ill-health. He complained of the 'Roman fever' which he contracted in Rome and which made summer visits impossible. This was probably malaria; he also suffered from catarrh and some kind of chronic bronchitis. Despite his reproaches to his nieces he consulted a celebrated doctor, Bartholomew, and was treated by Bernard, Dr Bartholomew's assistant, with a great variety of medicaments. (Constable, *Letters of Peter the Venerable*, 2: 247–51).

5   Hippocrates of Cos (c. 469–399 BC), 'The Father of Medicine' and reputedly the first to distinguish medicine from superstition. Babylon may refer generally to the Babylonian reputation for wisdom, and somewhat arcane, possibly sinful, knowledge, but possibly to Zachalias (or Zacharias), perhaps a Jew, who was a Babylonian follower of Hippocrates. This rather wary attitude to Babylonian learning was commonly contrasted to the pure and holy learning symbolized by Jerusalem (see Rev. 14 and 21).

6   Eccles. 38.1.

7   Luke 5.31.

8   Very little authentic is known of Agatha. She is said to have been a virgin martyr of the third century in Sicily. Among her tortures she is said to have suffered the cutting-off of her breasts. Initially refusing treatment for this she was divinely healed.

than you, and far more exalted than you? But your object in life is not incompatible with hers when you serve God by the witness of the same kind, and grace the splendour of the field of heaven with a virgin flower. Assuredly, I am glad; I shall rejoice and be exceedingly glad, if, from my family, from my blood, those virgins sublime throughout the whole world – Agatha, Agnes and Faith and she who is far more worth than the rest, the Virgin of Virgins – shall have you as followers in their footsteps.[9]

Indeed as I have said, if those worthy ones should hold you worthy to be as servants, I do not say as companions, I shall rejoice, rejoicing in the Lord, and my spirit will rejoice in Jesus my Saviour.[10] And you, my virgins, as I may call you, O handmaidens, O brides in very truth of the everlasting king; if indeed you are not of the foolish virgins but the wise, with what joy will you join in the dances, with what happiness will you exult.[11] With what joy, unknown to wretched mortals, will that be; with what a torrent of pleasure will you drink with insatiable satisfaction from him with whom is the fountain of life;[12] after what dense and detestable Egyptian darkness shall you see light in his light?[13]

What will be then, what will become of you when, after the prison of Marcigny, you escape into the free dazzling splendour of pure heavenly air and in 'Jerusalem which is above' and, according to the apostle, 'is the mother of us all',[14] you will say and sing rejoicing with heart and body in the living God, 'As we have heard, so we have seen in the city of the Lord of Hosts, in the city of our God.'[15] What will it be when Jesus, the king of the Heavens, in return for brief continence and gentle chastity, will greet his young girls, his hand-

---

9   Agnes and Faith: like Agatha, semi-legendary virgin martyrs. Agnes (d. c. 350?) appears to have been very young when she was put to death. Faith (third century) was possibly martyred at Agen in France and widely culted in France and England in the twelfth century; as a martyr, she provides another suitable role-model for Peter's young nieces.

10 Ps. 16.9; Hab. 3.18; Luke 1.47.

11 The Parable of the Wise and Foolish Virgins (Matt. 25.1) was one of the most frequently used by preachers to illustrate the fate of the thoughtless and unprepared.

12 Ps. 35.10.

13 See Exod. 10.21–23. 'Egyptian darkness': darkness was the ninth of the plagues sent to Egypt to punish the Pharoah who would not let the Israelites leave Egypt. Ps. 36.9; Ex. 10.21.

14 Gal. 4.26. The promise of heavenly freedom after a life of claustration is frequent in virginity and chastity letters.

15 Ps. 48.8.

maidens, his virgins, with his right hand? How great will that happiness be, unimaginable indeed, so that I should pass over it in silence? What will that happiness be for those, the greatest apostles, in that life which God, who does not lie, has promised them? Yet they will not follow Christ everywhere, but he promised you that, with the choir of virgins, you should follow the Lamb, the virgin's Son, wherever he goes.[16] Indeed, the virgins will shine like the sun in the kingdom of the Father,[17] and gleam like stars in unbroken eternity. They will gain glory that is greater by far, loftier by far, for the rewards of their nature. Yet they will not be able to equal you in this respect, nor will the privilege be granted to the uncountable throng of saints which has been promised to fortunate virginity, even though they shine like gold.

Augustine says: 'Press on therefore holy youths and maidens of God, men and women, single and unwedded; press on persevering to the end; praise the Lord more sweetly, the Lord on whom you meditate so fruitfully.[18] Hope with greater joy in him, whom you are the more eager to serve. Love him the more zealously, whom you are the more eager to please. With loins girded and lamps burning, wait for the Lord when he comes from the wedding. You shall bring to the wedding of the Lamb a new song to sing to your lutes. Not indeed such as the whole earth sings, to which it is said, "Sing unto the Lord a new song, sing unto the Lord the whole earth", but such as no one but you will be able to sing.[19] For thus he saw you in the Apocalypse, dear to the Lamb above all others, accustomed to lie on his breast, drinking and proclaiming wonderful thoughts on heavenly themes, the very word of God. He saw you, a hundred and forty-four thousand sacred harpists, untouched in virginity in the body, inviolate in truth in the heart.[20] And because you follow the Lamb "wherever he goes", he wrote this about you. Where do you think the Lamb goes, where no one has dared or been able to follow, save you? Where do

---

[16] Rev. 14.4.

[17] Matt. 13.43.

[18] Augustine, *On Holy Virginity* 27–8 (CSEL 41: 263–5).

[19] For the Marriage of the Lamb see Rev. 19. The Apocalypse or the Revelation is a series of visions of the end of the world. It was ascribed to St John 'the Divine', traditionally associated with John the Beloved Disciple; hence the reference to 'the disciple whom Jesus loved' (John 13.23; 21.20). There is a reference back to the wise and foolish Virgins who were bridesmaids. 'A new song' refers to Rev. 14.3 but also refers to Ps. 96, 'O sing to the Lord a new song, for he has done marvellous things.'

[20] For the 144,000 harpists, see Rev. 14.1–5.

you think that he goes, in what woods and fields, where, I believe, there are pastures of delight? Not the joys of this vain world and its deceiving frenzy; such joys as there are in the kingdom of God for others who are not virgins, but joys that are unlike all other joys. Joys which are fitting for the virgins of Christ, from Christ, in Christ, with Christ, after Christ, through Christ, because of Christ. Go then; in this you follow the Lamb, for the flesh of the Lamb is supremely virgin; though abundantly generous yet his integrity was untouched, for his conception and birth took away nothing from his mother.[21]

What is "to follow" but to imitate? "Because Christ suffered for us, leaving us an example", as says the apostle Peter, "so that we should follow his footsteps".[22] Each man follows him when he imitates him, not in that he is the Son of God, the one by whom all things were made, but in that he is displayed to the sons of men in himself and this we ought to imitate. Many things are set forth in him which all ought to imitate, but virginity of the body is not for all, for there is nothing that they can do to become virgins, when they have already ceased to be virgin. Therefore let the rest of the faithful who have lost their virginity of body follow the Lamb, not wherever he goes, but wherever they are able. For they are able to go everywhere, except where he goes in the comeliness of virginity.[23]

But see this Lamb walking in the path of virginity. How can those who have lost what they can in no way regain follow after him? You, therefore, his virgins, follow him thither, since because of this one thing you follow him wherever he goes. We can urge the married to any other kind of holiness in which they can follow him, except to this, which they have irreparably lost. Do you, therefore, follow him tenaciously, holding fast to what you have ardently vowed. Do this while you can, lest the goodness of virginity fade away from you and you will be able to do nothing to bring it back. The rest of the multitude of the faithful, who are unable to follow the Lamb in this will see you and not hate you; rejoicing with you over what they do not have themselves. They will possess it in you. For they will not be able to proclaim that new song which is fit only for you, but they will be able to hear and to rejoice in such a surpassing blessing. But you will

---

[21] 'Quod matri non abstulit conceptus et natus' must be literally translated 'which he did not take from his Mother when he was conceived and born'. This must refer to Mary's virginity and takes up the doctrine of the perpetual virginity of the Virgin Mary.

[22] I Peter, 2.21.

[23] Augustine, *On Holy Virginity* 27–8 (CSEL 41: 263–5).

both proclaim and hear it, since what you will proclaim you will hear in yourselves. You will rejoice more fully and will reign more joyfully.

But there will never be any lessening of your great joy. For the Lamb whom you follow wherever he goes will not desert those who are not strong enough to follow him as you do; he will go before you and he will not leave you when he shall be God, all in all. And those who have less than you will not shrink away from you, for where there is no jealousy, diversity is harmony. Take the lead then, be confident, take strength, persist in what you have vowed and fulfil the vow of everlasting continence which you have made to the Lord your God, not for this present world but for the kingdom of heaven.'[24]

How great my daughters, how great is the praise of virginity. If she perseveres, my Margaret will deserve what Mary Magdalene did not.[25] How so? Because neither patience, nor humility, not chastity itself, not any other virtue is said to be sister of the angels, but virginity. The blessed Jerome says: It was well that the angel was sent to the virgin, for virginity is always related to the angels.[26] Certainly to live in the body, but yet not in the body, is not an earthly life but heavenly. Whence it follows that to gain the glory of an angel in the body is a greater glory than to receive it; for to be an angel comes by grace, but to be a virgin has the angel by nature.[27]

Behold you are such now, because such you ought to be. These qualities added to virginity display the angelic life to men and the ways of heaven to earth. If therefore you have rejected the marriage of the sons of men, love with your whole heart what is, by nature, beyond the sons of men.[28] You are not bound; your heart is free from the chains of marriage. Consider the beauty of your lover; think that he is the equal of the Father, subject also to his mother, ruling in

24 Ibid. 29–30 (CSEL 41: 266–7).
25 The Magdalen's cult was greatly developed in the twelfth century, and in medieval litanies and in other invocations of saints she frequently occupies a high place, often next to the Virgin herself. Yet, as Peter points out, she lacks what his nieces have – virginity. There is a play here on Margaret (*margarita* = pearl), the name of one of Peter's nieces and of one of the major virgin martyrs of the church, St Margaret of Antioch.
26 Paschasius Radbertus, *Letter on the Assumption* 27.69–70 (CCSL 56A: 121). Angels (from Greek *angelos*, a messenger) are attested in both Old and New Testaments as spiritual beings intermediate between God and man. See, for example, Isa. 6.1–8; Matt. 18.10.
27 Augustine, *On Holy Virginity* 53 (CSEL 41: 300).
28 Ps. 44.3.

heaven, yet serving on earth, creating all things, yet a creature among others. Consider how lovely is that very thing which the proud derided in him. With the light of your mind meditate on his wounds as he hangs on the cross, the wounds of him who rose again, the blood of the dying, the reward of the faithful, the ransom of the redeemer. Think how much these things are worth; weigh this in the balance of love, and weigh too whatever custom required that you should provide for your marriage; spend it on him.

It is well that he seeks your beauty of soul, when he has given you the power to become the daughters of God. He does not seek beauty of body from you. He is not one to whom someone can lie about you and deceive you about him, or make you serve him without reason. See with what confidence you can love him when you do not fear that he will be displeased by slanders about you. Husband and wife love one another because they see one another, and what they do not see they fear to discover in one another. Nor do they rejoice confidently because of what is in the open, since, in secret, they fear much that is not so. You do not see him with your eyes, yet you behold him through faith, but you have nothing to find fault with, nor do you fear to offend him by chance. If, therefore, you owe great love to your husbands, how much love do you owe to him on whose account you are unwilling to have husbands. He who was fixed to the cross for your sakes is wholly fixed to your hearts. May he hold entirely in your heart everything you have not wished to devote to marriage. It is not right for you to love meanly the one for whose sake you have rejected what you had a perfect right to love. Loving what is gentle and humble from your heart, I do not fear you will be proud.[29]

The holy Ambrose also says: 'But for you, holy virgins, there is the special defence against pride, that you serve the holy chamber of your Lord with inviolable modesty.[30] Nor is it to be wondered at if the angels fight for you who yourselves do battle in the manner of angels. Chaste virgins deserve as defence the angels whose life they imitate. And what more shall I add in praise of chastity? Chastity indeed formed the angel. Whoever preserves it is an angel. She who has lost it is a devil. It is from this that he [the devil] received the name. She who weds the Lord is a virgin; she is a whore who makes gods for herself. For what shall I say about the Resurrection, for its

29 Augustine, *On Holy Virginity* 54–6 (CSEL 41: 300–1).
30 Cf. Matt. 22.30, and Virgil, *Aeneid* 8.412, '*castum ut servare cubile coniugis*' ('to guard her marriage in purity', trans. W. E. Jackson Knight, (Harmondsworth: Penguin, 1956).

rewards are now within your grasp? In the Resurrection they will neither marry nor be given in marriage but they will be like the angels of God in heaven.[31] What is promised us is near at hand for you. You have the benefit of our prayers. You are in this world and not of this world. This age is entitled to have you, but it has not been able to hold you. For it is well-known that angels fell from heaven into this world because of their excesses, but virgins have passed from this world into heaven because of their purity. Blessed virgins whom no allurement of the body entices; no foulness of pleasures casts them down. The food of frugality, or rather abstinence, teaches them to be ignorant of vice and teaches them to be ignorant of the causes of vice.'[32]

Again Ambrose says: ' "A garden enclosed is my sister, my spouse, a fountain sealed",[33] so that there in a garden of this sort she is imprinted with the seal of the image of God as the waves of a pure spring should be clear, should not be stirred up, a wallowing place for the beasts of the spirit, spattered with mud. Because of this, modesty enclosed with spiritual walls does not lie open to ravage. So just as the garden shut off from thieves diffuses the scent of vines, burns with the olive and is resplendent with the rose, so religion grows in the vine, peace in the olive, and the modesty of consecrated virginity in the rose. This is the scent which Jacob the Patriarch smelled when he was found worthy to hear, "Behold the smell of my son is as the smell of a field which the Lord hath blessed."[34] For although the field of the holy patriarch was filled with almost all fruits that exist, yet that field produced fruits with great expenditure of effort, but this one produces flowers. Then, virgin, gird yourself, even though the rule of this kind breathes to you like a garden with prophetic injunctions to keep it closed: "Place a guard on your mouth, and on your lips" so that you will be able to say, "As is the apple among the trees of the wood, so is my beloved among the sons. I sat down under his shadow with great delight and his fruit was sweet to my taste. I found him whom my soul loves, I held him and would not let him go." '[35]

After such sublime and sweet words of the saints, listen, my dear ones, to Hilary, of outstanding fame and repute, preserving his

---

[31] Matt. 22.30.
[32] Ambrose, *About Virgins* 1.8.51–3, ed. F. Gori, Biblioteca Ambrosiana 14.1: 150–4.
[33] Song of Songs 4.12.
[34] Gen. 27.27.
[35] Ambrose, *About Virgins* 1.8.45–6.

daughter according to the flesh in virginity of both body and mind; he placed before her the divine vesture and a celestial pearl, inviting her with great effort and exhorting her: "In the first year (said Saint Hilary) I saw the garment, I saw it, my daughter, I saw it, I cannot express what it was like; was not the fineness of silk like hessian in comparison to it, do not snowflakes grow black in comparison to its whiteness?[36] Was not gold turned to lead by its brightness? For its many colours overpowered all other lovely things and, in short, nothing could be equal when compared to it. After that I saw the pearl. When I saw it, straightway I was prostrate, my eyes could not bear the fineness of its colour. For nothing seen in the sky, in the light of heaven, nor on earth was able to compare with its beauty." '

This indeed was written to Hilary's daughter. But last of all there may come the great Cyprian of Carthage, equal to all his predecessors in the performance of his office, equal in preaching, greater in his martyrdom.[37] For he says: 'Now our talk turns to virgins: so much the greater their glory, so much the greater [our] concern for them. That flower is the glory of the stem of the Church, the splendour and ornament of spiritual grace. A happy innate gift of praise and honour, the work of God whole and incorrupt, the picture which reflects the holiness of God, the more splendid part of the flock of Christ; through them, and in them, the glorious fruitfulness of our mother the Church flourishes more abundantly, and how much more abundantly does virginity add to its number. The joy of our mother increases. We speak about these virgins, we urge these things, with affection rather than authority. They are the equals of the angels, since they are daughters of the resurrection. What we shall become, you now begin to be. You already touch the glory of the resurrection in this age. You pass through this age without the contagion of the worldly. Since you persevere chaste and virgin you are equal to the angels of God. May virginity remain and live unimpaired and unharmed as it started boldly and perseveres perpetually. Since we

---

36 Pseudo-Hilary, 'Letter to his daughter, Abra' (CSEL 65: 239). *Anno primo*: this might appear to mean 'in the first year' or 'at the beginning of the year' – not very meaningful in this context, but CSEL offers the alternative reading: *primum vestem vidi*, 'I first saw the garment'.

37 Cyprian, *On the Dress of Virgins* 3 (CSEL 3.1: 189). Cyprian, Bishop of Carthage (c. 200–258) engaged in many controversies but was greatly loved by his flock. He comforted them through a plague but died in the persecution of the Emperor Valerian.

carry the image of him [Adam] who comes from the slime, let us also bear the image of him [Christ] who comes from the heavens.'[38]

'Virginity bears this image, it bears integrity, it bears holiness and truth, and so do those who keep in mind the teachings of God, holding fast justice with religion, steadfast in faith, lowly in reverence. Brave in all endurance, gentle in bearing injury, quick to show pity, united and harmonious in sisterly love. These things, good virgins, you ought to keep in mind, to love, to persevere to the end, you who are ready for God and Christ, to the Lord to whom you have made your vow and have dedicated your greater and better part. As you are carried on by the years, act as instructors to the younger ones. Though lesser by birth, provide rivals for an incentive. Urge one another on with mutual encouragement, by striving earnestly, give examples of virtue, incite to glory. Persevere boldly, press on spiritually, arrive happily, and be mindful of us when you begin to be honoured for your virginity.'[39]

These, my dearest ones, from whose books, as from flowery meadows, I have gathered these delightful blossoms, are among the highest priests of God; after the apostles they are the most outstanding teachers of the faithful, doctors of the Latin Church; in truth if the many barbarities of various tongues did not prevent it they would stand out in the whole Christian world. I hold out their pearls to you from every side; I have poured out for you from their treasure valuables precious and desirable beyond gold and topaz.[40] It remains for you to take up with eager heart what is freely offered, and keep it safe with greatest zeal and care, and, with angelic virginity, with the deepest humility, with sublimest love so that you should be made handmaidens of Jesus Christ, or rather his brides, worthy of his love, and make me, who am concerned about your salvation more than of all people in the world, rejoice with you.

Remember my blessed mother, your saintly grandmother.[41] Remember, I say, with what great faith and what unimaginable fervour of love (which she took from above), when you were still little girls not knowing your left hand from your right, she fled the

38   Ibid. 23–4 (CSEL 3.1: 203).
39   Ibid. 23–4 (CSEL 3.1: 204–5).
40   Topaz: a yellowish, precious or semi-precious stone; one of the stones in the breastplate of the Jewish High Priest (Ex. 28.17). Peter may be implying the superiority of the Christian virtue of virginity over the virtues of the Old Testament: Ps. 119.127.
41   Margaret and Pontia were granddaughters of Maurice II of Montboissier, far lower in rank than many of the inhabitants of Marcigny.

world, carried you away from the devil, presented you to God and attached you to the lay sisters. As I have often heard from her own lips at Marcigny, she was afraid that she might by chance be carried off at the will of the Lord from this wretched vale of tears[42] when he summoned her, and you would be left to survive her before she could snatch you from the snare of the hunters,[43] and join you to the number of saints in the school of virtue. The blessed Saviour had regard from on high to the humble prayers of his handmaiden and he who fills with good things the ardent desire of his people,[44] and will fulfil the desire of them that fear him,[45] at length fulfilled her desire. He has made you members of the virgin choir while you are still in the body. See how he will make you members in the mind. Not all your sister members are virgins in the flesh, but they are, as says our father Augustine, virgins in the faith. About them he makes a solemn pronouncement on the holy day of the birth of the Lord. For when the flesh is not untouched by intercourse, let it be considered (by common understanding) virgin in faith; according to this the whole Church is virgin.[46] In accordance with this idea the trumpet of the apostle often sounds out about those who live chastely and holy, as about those who are virgins. I have promised you to one husband so that I may present you a chaste virgin to Christ.[47] Placed by a happier fate, not only in the spirit, that is, but with unimpaired bodies, in the virgin chorus of those saints whom I have set before you, order your life, regulate your behaviour, fight the good fight, finish the race[48] successfully by running earnestly the race begun for you in your tender years.

Copy the sisters and mothers with whom you serve God and, in particular, as I have reminded you, your happy grandmother who has gone before you and summons you (as you follow her), as she did not only while she lived but now too, even when she is dead. Give me, I entreat you, the voice of the great apostle, so that I may say confidently to each of you what he wrote to his disciple, Timothy, 'I may

---

[42] Ps. 84.6.
[43] Ps. 91.3.
[44] Ps. 103.5.
[45] Ps. 145.19.
[46] Augustine: *Commentaries on the Psalms* 147.10 (CCSL 40: 2146) and *Sermon* 213, ed. G. Morin, *Sancti Augustini Sermones post Maurinos reperti, Miscellenea Agostiniana* (Rome, 1930), 1: 447.
[47] II Cor. 11.2.
[48] II Tim. 4.7.

be filled with joy when I call to remembrance the unfeigned faith that is in you, which dwelt first', not indeed as he says, 'in your grandmother Lois and your mother Eunice',[49] but in your grandmother Raingard.

49 II Tim. 1.5.

IV Osbert of Clare to his Nieces Margaret and Cecilia in Barking Abbey: Heavenly Rewards for Virgins in Barking (Letters 21 and 22)

At the end of Osbert's letter to the abbess Adelidis (I above) he commends his two nieces, Margaret and Cecilia, to her; he calls them daughters of his sister, and they were presumably already nuns of Barking, but apart from this we know nothing of them. However, the two letters to Margaret and Cecilia differ in style and though it is dangerous to read personal feelings into such letters, it is tempting to imagine that the young women were different in character and Osbert perceived that they required different kinds of exhortation.

The letter to Margaret was written before Osbert's journey to Rome, probably in 1139. It is characterized by a feeling of personal interest and affection, and omits all reference to the spectacular accounts of St Margaret and the dragon and the tortures of her passion in the contemporary lives of this well-known saint. Osbert confines himself to the gentlest account of the meaning of the name, Margaret, and its beauties as 'pearl' (Latin *margarita*). The use of precious stones as symbols of virtues is common, and a special theme of virginity and chastity literature. The name Margaret was a favoured occasion for symbolic etymology among writers of saints' lives and devotional literature. Here, the use of the pearl as a symbol of virtues serves to distance Osbert's niece Margaret from the harshness of life. Sinners draw upon themselves the punishment of heaven, but there is scarcely any suggestion that the nun, Margaret herself, could have been touched by sin. Osbert's advice, 'as often as any troublesome thought comes to you, set this letter before you' is mild and gentle by comparison with his letters to Adelidis and to Cecilia.

Although it was probably written only a year later, in 1140 after Osbert's return from Rome, the *Letter to Cecilia* is different in tone from that written to Margaret. Where the *Letter to Margaret* focuses on the spiritual virtues symbolized by the pearl of virginity, the *Letter to Cecilia* presents the virgin life as a form of spiritual marriage. The profession of virginity or chastity is taken as a solemn nuptial vow and the joys of heavenly marriage are opposed to the disadvantages of union with an earthly bridegroom. We are reminded very strongly in this letter in particular that chastity was seen as a positive and desirable thing, a privilege and not a misfortune. On the other hand, the ecstatic joy of the beatific vision of God was sometimes converted by less spiritual minds into the more mercenary reward of a high place in heaven. Though Osbert does not specifically say this, he has little to say of the joys of heaven except for the robes and the jewellery.

Writing to Adelidis, Osbert encourages her by describing the joys of spiritual motherhood as abbess and does not dwell much on the other side of the picture. To Cecilia, however, he goes into horrifying detail about the sordid aspects of pregnancy and childbirth. The *molestiae nuptiarum*, woes of marriage, is a common topic among twelfth-century churchmen, and special emphasis on the dangers of pregnancy is particularly a feature of letters on virginity addressed to young women. Osbert writes here as though his audience (Cecilia or others) need warning off from any regressive longings for earthly marriage.

In keeping with Osbert's presentation of chastity as a prized possession, Cecilia is invited to see herself as a royal bride, chivalrously defended by a heavenly bridegroom 'girt with a sword to fight on your behalf' (p. 115 below). Moreover, Cecilia is not commended to her name saint, but to St Lawrence, the young martyred deacon of the early Roman church. When writing to Margaret, Osbert had apparently delighted to dwell on the gentler virtues of St Margaret; to Cecilia he has nothing to say of her patron saint. St Margaret's Antioch was remote, and places associated with St Cecilia were all around Osbert in Rome, but his account of this saint is reserved for his letter to Adelidis (I above) where he presents St Cecilia as a model for a chaste and authoritative woman; one who was virtuous, humble, learned, but a leader. Such a person was not a suitable model for a young nun and he offers something different – a heroic male figure to guard her. St Lawrence was a popular saint in England and frequently taken as protector by women. He had himself endured much suffering in his fiery torture on the gridiron, and might be pictured as being heroic in Cecilia's defence. In this letter, Osbert recounts a new vision of St Lawrence which stresses his sanctity and heavenly perfection. No doubt Osbert's personal contact with this new vision of Lawrence gave it special value both for him and for Cecilia: the second half of the letter is given up to it. Osbert stresses Lawrence's particular value as a heavenly intercessor: he also suggests that the image of Lawrence's steadfastness amid the flames can be used to quench the 'flames of sin' in his niece. In keeping with the contemporary tendency to value women if they could be perceived as acting manfully (*virago*), Osbert proposes Lawrence as a virile remedy for the inflammability of the 'weaker gender'.

Osbert of Clare to his Nieces Margaret and Cecilia in Barking Abbey: Heavenly Rewards for Virgins in Barking. Letter 21 to Margaret

Osbert of Clare having, by the grace of God, become a new missionary of Jesus Christ in his travels, to his dearest niece Margaret, consecrated a holy virgin to God

By the splendour of her virtues and the lamp of her good deeds she shines so brightly that she is worthy to glow in the crown of the everlasting king among its gold and precious stones.

The toils of the journey to Rome which have occupied my mind, and other cares and worries, call me to give a hand to others so that I am forced to draw back from writing and exert myself in the repairing of my companions' wallets and staves.[1] But your pure and shining watchfulness and prayer urge me to set forth some words however brief for you, although the business of preparing equipment for my household urges me to be silent. Listen then to what I say, and hide it devoutly in your soul.

Your name is called Margaret so that the brightness of perfect sanctity might be shown to grow in you.[2] This is the pearl, namely precious virginity, about which you have already had dealings with the greatest merchant so that you might obtain palms of dazzling rays in heaven.[3] Among all other pearls this alone is brighter; among all the rest this only is more brilliant. I have found it in the field of the Lord's blessings; be zealous and diligent to keep it hidden in the trea-

---

1   This letter was probably written in 1139 when Osbert was preparing to go to Rome to ask the Pope to canonize the last king of the Anglo-Saxons. See J. Armitage Robinson, 'A Sketch of Osbert's Career', in E. W. Williamson, *The Letters of Osbert of Clare*, p. 18.

2   See Matt. 13.45. The etymology of the name is obscure, but according to the *Oxford English Dictionary* both 'pearl' and 'Margaret' are connected with the shell in which the pearls are found. The Old Testament use of the word in Job 28.18 is equally uncertain, but in the New Testament 'pearl' is frequently used for a very precious jewel, and thus for anything of great value. *The Peterborough Lapidary* says that pearls are formed from the dew of heaven which falls into the shell at certain times of the year. It had many medicinal virtues, and 'Margarita is chef of al stons that been wyzt and preciase' (Evans and Serjeantson, p. 107). See I above, n. 37.

3   Matt. 13.46.

sury of your heart. See that that precious gem is not dashed to pieces by your enemy nor brought into the open to be broken up by your adversary. Your enemy is the spirit of fornication: your foe is the corrupter of chastity. 'If any man,' says the apostle, 'defile the temple of God, God will destroy him.'[4] I cannot say anything to you except what the Holy Spirit wishes me to be inspired with.

There are certain virgins, but foolish ones, to whom, indeed, the evidence of Holy Scripture is unwelcome when the lightning of heaven's threats against them terrifies and strikes their obstinate hearts in their sins.[5] For the sinners seek warrant by which, as with a shield, they can protect and arm their foulness. For love of this world has made fools of them in the allurements of the flesh; they do not know the sweetness of heavenly savour and have no wish or desire for the longed-for beauty and grace of the heavenly bridegroom.[6] Beware, therefore; do not be counted in that number; do not carry around a lamp empty of oil; be a virgin, but wise; be lovely, but prudent.

What, then, is written? 'Wisdom has built a house.'[7] What house? Your uncorrupt body; your stainless spirit. This is the house the apostle speaks of; it is built as a temple for God. He who assails that house to profane it, God will drive him too from the land of the living.[8]

Therefore be the guardian of his house for your Bridegroom and of his temple for your God and Lord. As long as that pearl remains whole you shall not lack the splendour of your beauty; you shall be deprived of no honour or glory. All other virtues are servants to this virtue, since they all serve her as mistress and queen. To her the heavenly bridegroom cries in the song: 'You are wholly beautiful, my love and without a blemish.'[9] She is said to be beautiful in every way, she is proclaimed totally fair and comely. She is not convicted of blame in any way, for the stinking rot of corruption has no power over her. A shattered vessel does not possess this glory, nor can filthy bodies keep their right of precedence. So to this queen amongst the daughters of Jerusalem and the maidens of Syon, surrounded by virtues of every kind, the Bridegroom sings in the marriage song: 'Come with

---

4   I Cor. 3.17.
5   Matt. 25.1–12.
6   Song of Songs 5.10–16.
7   Prov. 9.1.
8   Cor. 3.16, 17.
9   Song of Songs 4.7.

me from Lebanon, come and you shall be crowned. Come by faith, come by the purity of virginity, come by love, come first in the body then freed from the flesh, come glorified in the resurrection. Come from Lebanon, that is the white-robed glory of virginity and you shall be crowned with the everlasting laurels of immortality.'[10]

The blessed virgin Margaret strove for this; the martyr contended in the purple of martyrdom.[11] Just as you bear her name, so strive to imitate the achievements of her prowess. May the fine flower of the brightness resplendent in her mind strike roots in yours so that you may advance, accompanied by an angel of God as bridal attendant, to the heavenly Bridegroom. As often as any troublesome thought comes to you, set this letter before you like a reproachful figure in a picture, and, in spite of the fact that I am within the walls of Rome, yet you will be able to see a likeness of your uncle writing this.[12] And when, returning with the grace of God accompanying me, I have lovingly received welcome reports of you, I shall return relieved from anxiety to the land of my birth, and I shall love you more entirely to the end of life without interruption.

Acquaint the chapter of consecrated virgins with this letter so that their daily prayer for me may ascend to God above.[13] I do not fail to trust that I shall be borne through the ocean waves by their prayers and shall reach the threshold of the greatest apostles and shall visit the city, mistress of the world, who shows forth purple clad memorials of a thousand martyrs.[14] I cannot seek for the blessed Margaret

---

10 Song of Songs 5.4–8.

11 Margaret of Antioch, an immensely popular saint, especially in England, had no existence as a historical person. According to her legend she became a Christian and refused the advances of the pagan governor. She was swallowed by a hellish dragon, tortured in various ways, and was finally beheaded. She gave aid in various kinds of sickness and in childbirth and was frequently depicted in wall-paintings and stained glass windows. 'Purple of martyrdom' refers obviously to her purple blood, but perhaps also to the royal purple of the triumphant martyr.

12 'Picture' may also refer to a mnemonic system of calling to mind concepts and facts by picturing them in an imaginary building or landscape. See Frances Yates, *The Art of Memory* (London: Routledge and Kegan Paul, 1966).

13 'Chapter', meaning the governing body of a cathedral or monastery, seems the best translation for *senatus* but the word was not in general use at this time. Latham cites 1147 and c. 1160 as the first uses of *capitolium* meaning 'chapter', 'chapter meeting' or 'chapterhouse'.

14 Purple-clad may have reference to Margaret's suffering and glory referred to in note 11 above, but may well refer also to hangings in the churches of Rome; a regular use of liturgical colours is not recorded until the beginning of the twelfth century in Rome.

at Antioch but I shall endeavour at Rome to worship Cecilia the glorious bride of God with bended knees. Meanwhile let these things remain firm in your memory until I return; until, like a giant of the Church, I return rejoicing from the toil of my journey.

May this grace of which I speak be with me; for his love I receive the first-fruits of my Roman travels.[15] May he protect you who remain in your native land and guide me, an exile from my compatriots, Jesus Christ, our Lord God who, with the Father and the Holy Spirit, lives and reigns for ever and ever. Amen.

Osbert of Clare to his Nieces Margaret and Cecilia in Barking Abbey: Heavenly Rewards for Virgins in Barking. Letter 22 to Cecilia

Osbert of Clare, servant of the Church of God, sealed with the sign of Christ, to Cecilia, his dearest niece, reaching out in contemplation to the beatific vision of God among the daughters of Jerusalem

Be mindful, O daughter of Syon, that the celestial Bridegroom, to whom you have made a promise in bonds of love, deems your soul worthy of adorning with everlasting splendour.[16] For the king of peace calls you to the realm of heavenly life. He gives you hope of the gift of perpetual youth and the joy of everlasting springtime by the grace of God. For in those halls of the supernal ruler there will be angels, your bridal attendants, the citizens of God, to lead you into the king's chamber and to clothe you in purple and fine linen dyed with colours, the sure sign of holy reward.[17] Truly, your virginity, which has not experienced the loss of chastity in this holy marriage, will be crowned with a diadem and will gleam with gold, and precious stones will be skilfully set in your garments. Indeed your maiden hands will shine more beautiful than sapphire: wedding torches sparkling with lights of your good works. Your body will be robed in fair linen and fine garments. Nor will you have further need of anything else in this blessed state: the immaculate garment of chastity will adorn you for ever. For in truth it is sufficient that you are pleasing to the author of all purity and virtue; he leads you into

---

[15] 'First fruits' must refer to Osbert's own safe return and the joy of finding Margaret well; the canonization of Edward the Confessor had, however, been refused by the pope.

[16] Syon (Sion, Zion), the fortified citadel of Jerusalem captured by David, frequently standing for Jerusalem and so for the heavenly city.

[17] Esther 8.15.

his wine store in which the delightful pleasure of his love shall so intoxicate your mind that you will succeed in putting out of your thoughts whatever the vain glory of the world presents as so desirable, and it will fail.[18]

Those, then, who imbibe much wine are accustomed to forget other things quite completely; contemplation of this raises them to higher things, and whatever they delighted in in this world is emptied from their memory. Behold, he stands behind your wall, looking forth at the windows, watching through the lattice.[19] For he stands in our human nature girt with a sword to fight on your behalf against the tyrant who strives the more actively to spread these wanton desires before you. He looks in through the windows: that is, through the prophetic and apostolic teaching in which the pattern is stamped on you, and the purity of a yet brighter virtue is imprinted. Moreover, your chosen one looks through the lattice, since he shone forth through his miracles and was apparent to us, though on account of the weakness of the flesh he was hidden from us by his Passion.[20] Reverence these things and love them; for what was hidden under the shadow of the Old Testament was made manifest in the mystery of his Incarnation.

In the blessed Jeremiah and in John the Evangelist, the loveliness of virginity is set forth for you.[21] In their writings, a life made lovely with modest celibacy is a model of chastity prepared for holy virgins. Contemplate the glorious ever-virgin in converse with the angel in her room apart, consider her talking in Nazareth, so that you may learn that your dwelling place is fixed among the flowers of modesty, and in internal quiet learn to join your conversation with the messen-

---

[18] Song of Songs 2.4. Jerusalem Bible: 'in the banqueting hall', AV 'in the banqueting house'. *Cella* implies a place of concealment, 'chamber' or 'closet'.

[19] See Song of Songs 2.9: Vulgate: *ipse stat parietem nostrum respiciens per fenestras, prospiciens per cancellos*. Jerusalem Bible: 'See where he stands behind our wall. He looks in at the window, he peers through the lattice.' AV 'Behold he standeth behind our wall. He looketh forth at the windows, shewing himself through the lattice.'

[20] St Ambrose interprets the windows as the prophets. All other authors down to Anselm of Laon (fl. 1100) seem to interpret the windows as the dubious light of the miracles. Osbert regards them as both apostles and prophets.

[21] If *exprimitur* is to be translated 'is shown' and taken to mean that Jeremiah and John the Evangelist are models of virginity, this would be convincing in the case of John who is often represented as a model of devotion akin to a woman's. Jeremiah's tender grief for the sufferings of the Jews has been regarded as womanly; and, by exegetical tradition, his tears over the city of Jerusalem 'have traditionally been interpreted as figures of the life of Christ'.

gers from above. Because Nazareth is called 'flower', it is seemly for those who are consecrated to the Lord to dwell there.[22] For while they live together in the inner rooms and do not go rambling about, full of pride, out of doors, they speak to the Lord through secret inspiration and respond delightfully with inward sweetness. Consider how many women have died when their chastity was defiled, and how many purchased danger of death in exchange for the dowry of marriage settlements. For when the womb is swollen, the face grows pale, the blood vessels are enlarged, the eyes are hollow, the fingers grow thin, the skin grows sallow, the breasts are distended. The inward parts are rent apart and the outward parts are all misshapen in giving birth. You can consider how much more sweet and pleasant is that parturition in which no woman dies while she is giving birth. How noble are the offspring which the virtues bear; in which chastity does not suffer the expense of modesty and the woman giving birth is not defiled in the chamber of the bridegroom.[23]

Remember, O daughter of God, with what care rich men of this world guard their wives; how they appoint men whom they trust to guard their wives lest the weaker gender should fall into error. Pray then to Christ, the source of life, that he will appoint as guardian of your chastity the blessed martyr Lawrence who was strengthened in his glorious passion by calling on the name of Christ and who, with those above, was graced with the beauty of perpetual love in his presence.[24] Let this in particular be imprinted daily on your remembrance so that when you call to mind how so great a man triumphed over the fires that he scorned he may extinguish the flames of sin in you; for the fire of lust in the flesh is wont to burn maidens and young men;

---

22 'Those who are consecrated to the Lord': people who were consecrated for life or for a shorter period, and observed certain restrictions in life were known as Nazarites, but the word could also be used for inhabitants of Nazareth and is particularly suitable for nuns whose life is restricted but sheltered and fertile.

23 Emphasis on the evils of marriage, as well as on the anxieties and griefs of parenthood, was present in Christian thinking from early times. See Ambrose, *On Virginity* 6, 31–2; Jerome, *Against Helvidius* 20 (PL 23: 213–14). Origen, *Commentary on the Song of Songs* 4.13.191 and elsewhere.

24 Lawrence (d. 258) was chief of the deacons of Rome and so in charge of the relief of the poor and sick (see Acts 6). When ordered to produce the treasures of the church for the Prefect, he is reputed to have presented the poor saying, 'These are the treasures of the Church', and in punishment was slowly roasted to death on a gridiron. Modern scholars are of the opinion that he was beheaded like other contemporary martyrs. He was buried in a catacomb on the Via Tiburtina. A basilica was later built over the grave and is known as San Lorenzo fiori le Mure (St Lawrence-outside-the-Walls).

the injurious heat of tinder of sin can inflame the weaker gender more powerfully. For indeed this deacon overcame the fire in himself with the fire of heavenly love; the heavenly dew of grace has driven away evil humours, and oil will not consent to live in the same pot with ink, no matter where.[25] At any rate, [Lawrence] is certain to supply you with wholesome food and to pour down showers of heavenly dew if he sees your strong desire to master the troublesome heats of the flesh.[26]

In a certain church of his in Rome, a marvellous event has occurred, unheard of in our time in connection with any other saint. You ought to study it with eager attention so that you imprint it on your mind; do not fail to share it with the fellow citizens of your virgin life.

One night the sacrist had been extremely late in waking the brothers for the holy vigil and was lying awake in his cubicle (I do not know what he was waiting for in this space of time) when suddenly he saw the whole church shining with a flash of lightning, and through the east window of the blessed building, from near the Lord's table, there entered the magnificent figure of a king accompanied by a host of young men dressed in white.[27] There was an innumerable crowd of this glorious company, clad in purple and jasper with fine linen and lawn and with gold. Indeed, the hero, bearing a sceptre, stood pre-eminent, renowned for his merit; glory had crowned him with a diadem of indescribable splendour, and grace embellished him with unfading youth.

When the sacrist gazed in astonishment at his approach and marvelled at the unaccustomed splendour of such an unexpected sight, the heavenly chief of deacons came to him in his fear and, as he marvelled, spoke to him in this manner, 'Why', he said, 'have you been detained by such delay in your holy vigils? Why do you not show greater zeal in your nightly watching? Now', he said, 'that

---

25 Probably 'oil' is the 'heavenly grace', which suggests the holy oil used in anointing the sick and other ceremonies; 'ink' is the black and defiling element of sin.

26 'Wholesome food' and 'heavenly dew' refers to Lawrence's blessings to his followers but more particularly to the bread and wine of the Eucharist.

27 The sacrist had charge of the service of the altar – linen, silver, wine, bread and candles. If candles were used for measuring time, the sacrist would naturally be responsible for giving the time for services. See C. H. Lawrence, *Mediaeval Monasticism* (London & New York: Longman, 1989), p. 301.

solemn hour has passed when your duty was to rouse the brothers from the sleep of idleness, from their nightly rest.'

And when the sacrist, frightened and dumbfounded, remained transfixed by his voice and appearance the beautiful figure spoke once more to the man who was attending with heart and soul to the words of such a person, 'Do not be fearful at the sight of my glory which is before you, since I have not come here to strike you with terror, but to show you the grandeur of my immeasurable glory. Perhaps you are in doubt as to who it is who speaks to you, whose great beauty you gaze at, which seems to surpass the brightness of the sun. You marvel even at my companions, whose beauty, splendour, and great numbers are, till now, strange to you. But so that you may be more at ease in your mind and firmer in uninterrupted allegiance to me, I will tell you my name without any doubt. I am the holy martyr of God, Lawrence, under whose name the church here is consecrated and for whom the zealous devotion of the community here is employed.[28] I am your lord, in whose name you are accustomed to rejoice and to applaud the glory with which he is resplendent among the fellow citizens of the angels. For I am the athlete of Christ who, for his name, stood bravely and endured fire and iron, and I have always assisted in prayers before the face of God in heaven all those who venerate my memory on earth.'

'For you know yourself that you too are commended in my prayers because I have always perceived that you are devoted to me. I have discovered the zeal of your faith and love, both on every weekday and the same on the feast day when the triumphant victory of my martyrdom is celebrated. This privilege God has given me by grace: that I should be deemed worthy to free many who have been given up to punishment. For I descend to penitential prisons, and those who before my coming were never free from torture, were straightway freed from their burden with joy at the sight of my face. For as many as are able to cling to my sides rise with me from their punishment to the glory on high. Hence it is that they whom you see flowering in immeasurable beauty were led this night from the place of punish-

---

28 *Familia* means properly the household slaves or 'domestics', and thence the whole household – the head of the family, his wife, children, servants and others living under the same roof. It came to mean any group bound closely together: gladiators, philosophers, etc. In Christian usage it might be a bishop's household, a ship's company, or even a set of chessmen. Here it is translated it as 'community', but later as 'family' when Lawrence is taking affectionate leave of the worshippers.

ment by my potent virtue. Then love my memory with deepest devotion in whatever way of life you have undertaken, for I always stand
close before the face of God on behalf of those who are assiduous in
prayers and who habitually venerate with delight the memory of my
name.'

'Rise then, and rouse the brothers for the night service, for you
should have done it long since if the welcome joy of my words had
not kept you. For you must know that this famous place belongs especially to me and I am in the habit of often revisiting it with the
greatest affection, since my family has wisely done what pleases
God. But now I say farewell to you and to all of them, and ascend
victorious to my Lord with spoils of triumph.'

And saying this, the holy martyr of God, Lawrence, returned by
the wonderful power of God by the same course by which he came,
for he was seen to be raised from the earth, to go steadfastly in the air
and to pass over the Lord's table just like the Eucharist of Christ's
body.[29] But when he reached the eastern window, the unconquered
martyr passed through it just as the rays of the sun go through glass.
Ascending, indeed, to the glory above with the joyful multitude of
captives, with raised voice he began that antiphon which the
universal Church, glorifying God, sings in his praise, 'I did not deny
you, O God, on the gridiron, and when I was put to the flames, I
confessed that you were Christ.' For the rest, in truth, all that multitude sang with raised voices and that chorus arose happy and
glorious with such great melody as far as the heavens.

Consider, then, my dearest child, how many they are who are
protected by the blessed martyr Lawrence, and make him your advocate, lest you should fear as a harsh judge him on whom you ought to
look with a chaste conscience as your Redeemer. If you have had the
will to commit the more secret devotion of your heart to him, he can
and will care for the diseases of your soul with heavenly remedies.
For he has influence with your Lord, and God has power to cause
grace to abound in you through him, so that virgin glory under the
discipline of rule will be pleasing to you and you will not be separated from the will of God. Be mindful then of those who give birth

---

[29] A vision in which the Eucharist is brought by doves or angels or soars by itself
through the air seems to have become common among religious women in the
thirteenth century. See Caroline W. Bynum, *Fragmentation and Redemption*
(New York: Zone, 1991), p. 123.

to offspring to the heavenly Bridegroom in untouched virginity and have not suffered the loss of their modesty by giving birth.

As example I offer one in particular whose name you bear, I trust, with integrity of flesh: I mean the blessed Cecilia who was accustomed to shine in gold and jewels and yet, for all that, in the eyes of the angels of God was dressed in garments of goat's hair. Imitate her faithfulness and take prudence as companion for yourself, so that by loving your Creator you may deserve his protection. May the Holy Spirit who wished to inflame her with love for himself deign to kindle your mind with his heat; may he deem you worthy to follow in the footsteps of the blessed martyr Cecilia, and through her to lay hands in heaven on the crown of everlasting virginity: while exalted above all is her spouse Jesus Christ, the Son of the Virgin, who is God and our Lord; to whom with the Father and the same Holy Spirit be honour and power through all generations, world without end. Amen.

V Abelard to Heloise: On Educating Virgins (Letter 9)

L etter 9 of Abelard's correspondence with Heloise, written probably between 1132 and 1135, is concerned with learning and education. As in Letter 7's history of women and the Christian Church, Abelard's aim is to reach the spiritual values behind the practical injunctions. Abelard appears to have felt an affinity with Jerome (c. 342–420), the fourth-century doctor of the Church whom he takes as his principal source and model in this letter. Passionate, deeply learned, quick-tempered as they both were, they also suffered from scandalous comment on their association with learned women. While in Rome, Jerome had been a frequenter of the circle of rich, learned and austere Roman widows among whom Paula was a leader. He wrote to Paula's daughter-in-law, Laeta, in 403, in response to her request for advice in bringing up her daughter Paula. He dealt with the training of the little girl from her weaning, and when we remember that many inhabitants of nunneries and monasteries were oblates, offered to the Church as children, it is clear that their education would begin, as Paula's did, with learning their letters. Abelard seems to have envisaged this training as what the nuns might give children in their care and also as what Heloise might arrange for the instruction of older members of her community where necessary.

The education which Jerome advised and which Abelard repeated is strict in its controls on pleasure and worldliness, but both writers show great tenderness for the young child, who must be encouraged to learn by success, praise, and emulation. So far the object was to enable the child to read the Bible and to sing the psalms and canticles. For Abelard, however, this was only the beginning. The children were to be introduced gradually to the different books of the Bible so that they could learn the appropriate spiritual lessons without being led astray by what they did not properly understand.

Unlike those writers, such as Osbert of Clare, who stress the rewards chastity will bring to young women in conventual life, Abelard assumes his readers are chaste and virtuous and shows them the way of scholarship as an escape from idleness, frivolity, and temptation. He repeats Jerome's praise of Marcella, one of the widows of Rome, whose devotion to study made her constant in her pursuit of knowledge of the Scriptures. He urges the value of knowing Greek and Hebrew for a real understanding of the Scriptures, knowledge which Heloise, most exceptionally among her contemporaries, is thought to have had herself. He points out the great advantage to the Paraclete nuns in having so learned a mother in religion as Heloise. He sets before them the ladies of Rome and their own abbess as models, and he strengthens Heloise by praising her achievements and by supplying the familiar but continuingly powerful image of the abbess as mother of rewarding children.

Abelard to Heloise: On Educating Virgins (Letter 9)

[St Jerome's concern for the education of nuns and laypeople]
As the blessed Jerome was greatly concerned with the education of Christ's virgins, among the other things that he wrote for their instruction, he recommended to them in particular the study of Scripture and he did not so much exhort them to this by words as attract by examples.[1] Certainly I remember the maxim which he pronounced when he was instructing the monk Rusticus; 'Love the knowledge of the Scriptures and you will not love the sin of the flesh.'[2] He thought the love of this study so much the more necessary for women as he perceived that they were weaker by nature and frailer in body. He does not adduce this argument, taken from the analogy of virgins, for the encouragement of virgins alone; from it he took widows and wives as examples for a comparison of lesser importance. He urged the brides of Christ to this study, and urging lay people through the lay widows he drove out and disconcerted the sloth of monks through the virtue of lay people. And since according to that saying of Gregory, 'Everyone begins from the smallest things in order to come to the greater,' it is helpful to set down in advance with what earnestness he devoted himself to initiating young nuns or little girls in

---

[1] Letter 9 lacks the formal beginning and ending of other letters and in its only extant manuscript is entitled 'Here begins the sermon of master Peter Abelard to the virgins of the Paraclete about the study of letters.' This letter both refers to Heloise and is addressed to her nuns: it is not hard to accept this as a letter of advice to an abbess for the benefit of those for whom she is responsible. It may be the continuation of Letter 8, Abelard's Rule for Heloise's convent of the Paraclete (see Betty Radice, tr., *The Letters of Abelard and Heloise* (Harmondsworth: Penguin, 1974), for a translation of Letter 8).

[2] Jerome, Letter 125 (CSEL 56: 130). Rusticus became a monk on Jerome's advice and was later Bishop of Narbonne. He and Jerome later quarrelled over the heresy of Origen.

sacred writing.[3] Leaving out other matters, he now goes on from this to the middle part which deals with this study of letters and sends [this letter] to Laeta on the education of her little daughter Paula.[4]

[The rudiments of reading and writing for the child Paula]
'This is the way in which the soul which is to be the temple of God is to be instructed. Let her have letters of box or ebony and called by their names. Let her play with them and let her play be learning. And do not only let her keep the letters in order but let the order often be disturbed; the last mixed with the middle and the middle with the first. And when she has begun to direct the stylus to the wax with her hand either let her tender joints be guided by the hand of another person or let the rudiments be formed on the tablet, so that the traces are drawn inside the margins, enclosed by the same grooves, and she should not seek to wander outside. Let her join the syllables to the first one and let her be encouraged to the minuscules which she is able to inscribe at that age. In her lessons let her have companions whom she envies and whose praise nettles her. She should be encouraged by praise so that she is pleased when she succeeds and grieves when she is unsuccessful. Care should be taken at the beginning that she does not hate her studies lest the harshness which she felt in childhood should last beyond her unformed years. The very words, by which she is in the habit little by little of constructing sentences should not be selected at random but planned and diligently accumulated: from the prophets, of course, and from the apostles and let the whole succession of patriarchs come down according to Matthew and Luke,[5] so that while she does something else the list is prepared for her to remember in the future.'

[In the master the smallest qualities are important]
'The chosen master must be of fit age and manner of life and learning. Nor should a learned man blush to do in relation to a noble virgin what Aristotle did for the son of Philip so that he transmitted

---

3   Cf. Gregory, *Moralia in Job* 31.34 (CCSL 143B: 1601–2); see Abelard, Sermon 8 (PL 178: 439C), 16 (498C), 26 (544D), 29 (555D).
4   Laeta was the daughter-in-law of Paula, one of the circle of ladies rich, learned, and austere whom Jerome instructed and inspired in Rome. Laeta had asked Jerome for guidance on bringing up her daughter the younger Paula. What follows is taken from Jerome, Letter 107 to Laeta, section 4 (CSEL 55: 293).
5   Matt. 1.1–17; Luke 3.23–38.

to him the usefulness of books and writing.[6] Even small things are not to be despised, for without them great things cannot exist. The very sound of the elements of the language and the first instruction is presented in one way by an educated mouth, in another way by an uneducated one. Nor ought she to learn in her tender years what ought to be taught to her later. It is difficult to get rid of whatever the mind has assimilated in raw youth. A Greek story tells that King Alexander could not get himself free from the bad habits of manner and gait of his tutor Leonidas which he had acquired when he was a small child.'[7] So that she can commit the pronunciation of Scripture to memory he wishes her to set a fixed amount of reading for each day and when she performs what she holds in memory, he advises her to take pains not only with Latin but also with Greek writing (since both languages were in common use at that time) and, particularly as regards the Scriptures, translated from Greek into Latin so that she should get to know them better from their original and be able to distinguish them more exactly.[8] For Latin Christendom was not yet using a translation of orthodox belief from the Hebrew. So [Jerome] said: 'Let Latin lessons follow immediately, for if the mouth of tender years had not construed it from the beginning the language would be degraded and turned into foreign pronunciation and the native speech would be defiled by foreign. As much as gems and silk let her love the holy books, in which it is not the picture decorated with gold and Babylonian parchment which pleases, but the fine judgement corrected and learned which satisfies faith.'[9]

[A reasoned progress through the books of the Bible]
'Let her learn the Psalter first; let her devote herself to these canticles; let her be instructed for life by the proverbs of Solomon; let her learn the habit of treading down the things of this world in Ecclesiastes; let her follow eagerly the examples of courage and patience in

6   Alexander the Great (356–323 BC), son of King Philip of Macedon, was taught as a youth by the philosopher Aristotle, whose writings later had a great influence on Christian thinking.

7   Apart from the virtually contemporary histories of Alexander by Arrian and Callisthenes, there were in circulation in late classical and early Christian times various magical and fabulous tales of Alexander which are now lost. It is probably from one of these that this story of Leonidas is taken.

8   Jerome, Letter 107.9.

9   *Vermiculata* originally means 'wormy', so 'in wavy lines' and so 'decorated'; Babylonian in the sense of luxurious and foreign. Jerome, Letter 107.9 (CSEL 55: 300).

Job. Let her go to the Gospels and never afterwards put them from her hands. Let her take in the Acts of the Apostles and the whole of the Epistles with willing heart. And when she has filled the whole storehouse of her breast with these riches let her put to memory the prophets and the Heptateuch and the books of the Kings and of the Paralipomenon, the books of Esdras and Esther.[10] Finally she may learn the Song of Songs without danger, and not be harmed by reading it at the beginning by not understanding that it was the bridal song of spiritual marriage under carnal words. Let her beware of all apocryphal books and if ever she wishes to read them, not for true dogma but reverence of the miracles, let her know that they are not what their title implies. Many evil things are intermingled there, and great care is needed to seek for gold in the mud. Let her always have the treatises and letters of Cyprian in her hand.[11] Let her hasten through the letters of Athanasius and the books of Hilary with unhindered feet.[12] Let her be delighted by the tractates and the way of thinking of those who do not waver in their duty to the faith in their books. Let her read others in such a way that she judges rather than takes them as guide.'

[The best place to bring up a young girl]
'You [Paula's mother Laeta] will reply, "How shall I, a laywoman, be able to observe all these things in such a great crowd of people at Rome?" Then do not try to undertake a burden that you cannot carry, but after you have weaned her, send away the grandmother and aunts, give back the precious jewel to the chamber of Mary and place it in the cradle of the crying Jesus.[13] Let her be fostered in a convent, let her be among the choir of virgins; let her know nothing of worldly affairs; let her live as an angel; let her be in the body without the body; let her think every human race like her own and, not to speak

---

10 The Heptateuch: the first seven books of the Bible (Genesis, Exodus, Leviticus, Numbers, Deuteronomy, Joshua, Judges). The Paralipomenon: the two books known as the third and fourth book of Kings or the first and second of Chronicles. Esdras and Esther: books appearing in the Greek Old Testament, but not in the Hebrew Bible.
11 Saint Cyprian (d. 258), Bishop of Carthage; during the Decian persecution he was forced to flee and continued to rule his church in exile by letters.
12 St Athanasius (296–373), Bishop of Alexandria; an implacable opponent of Arianism. St Hilary of Poitiers (c. 315–367) 'The Athanasius of the West': writer of histories and commentaries.
13 'The crying Jesus': an odd expression but presumably implying, 'the infant Jesus'.

of other things, she will release you from the difficulty of looking after her and the dangers of guardianship.[14] It is better to long for the one who is absent from you than to fear for her. Give the little girl to Eustochium.[15] She will admire her from her earlier years for her speech, and mien and carriage trained in godliness. Let her be in the bosom of the grandmother who has learnt by long experience to nourish, teach and protect maidens. Hannah, who had dedicated her son to the Lord, afterwards offered him at the Tabernacle and never took him back again.'[16]

[Jerome is willing to take responsibility for Paula's education himself]
'If you yourself are anxious for Paula I will assume responsibility as teacher and nurse. I will bear her on my shoulder; I, an old man, will pronounce stammering words. I should then be more famous in the world than the philosopher, since I did not teach the Macedonian king who was to perish by Babylonian poison [i.e., Alexander], but I taught the bride of Christ fit to be presented to the heavenly realm.'[17]

[Abelard commends Jerome's thoroughness]
Consider, also, my dearest sisters in Christ, and keep in mind how much care so great a doctor of the Church undertook in the education of one little girl, how he specified so particularly all the things that he laid down that were necessary, taking the beginning from the very

14 Angels were regarded by both Jews and Christians as spirits, pure and sexless, whose function was to worship God in heaven and to act as his messengers on earth. One explanation of the presence of evil in the world lay in the intercourse between Adam and Eve or between human women and fallen angels (cf. Gen. 6.2). The religious, especially nuns, who occupied their time in worship and denied the flesh in every way, but above all sexually, were of all inhabitants of earth the most like the angels in heaven.

15 Eustochium (370–c. 419): The daughter of the elder Paula (see note 4 above). The influence of Jerome on the family was such that the austerities that he encouraged were held responsible for the death of Blesilla, Eustochium's sister. At the same time he was accused of a scandalous relationship with Paula. Jerome left Rome, followed a few months later by Paula and Eustochium. They met in Antioch, travelled to Egypt, and finally settled in Bethlehem where they founded four convents.

16 I Sam 1.20–28.

17 *Balbuciencia*: babbling. Wright translates 'my old tongue shall train her stammering lips', thus jokingly relating the child and the old man; Jerome, Letter 107.12–13 (CSEL 55: 302). It is more probable that Alexander died of fever than by poison.

alphabet itself. He produced an example of pronouncing the syllables and distinguishing the words; he even produced an example of writing and also saw to it that there were suitable companions who would incite her by envy or praise. He even advises that she should be encouraged by kind words, and praise and even little presents in order that she should act of her own will and not under compulsion, and take up her studies with great delight. He also specifies those words which must be taken from Holy Scripture; and in quoting these words she should first occupy herself and particularly should commit them to memory, as that verse says, 'A shard freshly moistened will keep the scent for a long time.'[18]

He carefully describes the kind of teacher who should be chosen for this purpose, and he does not fail to mention that there ought to be a set amount of reading which she construes by heart each day. And since at that time the use of Greek scholarship was very common in Rome, he does not allow her to be lacking in Greek learning, particularly, as I think, since the handing down of holy learning from the Greeks to us has been neglected. She may from this study be able to distinguish what deserves less or different attention, and perhaps by the discipline of liberal arts she may learn something of use from those who press forward to perfection of doctrine. And he sets out this instruction in the Latin language as if our teaching began from that. But when her senses had registered the sounds made by the voices and she wanted to understand what she had learnt to repeat, she knew the difference between various versions of Scripture, both of the canon of the two testaments as of the lesser works of the doctors, and she was able to progress in learning from them to perfect knowledge.

[The supreme importance for women of reading the Scriptures]
Among the canonical Scriptures he commends the Gospels to her in such a way that he advises that they should never leave the maiden's hand, as if to say the deaconesses should be more attached to the reading of the Gospels: since the men had to read them in church, the women ought never to cease reading them. Finally writing to this mother about her daughter, lest the mother should offer as an excuse that a laywoman could not perform all these things at Rome in such

[18] Horace, *Letters* 1.2, 69–70, trans. by H. Ruston Fairclough, T. E. Page and others (London: William Heinemann, 1966) translates this: 'The jar will long keep the fragrance of what it was steeped in when new.' See Jerome, Letter 107.4 (CSEL 55: 295) and Abelard, *Dialogue* (45.113).

crowds of people, he gives as his advice that she should free herself from this burden and take her daughter to a convent of virgins where she could be educated without danger and instructed more effectively in matters about which he had spoken. Next, to prevent every possibility of the mother being anxious that the master should be as he had described, at length he offered himself as both teacher and nurse for the girl when she was sent from Rome to Jerusalem to her grandmother, that is the holy Paula, and her aunt Eustochium. And, what is marvellous to say, he kept his promise so well that such a doctor of the Church already weakened by age should say that he did not scorn to carry the girl on his shoulders like a porter. A thing which could not be said to be done among the suspicious without suspicion, and scarcely even among the religious without offence. But a man filled by God with all these qualities and long known by all for his purity of life used to reply boldly that, provided he could teach one virgin in this way, he would leave that one to teach others and she who had never seen Jerome should read Jerome in her.

[Jerome gives his reasons for teaching women]
To go from the little ones to the older virgins whom he always urges the most to the study of letters (as is evident from his writing in which they may read how he praises them for their application in reading and learning), we may hear what he says when writing to the virgin Principia on Psalm 44: 'I know, Principia, daughter in Christ, that many men blame me because I sometimes write to women and prefer the weaker gender to the manly, and therefore I must first reply to my critics and so come to the little dispute that you have raised.[19] If men perused the Scriptures I should not be speaking to women. If Barak had wished to go to battle, Deborah would not have triumphed over the defeated enemy.'[20] And a little later: 'Aquila and Priscilla instructed Apollos, an apostle and most learned in the law, and taught him about the way of the Lord.[21] If it was not shameful for an apostle to be taught by a woman why is it shameful for me to teach women too after the men? I have briefly glanced over these points in this manner, my daughter, so that your gender should not displease you, nor their name elate them, since the life of women is praised in

---

[19] Jerome, Letter 65 to Principia on Psalm 44 [AV Ps 45] (Paris: Collections des Universités de France) 3: 140; see also Jerome's Letters 127 and 65.

[20] Jerome, Letter 65.1 (CSEL 54: 616). For Baraih (Barak) and Deborra (Deborah) see Judges 4 and 5.

[21] Acts 18.24–28.

Holy Scripture in condemnation of men.'[22] After the virgins he
delights to consider how widows too should progress in the study of
sacred letters as he witnessed and praised them.[23]

[Wise and learned women]
So the same doctor writes to the same virgin, Principia, about the life
of Saint Marcella, as she had requested.[24] He records among the
marks of Marcella's moral perfection: 'She possessed unbelievable
zeal for the holy Scriptures and was constantly singing, "Your word
have I hidden in my heart, that I might not sin against You"; and thus
about the perfect man, "His delight is in the law of the Lord, and in
this law does he meditate day and night";[25] and, "Your precepts
endow me with perception."[26] Finally, when the needs of the Church
had drawn me too to Rome with the holy pontiffs and I modestly
avoided the eyes of noble women, she acted, as the apostle once said,
"in season and out of season", so that her zeal perforce overcame my
sense of propriety, and since I was at that time esteemed above all
names in the study of Holy Scripture it did not seem unfitting that
she should ask me questions about Scripture. She was not satisfied
immediately but presented other disputed points, not to quibble, but
by questioning to learn the answers which she saw could be made to
them. I hesitate to say what moral virtue and what intelligence I
found in her lest I venture beyond belief and stir you to greater
sorrow in recording how much good you lack. All I would say is that
she tasted whatever we gathered by long study and made it her own
by daily meditation; she learnt it and made it her own so that after
our departure, if any dispute about the evidence of Scripture arose,
recourse was had to her as judge. And since she was so very cautious,
she replied in such a manner when she was questioned that she would
even say that her sayings were not her own, but that they were mine
or some other person's, so that in the very matter in which she was
teaching she declared that she was a pupil. For she knew the injunction of the apostle, "I do not allow a woman to teach", lest harm
should appear to be done to the stronger gender and even to priests

22 Jerome, Letter 65.1–2 (CSEL 54: 616).
23 Jerome, Letter 65.1–2 (CSEL 54: 618).
24 St Marcella (325–410), a pious and cultivated Roman widow, the first of
Jerome's followers in Rome. She died as a result of her ill-treatment by the Goths
in the sack of Rome. What follows comes from Jerome's Letter 127 to Principia.
25 Ps. 1.2.
26 Jerome, Letter 127.4 (CSEL 56: 148); Ps. 119.11; 1.2; 119.104.

through women's enquiring about secret and debatable matters.[27]
When we were parted we solaced our separation with mutual encouragement and we kept in the spirit what we could not maintain in the
body. The letters always received replies, they surpassed formal
politeness, they went beyond conventional greetings. Absence did
not lack much when it was united by fresh and living words.'

[The rise of heresy]
'In this calm service of the Lord a storm of heresy arose in these
provinces; it unsettled everything and it was stirred into such
madness that it spared neither itself nor any of the good men. And if
it was not enough to have unsettled everything here, it carried a ship
full of blasphemies to the port of Rome.[28] When she discovered at
Rome the poisonous and filthy doctrines which the ship had brought,
the holy Marcella, who had long closed her eyes to this, fearing that
anything should seem to have been done out of a spirit of rivalry,
afterwards felt that her faith had been offended on many topics. For
the heresy drew priests and not a few monks too and very many
laymen into agreement with it, and made mock of simplicity, and of
the bishop who judges others by himself, so Marcella resisted
publicly, preferring to please God rather than men. This was the
beginning of the condemnation of heretics when Marcella produced
witnesses who were first taught by them and had afterwards been
turned away from their heretical errors. While she exposed the crowd
of deceivers, the *Periarchon* adduced impious things and volumes
were brought forth which were emended by a scorpion hand, while
the heretics, summoned by frequent letters to defend themselves, did
not dare to come. So great was the power of conscience that they
preferred to condemn those who were absent rather than to refute
those who were present. Marcella was the source of this famous
victory.'[29]

You see, my dearest, what delight rewarded all the faithful when
the heresies were repressed in the city through the laudable learning
set up in the mind of one matron, and by what great lamp of doctrine
one woman drove out the darkness of the doctors of the Church. That

---

[27] Jerome, Letter 127.7 (CSEL 56: 150); II Tim. 4.2; I Tim. 2.12.
[28] Jerome, Letter 127.8–9 (CSEL 56: 152). Blasphemy: the denial of Christ's
equality with God the Father. The heresy arose in Alexandria under the teaching
of Arius.
[29] *Periarchon: On First Principles*: A book by Origen. Pammachius and Oceanus
wrote to Jerome begging him to write a refutation of it.

same doctor, commenting on the first book in Paul's Epistle to the Galatians about the study of sacred writings by which she earned her victory, recalls, for your encouragement: 'I know her zeal, I know her faith, the flame she had in her breast to overcome her gender, not to speak of men, and to cross the Red Sea of this age at the beating of a drum of holy volumes. Certainly when I was at home she was never in such haste when she saw me that she did not ask some question about the Scriptures. She was not indeed, in the manner of Pythagorus, in the habit of thinking that every answer I gave was right, nor did authority prevail with her without her having come to a conclusion that she had previously thought out, but she considered everything and weighed everything with a wise mind so that I felt that I had a judge, not a pupil.'[30]

[Women's zeal to learn Greek]
'The ardour for the study of letters flamed in the holy women of that time, as in men too, so that they were by no means satisfied with those streamlets of Scripture which they possessed in their own language; they looked for the very sources and did not believe that the poverty of one language was enough for them. From this arises what was written among other things by the doctor referred to above, to Paula on the death of her daughter Blesilla, in outstanding praise of her: "Who would mention without tears her earnestness in prayer, her elegance of language, her tenacity of memory and her sharpness of wit? If you heard her speaking Greek you would think she knew no Latin; if she turned her tongue to the Roman speech her conversation would have no smack of a foreign tongue. But now Greece too marvels at what men marvel at in Origen. In, I will not say months, but in a few days she overcame the difficulties of the Hebrew language, so that she vied with her mother in learning the Psalms by heart and singing them." '[31]

Naturally the doctor did not fail to mention that the mother Paula, nor the other daughter of Paula (Eustochium, a virgin dedicated to God), were no less occupied in the same study of writings and speech. Thus when writing the life of that same Paula and recording this he says: 'No mind was more teachable than hers. She was slow to

[30] Jerome, *Commentary on Galatians*, Prologue (PL 26: 331B–332B).
[31] Origen (185– c. 254), probably born in Alexandria of Christian parents; he wrote many commentaries and homilies, many of which are now lost. At one period he undertook an extremely ascetic life. For Blesilla see note 15 above. Jerome, Letter 39.1 (CSEL 54: 344).

speak, swift to listen, mindful of that precept, "Hear, O Israel, and keep silence."[32] She retained an exact memory of the Holy Scriptures. Finally she urged me on so that she might read them through while I discussed them with her. I refused for modesty. I yielded to her persistence and repeated requests; I took it upon myself to teach what I had learnt. If I was at a loss at any point and confessed openly that I did not know, she was not willing to be content with me, but by persistent fresh enquiries pressed me to indicate which of many diverse readings seemed to me the more likely. I may say this which may perhaps even seem unbelievable to her rivals; I had learnt the Hebrew tongue from my youth with much toil and sweat and unwearying study so that now I do not forget it, nor does it forget me; but she wished to learn it, and reached such a standard that she could sing the psalms in Hebrew and she reproduced Greek speech without any Latin peculiarities. And we find this to this day in her blessed daughter Eustochium.[33] For they knew that the teaching of the Latin codices had come from Hebrew and Greek Scriptures and that the special character of each language could not be preserved by the translator in its journey. For both Hebrews and Greeks, too, boasting of their perfections, are often in the habit of despising the perfection of our translations, claiming that this is like an analogy in which, if any liquid was poured out into several vessels in turn, the volume would not be reduced, nor the same amount found in the remaining vessels as was there in the beginning. So it often happens that when we attempt to argue with the Jews on any evidence they easily show us, who know no Hebrew, to be in the wrong, from, as they say, the fallibility of our translations. And the very wise women of whom we have already spoken gave this matter great importance and were not in the least satisfied with the teaching in their own language, so that they not only instructed their own people, but were even able to confute others and satisfied their thirst with clearer water from the fountain.'

[Jerome's account of his own education]
Jerome himself, who was skilled in these languages supplied, if I am not mistaken, an example himself. He wrote in these words to Pammachius and Oceanus that he had gained perfection in this skill

---

32 Jerome, Letter 108.26 (CSEL 55: 344). There is no exact biblical source of 'Hear and keep silence', though the sentiment is frequently found, e.g., Job 29.21.
33 Eustochium: see note 15 above.

with great effort and expense:[34] 'While I was young I was drawn to learning with great devotion and taught myself without any suggestion of presumption. I frequently heard Apollinarius the Laodicean at Antioch: I cultivated him and when he instructed me I never accepted his controversial opinions beyond common sense. Now the dog's head was spectator and became the master rather than the pupil. I went on to Alexandria; I heard Didymus.[35] I give thanks to him for many things; I learnt what I did not know; when he taught me different things I did not lose what he taught me. Men thought I had reached the limits of learning. I came again to Jerusalem and Bethlehem. With what toil! At what price did I have Baramia as my teacher by night, for I feared the Jews and I showed myself another Nicodemus. I have often made mention of all these things in my minor works.'[36]

[The nuns of the Paraclete have an ideal teacher in Heloise]
Reflecting on this zeal for Holy Scripture of so great a doctor and of holy women, I advise you and long for you to pray without ceasing that while you can, and you have a mother [i.e., Heloise] skilled in these three languages, you should go on to perfection in these studies, so that, whatever dispute arises about the different translations, you may bring the examination to a conclusion. The title that was written on the cross of our Lord in Hebrew, Greek and Latin will appear to have prefigured, not unfittingly, the fact that in his Church there spread in every land the teaching of these languages which are the chief, and of which the writing of each testament consists. Nor do you need a long journey or great expense to learn these languages as the blessed Jerome did, since in your abbess, as I have said, you have a mother equal to this study. After that the virgins, too, the faithful widows, the married women show you encouragement by their teaching and either accuse you of neglect or increase your ardour.

---

34 Saint Pammachius (c. 340–410), a friend of St Jerome in Rome. When his wife, daughter of the elder Paula, died, he became a monk and gave her fortune to the pilgrim church at Ostia. A peace-loving man, he disapproved of Jerome's involvement in violent controversy. Oceanus joined Pammachius in asking Jerome to write a refutation of *Periarchon* (see note 29 above). In his reply Jerome addressed them as brothers.

35 Didymus of Alexandria (313–398), blind from birth, a teacher and writer.

36 Nicodemus: See John 3.1–15; Jerome, Letter 84 (CSEL 55: 122).

[Celancia's request for guidance in marriage]
The revered Celancia, also, stands out as an example for you: she, wanting to live in marriage according to a Rule, begged earnestly that Jerome would prescribe a rule of marriage for her.[37] Replying to her about this, he reminds her: 'I was encouraged to write by your letter; I was for a long time in doubt, for modesty demanded silence. For you ask earnestly, even urgently, that we should prescribe a sure rule from Holy Scripture by which you might arrange the course of your life. So that among the honours of the world, the attractions of wealth, you should love the customs of the marriage-bed more, and you should be able, when you are established in marriage, to please your husband, but also him who granted this marriage. If anyone is not satisfied with this virtuous request, what else is there indeed but not to love? I will answer your request, and, if you are prepared to fulfil God's will, I will strive to quicken your thoughts.'

[Virtuous wives]
Perhaps this married woman may hear what Scripture reports in praise of the holy Susanna. When she was declared first to be 'extremely beautiful and God-fearing', and that from those qualities came her reverence and true grace, it immediately adds, 'For her parents, being upright, instructed her according to the Law of Moses.'[38] Through the troubles of marriage and the disturbances of secular occupations Susanna was not unmindful of this education, and when she was condemned to death, her judges and presbyters deserved to be put to death for her sake. When Jerome expounded the passage where it is said in Daniel, 'Since her parents were just they taught their daughter, etc.', astutely taking the opportunity he said, 'Making use of this is an occasion for exhorting parents that they should teach not only their sons, but their daughters, too, according to the law of God and the divine teaching.'[39]

---

[37] *Letter to Celancia*, once ascribed to Jerome, is attributed by B. R. Rees, in *The Letters of Pelagius and His Followers* (Woodbridge: The Boydell Press, 1991), to Pelagius; he observes that 'nothing further appears to be known about Celancia (Celantia)'. See Pseudo-Jerome, Letter 148.1–2 (PL 22: 1204–29; 61: 723–36; CSEL 129: 436–59).

[38] Apocrypha, *History of Susanna*, vv. 2.3.

[39] Jerome: *Comm. On Daniel IV.* 13 (CCSL 75A: 945).

[The Queen Sheba]

And since riches are commonly accustomed to hinder the pursuit of learning as of virtue, let the Queen Sheba drive away all your neglectful sloth: that very rich queen who, despite the great fatigue to her feeble sex and the toil of a long journey, as well as dangers and very great expense, came from the ends of the earth to have experience of the wisdom of Solomon and to discuss what he knew of things of which she was ignorant.[40] Solomon approved so highly of her zeal and effort that he gave her as reward everything that she asked for, apart from what he had presented to her according to his royal custom. Many powerful men came together to hear his wisdom and many of the kings, and leaders of the world gave honour to his teaching with great gifts, and he is said to have rewarded no one of them more than that woman of whom we have spoken. From this it is clearly shown how much he approved of women's holy learning and zeal for instruction, and how much he thought it was pleasing to God. And a little later, God himself and the true Solomon (and far greater than Solomon), in condemning the learning of men, did not fail to make known his condemnation: 'The Queen of the South', he said, 'shall rise up in judgement with this generation, and shall condemn it etc.'[41] Be careful, my dearest ones, lest your neglect condemn you too in that group of people. It is not necessary to undertake a long journey in haste or provide for great outlay to excuse your ignorance. You have skill in your mother [i.e. Heloise] which can suffice for all purposes; that is, as an example of virtue as well as instruction in letters, for she is not unskilled in letters, not only in Latin but even in Hebrew and Greek; she alone in this age seems to have achieved practical knowledge of three languages, so that according to the blessed Jerome she is declared unique in grace by all, and is thereby specially to be included among the venerable women spoken of above.

[The significance of the three languages in Christian learning]

The two testaments come to our knowledge in three principal languages. For the title of the Lord was affixed on the cross in three languages, written, that is, in Hebrew, Greek and Latin. Clearly it implies that teaching about the Lord, the praise of Christ and the very

---

40 Solomon (I Kings 3.11), also the Queen of Sheba (I Kings 10.1–13 and 2 Chron. 9:1–12), but known in the Vulgate as Queen Sheba. Solomon's achievements of every kind were celebrated in history, but in the Middle Ages he was especially known as a paragon of wisdom.

41 Matt. 12.42. The true Solomon is Christ.

mystery of the Trinity, would be declared and affirmed in the three zones of the world, just as the wood of the cross, on which the title was placed, was threefold. For it is written; 'In the mouth of two witnesses, or three witnesses, shall every word be established.'[42] Accordingly, in order that the Holy Scriptures should be sanctioned by the authority of the three languages, and the teaching of each language should be confirmed by the witness of the others, divine providence decreed that both the Old and the New Testaments should be expressed in these three languages. The New Testament itself, which surpasses the old in grandeur as in usefulness, is known to have been first written in these three languages, as if the title placed on the cross signalled in advance what was to happen. For certain things within it written in Hebrew need that language to express themselves; likewise those in Greek, and some are characteristic of the Roman tongue and it is necessary that the scribes should be directed in that language. In fact, the first Gospel, according to Matthew, since it was written for the Jews, was originally written in Hebrew. It is also certain that the epistle of Paul to the Hebrews, and of James to the twelve tribes now dispersed, and perhaps not a few others, were written in Hebrew for the same reason. Who doubts that the three Gospels were written in Greek to the Greeks, as well as whatever letters of Paul and the others that were destined for them; and the Apocalypse, too, was sent by him to the seven churches? We do indeed know of one letter of Paul written to the Romans so that we Latins boast a little but we are aware how the teaching of others is necessary for us.

[The difficulties of translation]

But if we were to study to translate them fully we should have to seek in that fount itself rather than in the streamlets of translation, particularly since the varying translations create ambiguity rather than certainty for the reader. For the idiom – that is, the peculiar expression of each language – is not easy, so that (as we have mentioned above) it is possible to keep the translation faithfully and adapt each interpretation in turn so that we can express them in a foreign language as they were expressed in their own language. For when we wish to set out some thing in another language we often fail when we do not have the right word to express it precisely.

42 Deut. 17.6; Matt. 18.16.

[Jerome's difficulties and successes as translator]
We know also that the blessed Jerome, outstandingly skilled among us in these three languages, sometimes varied very much from himself in his translations and in his commentaries on them. For often he says in his expositions, 'thus it runs in the Hebrew', but what he claims in his translations to be according to the Hebrew cannot be found when they are completed. Then what is remarkable if different interpreters differ in turn, when one is sometimes found to differ from himself?

[The pure rivers of learning]
If anyone wants to be sure about these things he must not be satisfied with the water of rivulets, he must seek the purity of the spring and drink from it. By this procedure the blessed Jerome's translation, which was very novel and taken from the Hebrew or the Greek as far he himself was able, just as though he had sought diligently from the source of the spring, surpassed the old translations which we had. 'When new things supersede', thus it is written in the law, 'old things are thrown out.'[43] And also Daniel: 'Many people shall run to and fro', said he, 'and knowledge shall be increased.'[44] Jerome in his own time did what he could, though as it were alone in a foreign language, having no reliable interpreter but a Jew (with whose help he shone brilliantly). As he himself bore witness, many were displeased because he did not believe that the translations already made were adequate, and because he stood firm in his intention, like that quotation of Ecclesiastes, and with the help of God accomplishing it: 'To the fountain whence they came, the rivers return that they may flow again.'[45] Like the sources of fountains, the sources of the translation of Scripture provide the origins from which they are derived. Translations which, as it were, are lying can rapidly be proved wrong if, when they have deviated from their original, they cannot be shown to be in agreement with its underlying meaning. But lest we should

43 Lev. 26.10. The quotation has little connection with the text, being a promise of prosperity for those who keep the Law. 'You shall eat your fill of last year's harvest, and still throw out the old to make room for the new.'
44 Dan. 12.4 (AV, following the Vulgate). The Jerusalem Bible follows the Septuagint ('Many will wander this way and that, and wickedness will go on increasing').
45 Ecclesiastes 1.7: 'Into the sea all the rivers go, and yet the sea is never filled, and still to their goal the rivers go' (Jerusalem Bible). 'All the rivers run into the sea; yet the sea is not full; unto the place from whence the rivers come, thither they return again' (AV).

believe that this one interpreter is enough for all occasions, as if he had acquired skill in each language by training, particularly in Hebrew, in which he is said to surpass any of us, let us hear this witness himself on this subject; let us not presume to ascribe more to him than he possessed. He wrote on this subject to Pammachius and Marcella against his accuser in these words: 'We who have at least a little knowledge of the Hebrew language, and somehow or other do not lack Latin speech, we are more able to judge and to express in our own language what we understand of others.'[46]

Happy is that soul who meditates 'on the law of the Lord day and night',[47] and for whom it is sufficient to drink each passage of Scripture as though it were purest water from the source of that fountain, and not through ignorance and inability to take those streams for pure ones as they run away confusedly in different directions, and so be compelled to vomit up what it had drunk. This study of foreign tongues has been lacking among men this long time and with neglect the knowledge of those languages has been lost. What we have lost among men we regain among women, to the condemnation of men and the reproach of the stronger gender. The Queen of the South again seeks the wisdom of the true Solomon in you. You are so much the more able to take over this since nuns are less able to toil in physical exertion than monks are, and because of their quiet inactivity and by the weakness of their nature it is easier for them to fall into temptation.

From this the aforesaid doctor, outstanding in teaching, and exhorting you both by his writing and his example, urges your effort towards the study of letters; especially so that it should never be necessary to call in men on a matter of learning, or that the spirit, concentrating uselessly on the body should wander out of doors and, abandoning her spouse, should fornicate with the world.

---

[46] Jerome, *Against Rufinus* 2.28 (CCSL 79: 66).
[47] Ps. 1.2.

VI Goscelin of St Bertin: Lives of the Abbesses at Barking (Extracts)

Abbesses had a wide range of responsibilities in the spiritual and practical care of their monastic estates. These are demonstrated in this section through the example of the concern of successive abbesses of Barking with arrangements for various kinds of burials. The organization and maintenance of cemeteries and shrines are matters of practical concern and symbolic importance: they reflect earthly concerns with hierarchy, prestige and ritual as these shaped the identity of the living community. The dead themselves, as the following extracts show, were seen as vigorously participating in and guiding this sense of identity: their status and reputation continued to provide patronage from heaven.

The source of information here is the rewriting of the lives of the abbesses of Barking, most probably carried out between 1086 and 1100, by Goscelin of St Bertin. This Flemish cleric travelled widely in England and seems to have been in demand as a refurbisher of the histories and cults of monastic houses.[1] In updating the Barking lives, Goscelin drew on earlier Latin lives, especially the accounts in the prestigious *Ecclesiastical History* of the Venerable Bede (AD 673–735). He supplemented written sources with the nuns' own memories and knowledge of the house's traditions.[2] The occasion for this updating at Barking was probably Abbess Elfgiva's desire to re-bury the bodies of her predecessors in a larger and grander shrine. Goscelin's *Life of Ethelburga* is dedicated to Bishop Maurice of London (consecrated April 1086), and Elfgiva seems to have asked Goscelin to prepare the new life in addition to the two extant narratives of the creation of new shrines in the abbey church (probably to

---

[1] For Goscelin see *The Liber confortatorius of Goscelin of St Bertin*, ed. C. H. Talbot in *Analecta monastica*, series 3, Studia Anselmiana 37, ed. M. M. Lebreton, J. Leclercq, and C. H. Talbot (Rome: Pontifical Institute of St Anselm, 1955), 1–117 (Introduction).

[2] See further Elisabeth M. C. van Houts, *Memory and Gender in Early Medieval Europe 900–1200* (Basingstoke: Macmillan, 1999), esp. p. 97.

help persuade the new Norman bishop to support the translation of these Anglo-Saxon saints).[3]

Re-burials, or 'translations' are a frequent feature in the cult of saints and in the development of monasteries: they often created increased prestige, pilgrimage, and revenues and accounts of them constitute a sub-genre of hagiographic writing. The royal and noble foundresses of the major Anglo-Saxon nunneries were usually culted as saints by their successors, both before and after the Norman Conquest. Continuity became very important to the Normans, who, after the first post-Conquest generations, reinvented cults and histories of Anglo-Saxon saints and institutions as their own history in Britain.

Goscelin's lives reveal disruptions in Barking's history as well as a concern for continuity among its abbesses: the abbey church and community may sometimes have defied Danish attacks (as in [a] below) but was destroyed in the Danish raiding of the ninth century (see [c] below). Like many other notable religious houses, Barking seems to have been in at least partial decay after the ninth-century raiding.

Nunneries were seldom as well-equipped in libraries as male houses. Barking, however, was wealthy and prestigious enough to maintain and renew its traditions and it can offer us some sense of how abbesses could draw on their house's history and precedents in planning their own administrations (even if they could not always, as extract [e] makes clear, rely on the cooperation of the churchmen of their diocese). Elfgiva's inspiration to continue with the rebuilding work in spite of difficulty and uncertainty comes both from the convent's collective will and from her predecessor's appearance to her in a dream. The metaphors that make Elfgiva pupil and nurse, daughter and new mother of Barking are Goscelin's, but his narrative is nonetheless a good example of the value of female precedent so often lacking in women's administrative and managerial careers. Goscelin's biographies show us a nunnery well capable of reconstructing its own heritage and traditions for its contemporary purposes in the eleventh century.

The abbesses of Barking mentioned by Goscelin are (in their chronological order):

---

3   Paul Antony Hayward, 'Translation Narratives in Post-Conquest Hagiography and English Resistance to the Norman Conquest', *Anglo-Norman Studies* 21 (1999), pp. 67–93 (81–3).

(1) *Ethelburga* (d. 675), co-founder, with her brother Erkenwald, Bishop of London, of the abbey. She was venerated for her saintly life and good organization of the community. Bede says 'She always bore herself in a manner worthy of her brother the bishop, upright of life and constantly planning for the needs of her community, as heavenly miracles attest' (Bede 4.7). When an epidemic killed many of the brothers (pre-Conquest Barking being, as was customary, a double monastery with monks and lay brothers as well as nuns under the charge of the abbess) Ethelburga prudently planned a cemetery, asking her nuns where they would wish to be buried if they too succumbed to the disease.

(2) *Hildelitha* (d. c. 712), also celebrated by Bede.

(3) an abbess of unknown name during whose tenure the monastery was sacked by Danes (after which it seems to have remained in a ruined state for the best part of a century).

(4) *Wulfhilda* (d. c. 1000), re-foundress, in about 970, of Barking. Wulfhilda was ejected by the Queen Mother Alftrudis, but was subsequently reinstated and died about 990 in London, whence she was brought to Barking for burial beside Ethelburga. The three saints lay there together: Wulfhilda to the right, Hildelitha to the left and Ethelburga in the centre. Goscelin describes them as being in the prominent position of the middle of the choir of the abbey church ('in medio choro': see further 'Archaeological Evidence' below).

(5) *Lifledis*, presumably abbess during the early eleventh century, but known only from this life by Goscelin.

(6) *Elfgiva*, who became abbess some time between 1051 and 1066, and died in the late 1080s. She was confirmed in office by William the Conqueror, and was his host while the Tower of London was being prepared for him. She seems to have instigated the largest building programme at Barking before the complete rebuilding of the nunnery in the 1180s. She swept away peasant holdings round about the abbey and it may be she who established tanneries and encouraged the wool trade noted later in the century.

Archaeological evidence for burials at Barking
The Abbey of Barking was excavated in 1913 by Sir Alfred Clapham, from whose work the accompanying plan is reproduced.[4]
It will be seen that there is no recognizable Anglo-Saxon work

4   See A. W. Clapham, 'The Benedictine Abbey of Barking', *Essex Archaeological Transactions* 12 (1913), 69–89.

BARKING ABBEY

12th CENTURY WORK
13th CENTURY WORK
14th & 15th CENTURY WORK

1. St. Ethelburga's Shrine (probable position.)
2. Tomb of Abbess Maud.

CHAPEL

INFIRMARY HALL

MISERICORD

WARMING HOUSE

PASSAGE

PASSAGE

CHAPTER-HOUSE

PASSAGE

PASSAGE

FRATER (REFECTORY)

CLOISTER

DORMITORY

PASSAGE

RERE DORTER

SEWER

NUNS' CEMETERY

SAINTS' CHAPEL

PRESBYTERY

NORTH TRANSEPT

TOWER

SOUTH TRANSEPT

PARISH CHURCHYARD

NAVE

PARISH CHURCHYARD

N.W. TOWER

S.W. TOWER

25 metres

100 feet

surviving; this is not surprising since Goscelin records the destruction of the buildings and the slaughter of all the nuns by Danish invaders ([c] below). Possibly the only indication of an Anglo-Saxon foundation is the fact that the cloister is to the north of what might conveniently be called Clapham's church. This practice seems to have been not uncommon in double monasteries as Barking originally was.

The main layout is described as twelfth century or later and may or may not represent Wulfhilda's rebuilding with Elfgiva's extensions, but there is evidence that there have been alterations where the apses at the east end of the north and south aisles have been replaced. The lines stated to be twelfth century are, interestingly, chiefly on the periphery so that the extent of the buildings is vouched for, and corresponds to the wealth and importance ascribed to Barking. Very little of the buildings survives, except for the church which is late medieval or modern; one must assume that the plan represents foundations or walls that have virtually disappeared under later building. What can now be seen as outlines of buildings are laid out in modern rag-stone.

The modern situation of the ruins is relevant. The Abbey ruins and the modern church lie to the west of the modern town at the foot of a modest slope and occupy an island site within the roads of a one-way system. To the west of the ruins and just beyond the road is Barking Creek. It seems strange that the nunnery was not founded on the higher and probably drier site of the modern town, but the convenient proximity of the creek to the abbey sewer may help to explain this. Moreover, from the beginning, Barking was rich, and nunneries depended on rents and dues, rather than on agriculture: dues from fishing and shipping rather than profits from farming. If we accept this plan as providing a fairly accurate representation of the site and buildings, there is no discrepancy with Goscelin's history of events in the nunnery. The light observed by Ethelburga and her nuns which had been overhead above the monastery moved to the east and set there in a position which could very well correspond to the nuns' cemetery of the plan. Though no scale is given, the cemetery is not very large by comparison with the buildings that surround it and may very well have become over-crowded as Abbess Hildelitha feared ([b] below).

It is possible to think that the 'choir' was the area labelled 'Presbytery', i.e., area reserved for priests while lay people remained in the nave. If that is so, Clapham's 'a' on the plan represents the altar, backed perhaps by a solid wall at that time, and the tombs were probably to the west of the altar. Since Goscelin describes them as 'aedicula', literally 'a chapel or small dwelling' it is likely that whether in front of or behind the altar, they might well obstruct the priest at mass and the nuns' choir-work.

Goscelin says *extendit curiam Christi et atria* (below, p. 151: Colker, 4 iii, 26). 'Atrium' properly means 'an open area and its surrounding portico' as at St Peter's in Rome; 'curia' is similarly 'an open space for assembling the people' but was also the meeting place of the Romans. Osbert of Clare sometimes uses 'curia' for Barking's chapter house, but the chapter house is not very accessible at Barking; extended, it would only infringe on the already crowded cemetery. The continuous line b–c on the plan is probably the modern boundary wall and the church extension certainly does pass it, so one is almost bound to conclude that Goscelin was using 'curia' and 'atrium' in a general sense, looking for a Latin equivalent for a native idea, and that there was an open space perhaps accessible to the townspeople outside the east end of the church. It does not seem likely that Elfgiva made extensions at the west end of the church, though that would be the most probable public open space by ordinary usage.

Goscelin of St Bertin: Lives of the Abbesses at Barking

(a) Abbess Ethelburga
[The Abbess and the plague]
Behold the tempest of death, laying waste everything far and wide and turning what was expended on earth into the riches of heaven. On every side he even carried off the male choir of priests and ministers of the monastery of the blessed Ethelburga. The wisest of virgins understood that the same thing was menacing her people, according to that poetic saying, 'It becomes your affair when your neighbour's wall burns.'[5] Hope or dread struck all the house, as if the evangelist raised the cry, 'Behold the bridegroom comes. Make way for him.'[6] Then with what exhortations did that mother most attentively strengthen her fortress in the final struggle, so that they should stand clad in the invincible armour of faith in God against all the weapons of the hostile ambush: their lamps were prepared with an inextinguishable light of oil so that all wakefulness of prayers and good

---

5   Horace, *Epistles* I.18.84.
6   Matt. 25.6.

works were made ready against the coming of the Lord.[7] This best of guardians, not only of their immortal souls but also of their resurrected bodies, often asked in the chapter of virgins where they should decide upon a cemetery for their remains when they were to be buried.[8] But since they gave no definite answer when she asked them frequently, and they left everything to God and to herself, she, with the others, finally received a reply from providence.

She held it a very sweet thing after lauds and vigils to lead the choir not to their beds but to the tombs of the brothers and to commend the souls of the dead to God in sacred hymns. When on this very night, according to their custom they were singing psalms with this devotion in the same place, behold a glorious miracle, behold an amazing brightness from heaven above them was poured down like a huge sheet of linen and covered them all completely. Then extreme fear and trembling drove the song from the mouth of all of them, and a stroke of lightning in addition almost terrified them, if the faith of their mother and the joyful beauty of the light had not soothed them in their fear. So great was the power of this splendour that it seemed, to their mind, that the blaze of the whole of the midday sun might be darkened. Night was turned into day and day was the conqueror of night. So indeed this light of God poured around those watching and praying with the mother like that which once poured on the Bethlehem shepherds guarding their flock in the watches of the night and seeing the celestial messengers glorify the new child. Not long after this, when they all stood amazed with exultant spirits and glowing faces in the radiance of that scintillating splendour, the same light which was raised to the south part of the monastery moved to the east and, having delayed for a while in that very place, sank by God's grace, and thus finally, as though inviting to the heavenly home the souls who undertook to go thither, it faded away as they all watched. By this was shown to them all that same light which was to lead and encourage the souls of the virgins to eternal blessedness, even by indicating the cemetery for those who would rise in glory.[9]

7   Matt. 25.4.
8   Chapter: the ruling body of a cathedral or monastery.
9   Not long after this vision, Ethelburga herself died (in 675) and was succeeded by Hildelitha.

[Ethelburga's death]
Meanwhile, the body of the most holy virgin was put in the church and was continually attended with holy songs until it could be established permanently in the church itself where it is, raised above the earth, to this day.

[Ethelburga continues to protect her convent after her own death]
The nun named Judith, who was sacristan of this monastery and whose faith was eloquent, who lived into the times of this present king, claims to have heard of the following miracles from the ealdormen by whom they were performed, and the closest witnesses survive to this day in this very church.[10] Under King Ethelred, when, by the testing of God who weighs all things in the balance, the army of the Danes laid waste the English realms with continual wars, there came an enemy troop to the monastery of the blessed Ethelburga, not so much to fight as to pillage.[11] For everyone had fled to the nearest city, London, as they were in the habit of doing as often as they feared the violence of war, and they left the church and the bodies of the saints without protection, abandoning everything to the care of the God of heaven. Drawing near to the holy place, the Danes saw a huge wolf before the doors of the church instead of a doorkeeper, on guard like a picked soldier, terrifying in appearance, and of itself it made an unprovoked attack on the mob. It suddenly leaped on them as though they were so many cattle and with huge gaping jaws and gnashing teeth frightened them all far off and drove them headlong in flight, not daring to resist. They looked for a safer entrance but a bear as defender drove them away more fiercely from the other door. Next, a huge lion stood in the way when they were trying a third entrance and, growing savage, kept them at a great distance as they fled from its roaring and attack. At length, tamed by beasts from beastly savagery, and perceiving that they had been driven out by divine influence, they prayed to the guardian saints of the place to let them go in peace. Straightway, the guardian beasts allowed them

---

10 Goscelin here leaves following Bede's *Historia* and depends on the recollections of the elderly nun Judith (whose former name had been Vulfruna). 'Ealdormen' is used to translate Latin *ducibus* here because it is the standard Old English term for a nobleman or ruler, and Vulfruna's maternal tongue was presumably English.

11 King Ethelred II the Unready, 968–1016. During his reign Danish raiding on England began again after many years of comparative peace.

entrance, now bringing peace to the cherishers of peace and they who had by no means been able to enter by violence, now entered with devoutness. Where they had sought booty they offered as sacrifice copious gifts as long-lasting supplies that were enough for the sisters for a whole month. And so, when they had left the sacred building, the beasts never reappeared. So thus, the holy Ethelburga who watched with her lamp for the coming of the Lord was worthy to guard vigilantly her own dwelling and in the beasts to have the Lord as her defender.

(b) Abbess Hildelitha
[Abbess Hildelitha removes Barking's dead from the cemetery to the church]

After the triumph of the venerable Ethelburga's translation to heaven, her disciple, Hildelitha, was advanced to the superintendence of the nuns and the monastery. She followed the footsteps of her mother, she oversaw everything completely as though seeing with her own eyes that nothing could be lacking within for religious concord, nothing without for bodily needs, and she continued for many years diligently to administer everything; she was as energetic as she was devout. But, like the most blessed Ethelburga, who not long before used to ask during the harvest of mortality where she should make the cemetery, Hildelitha discussed how this space which was already full could be cleared when remains were to be buried, for no room remained because of the congestion. And at length it was clear in discussion that all the bones of the brothers and sisters buried there should be moved from there into the church of the holy mother of God. And this was done with devout solemnity of funeral rites and thanksgiving as is natural in the moving of so many holy bodies. For we believe that this was ordained by divine grace when flowers of roses, lilies of the valley and incense of spices should as it were surround her, herself the mother of so many signs. For the whole of this most holy burial-place, the treasure house of this holy dust overflows perpetually with the grace and glory of spiritual gifts from heaven. For so many times that ethereal brightness, formerly displayed in the life of the bountiful Ethelburga, shone forth manifestly from the heavenly dwellings and many times the sweetest scent of fragrant odours flowed forth, and the sense of miracles and healing was frequently felt.

(c) An unnamed Abbess
[The abbess and nuns of Barking perish in Danish raiding]
But we have passed over many things of value for succeeding generations: for on one occasion the whole assembly of sacred virgins with
their mother abbess were burned together by the heathen in this holy
church; that was at the very time when the blessed King Edmund was
sacrificed by the heathen as an offering to God.[12] Oh, how we ought
to consider and bear in mind that, as the lead of the burning monastery was pouring down, the mother of that holy family spread out
both her tunic sleeves, like wings of supporting promises, and,
wounded by love and strengthening all who were joyful in their tears,
she said, 'Endure, my dearest daughters, O endure this passing bird
of fire as long as we run for the everlasting reward. Now heaven lies
open for you, now the martyr's palms and everlasting glory are
exchanged for momentary pain.'

(d) Abbesses Wulfhilda and Lifledis
[The burial of Abbess Wulfhilda]
Wulfhilda, dear to God and famous for her miracles in her life and
after her death, departed to the stars having stayed until her last day
with her flock in the city of London because of the foreign troops.
When they prepared to carry her sacred body to her convent of
Barking which was seven miles from the city, a certain man, with
whom the holy mother had been angry because of his sins, placed his
hands, with others, on the bier and directly it was so rooted to the
ground by its weight that it could not be moved by any strength of the
crowd. The wicked man was known to everyone and he fled in fear,
blaming himself, and immediately the healing burden was carried
away with amazing lightness. But with great grief he bitterly
bewailed the departed lady whom he had offended, and followed the
funeral procession with life-threatening groans. At length, after he
had wept, he was called by divine care from his companions and took
his turn with the honoured bier and thus he carried the beloved
burden for almost two miles to the convent of perpetual peace. When
she was buried by the head of Ethelburga, the most blessed first

---

[12] St Edmund 841–870, king of the East Angles, who resisted a great invasion of
Danes in 866. After a fierce battle, Edmund is said to have been so moved by the
sight of the carnage that he gave himself up to the Danes to save his people. The
Danish leader commanded him to renounce his religion and become his vassal.
Edmund refused and was tortured and finally beheaded.

mother of the Church, she showed with undoubted miracles that she could bestow the blessings of heaven on those who asked.

[The translation of Abbess Wulfhilda by Abbess Lifledis]
Now that about thirty years from the mother's burial had passed, she [Lifledis] decided on a set day to translate her most sacred body and to re-site it with greater honour near the main altar. Then the glorious Wulfhilda appeared in the sight of a certain woman in that monastery; she was recognizable by her sacred habit and by a clear sign showed what she wanted them to do. 'Soon, when my tomb is to be opened for my translation you will please me if it is covered with your habit so that my body is not seen outside of the tomb.' This vision she repeated with firm assertion to the sisters of the convent. At once the sister Wulfruna of marvellous faith, who had been given the name of Judith, supported her with the petition, 'I beg of you, dearest one, grant me a very small favour. Fulfill this wish of mine.' And not understanding the living significance of this obligation, she [Lifledis] spontaneously agreed.

So the virgin Judith rejoicing, like Jacob, at the promised blessing, carried out the instruction as though it had been laid on herself and prepared the best and finest head-dress that she had by way of votive funeral rites. And when the crowd was religiously hastening to move the stately tomb, and the cover was moved, Judith, consecrated in advance, went before them all and with a few of the faithful helping her she spread out a pure white cloth and wrapped the holy remains and covered them from the unworthy sight of the worldly. In truth when the tomb was opened, the marvellous grace of God was apparent for she [Wulfhilda] was found uncorrupted in the whole body and garments; she seemed as though she was sleeping and not dead after, as has been said, thirty years. Judith, the most devout, alone dared to touch her and knew that the body was marvellously sound and whole, and the rest of the sisters with the abbess Lifledis herself saw this. Indeed, such fragrance of paradisiac sweetness flowed from it that the whole church overflowed with it.

But when the crowd of men struggled to carry the tomb of the bountiful lady, it was held fast there by its weight, as is reported above to have happened when she died, so that it could not be moved an inch by all the crowd who ran to help. And when they were all dumbfounded and bereft of their strength and the assembly of sisters sang together the seven penitential psalms, they saw reaching for the holy body and staying in the same place like a humble supplicant, a woman whom the abbess herself had condemned to slavery because of her deceit in heaping up gold. Then they all understood the matter and prayed for forgiveness from her sins for the sinner, and Wulfhilda, guided by her maternal feelings, at last was willing to free her. When this was done, immediately, while the crowd was standing by, four attendant priests carried the virgin tomb with great ease so that they seemed to run, driving it forward to the destined place. And thus, the blessed Wulfhilda was placed at the right side of the altar, with the blessed Hildelitha, sheltered by a similar little chapel with the blessed Ethelburga in the middle of the chancel embraced by her choir, and the whole church raised their thanks to these three luminaries. We therefore celebrate devoutly the festival day of her translation in as much as we, too, translated from our paths to the high place of virtue, shall be worthy to see with her the Lord in the Galilee above.

(e) Abbess Elfgiva

[Abbess Elfgiva enlarges Barking church and re-buries her predecessors]
The right order of events and the heavenly praise demand that we must begin as though we were walking in procession, with the upbringing of that mother of the convent who carried out the translation.[13] The little girl grew up in mind and body in the convent according to God's will so that she bloomed, full of favour, alert in understanding, filled with all kindness, full of milk and honey for everyone, so much so that everyone called her the grace of God, or dear Grace.[14] Then a heavenly revelation blessed her. During the reign of King Edward, when she was a maiden of fifteen, she took on the care of the monastery which, as a mother of fifty, she retains till now.[15] When the bishop, being absent in London, had delegated the consecration to another, by a great blessing William, the bishop of the diocese, came in at the door.[16] He consecrated her and this was esteemed by all to have come about by the will of God when it was unlooked-for. She was blessed on July 31st, the triumphal day of the blessed Germanus, the bishop of Auxerre.[17] The remains [of

---

[13] Elfgiva translated the saints of Barking in her adulthood after she had herself become the abbess or 'mother' of the convent.
[14] Cf. 1 Corinthians 15.10.
[15] Edward the Confessor, last Anglo-Saxon king of England, reigned 1042–1066.
[16] William was bishop of London 1051–1075.
[17] Saint Germanus (c. 378–448), trained originally as a Roman advocate, was sent to Britain to combat the heresy of Pelagianism in 429. He silenced the heretics at

Ethelburga] were unknown to all of this generation, but when [Elfgiva] had the shrines of the saints opened, to the great joy of her heart she found them, surrounded by the sure evidence of writings, so that you may claim that the blessing of the rejoicing father smiled upon this devoted guardian.[18]

Since this monastery of hers was closely beset by peasant holdings, she rooted out the dwellings on all sides and cleared it extensively; they extended the church of Christ and the churchyard and the tents of Israel by a great extent when the Lord Iapheth enlarged them.[19] She rebuilt the cloister wall and made domestic offices of convenient size and height. Full of energy and power, she founded a church which rivalled the heights of the country. It was not with such grace of God that Semiramis founded Babylon, nor Dido founded Tyrian Carthage, for their pride was sunk in the foundations, but this one rose from the depths to heaven by Jacob's ladder.[20]

So we may now unfold the reason we have been given for the translation: the church rose up above the other, baser, buildings, but the size of the new works made it impossible to proceed to the intended end because the old church of the first founder, Ethelburga and her older brother Erkenwald, obstructed it. It was even necessary to remove the chief lady, with her previously mentioned companions, from the very church to which Hildelitha and Wulfhilda had been brought; but who would take such a presumptuous deed upon herself?

While she was undecided in these difficulties, the author of the works previously mentioned assailed the armoury of God with her sisters and the people when Maurice, the bishop of the province, and

Verulamium, but was obliged to return for the same purpose in 447; he also led the British troops to victory over the Picts and Saxons, teaching them the war-cry 'Alleluia'.

18 Probably writings placed in the tomb at Ethelburga's burial.

19 See above pp. 143–4 for details of the building. Colker's reference to Exodus 19.2 implies a false reading, probably by Goscelin. Iafeth is not otherwise known. The Jerusalem Bible reads 'From Rephidim they set out again . . . in the wilderness they pitched their tents.' The Latin reads *de Rephidim*; since *De* could be misread as *Dno*, the abbreviation for *Domino* – by or for 'the Lord' – it is not unlikely that *Domino Iafeth* was misread or misheard in dictation for *De Rephidim*.

20 Semiramis, the legendary woman builder of Babylon. See Ovid, *Met.* 4.59; for Babylon, see Gen. 18.12. Though Goscelin is probably speaking of the literal foundations of Babylon, he implies a contrast between the infernal origins of Babylon (a by-word for wealth and corruption) and the Church which, like Jacob's ladder, provides a means of access to heaven (see Gen. 28.12).

all the church fathers obstructed her.[21] At that time, that is the forty days observance which was set up for all Christians by divine institution, it was pleasing to them to add something of fitting abstinence to the rule of the convent. They fasted three Fridays with bread and water before the middle of Lent (with these luxuries the life of the first men is said to have been satisfied from the beginning). But when the fathers of the church were invited to remove these holiest of objects, they replied that they were unworthy and did not dare to remove the holy bodies from sepulchres that were the temples of God. Thus constrained, with bitter tears the mother of the daughters reported her grief to the convent of all the sisters: with most grievous groans she accused herself of undertaking this building when the saints seemed, through so many difficulties, to regard this as unwelcome and not to wish to change their first position and dwelling. While the others were shaking their heads or groaning together, one sister said in reply, 'Perhaps strangers are forbidding this undertaking to us because those saints of ours wish so much to be moved by their own family; so it is enough for us to rely on the help of the Lord, and if we trust ourselves to God's help we shall do more than we can do with their patronage.'

The following night the most supportive and tranquil lady Ethelburga strengthened the fearful abbess with a very clear sign. For she appeared to the steward of the convent with shining countenance and, telling her her own name, spoke with this encouragement, 'The ruler of the church is sufficiently disturbed with anxiety and doubt about the desire for our translation. Do you therefore tell her our message without any uncertainty that since we wish this carried out without delay, after the destruction of the old convent, a new one should be produced and we should be replaced in the spot where our resting place has been prepared.' So having received such an assurance, the lady abbess, after deep discouragement, rejoiced with extreme joy as if the translation was already completed. But in truth with prudent foresight she considered what resources lay hidden in the treasury for the tomb of the bountiful Ethelburga, before it became public consideration and knowledge. Hence she encouraged the sisters to their prayers for, however intent they were in the forty days (and for the most part of the year before had taken pains together and alone, in psalms and prayers), now they prayed that they

---

[21] See Hayward, 'Translation Narratives', pp. 81–3. Maurice was Bishop of London 1086–1107.

might continue steadfastly until they obtained the sign of heavenly approval. She also ordered architectural instructors and reliable assistants and others skilled with iron tools to be present and prepared.

Now the night of the Sabbath was at hand when the third fast of the sixth day would have been accomplished and the Sunday intended for the translation drew near. On the night of this Sabbath, ever-watchful, the mother with chosen sisters and the previously mentioned assistants came to the most holy mausoleum of the bountiful Ethelburga. There with fear and faith she bowed herself to the sign of heavenly approval and with all the others stretched out in secret piety to the anticipated achievement. With her nuns and faithful priests she contended in prayer and equipped the hand of the workman with a pearl to offer to God. May it be sweet and lovely for succeeding daughters to know clearly of the marriage settlement of this most blessed and loving woman, their mother.

The tomb was of white Parian marble, with four sides raised from the floor beyond the average height of a man, and above a roof angled in the style of an extremely beautiful little chapel. Indeed, both sides and roof of the holy places were carved with figures and actions in relief. When it was opened with iron and the excavated floor had been taken up, there were found, as the traces of the blessed foundation of the two holy virgins, their caskets and bones of dazzling white, the likeness of milk. Sandy earth was dug out from here, touching the blessed Ethelburga's shrine; first black, then white and clayey, and lastly shiny chalk was thrown from the stony earth. Doubtless, on account of the frequent incursions of the pagans, the most faithful preservers of such a treasure had made the walls so high.

[Abbess Ethelburga encourages Abbess Elfgiva in a vision]
The hallowed dust of the blessed virgins was given a lodging when it was transferred to the basilica of all the saints, willingly yielding place when the old church was destroyed and rebuilt anew, as we have set forth in their translation.[22] They were kept there for seven years and the new chamber where they could take their rest appeared to be ready prepared. Here the mother of the convent [Elfgiva] was disturbed and warned by pleasing but reproachful visions. On a certain night, it seemed to her that she came to the grave of the most

---

22 I.e., Goscelin's separate account of the reburial (pp. 150–3 here), not his life of Ethelburga.

beloved lady with offering of prayer, as she was accustomed to do, frequently visiting her and surrounding her with the incense of prayer. There was at that time a mistress of the young girls and of the convent pupils of the same age, of good memory, a woman of sound intelligence who loved Elfgiva especially as the great hope of the grace of God. So this woman who had now been taken up to the blessed world was being gazed upon by Elfgiva: in this vision she was standing by the monument of the blessed Ethelburga and said something like this to Elfgiva: 'See', she said, 'our lady Ethelburga whom you have always longed to see is near you. Look, you can see her and ask what you wish of her.'

And so while our celebrated mother [Elfgiva] lay in prayer near the mother's [Ethelburga's] tomb she felt that the very tomb moved of itself; coming near the right side where she lay praying, it pressed on her, and, as she prayed, pushed her up to the nearby wall of the choir and thus the stone tomb and the stony wall cramped and squeezed her so as to restrict her. Exhausted and severely shaken she cried out, 'Spare me, my lady! I am overwhelmed, I am crushed. I can scarcely draw breath or gasp because of the force of your pressure.' Then she drew back, trembling from the constriction, from that place to her position at the burial site of the virgin dust, and what had seemed to her to be narrowed was, thanks be to God, widened. Let us consider what the mystery of this vision means, namely, what the blessed virgin of the household of the Lord would teach its nurse [Elfgiva] by the dashing down and destruction of her sarcophagus. She wished that Elfgiva should remove her from the restriction of that dwelling which cramped her to the new house which had been prepared and she said to Elfgiva, 'Learn from this pressure which I put on you how you should take me from this narrow lodging in which I am confined.' We say this not because the urn of the saintly body had need of greater space compared with the cave of the Saviour whose spirit reigns in heaven, but because the choir singing round it was being oppressed by the narrowness of the space, for it was scarcely possible to pass between the seats of the singers and the tomb of the virgin.

Then, to continue with our narration of the vision, after the pious abbess ceased her prayers the vision seemed to her to rise to the lowest step of the altar opposite and sat opposite the traces of the virgin's dust, to the sound of psalm-singing. Here, Elfgiva suddenly saw the altar cloths and the pall of the holy tomb as it were set on fire and blown about as though by a whirlwind; soon the coverings were raised, the lid of the tomb was opened, the shining virgin rose from it, she came down to her and stood there white as snow and of natural size. She spoke to the abbess who was watching her, she comforted the trembling woman, she reproached her for her idleness, she upbraided her carelessness. 'You see', she said, 'the helper of your prayers whom you have longed to see, the consoler of your sadness. Now make haste to take us from here and set us in the place you have prepared. This lodging oppresses us; the narrowness of the place binds us tightly; the coarse couch dishonours us.'

Then the abbess, trembling as though at a message of the Lord's command and an angelic embassy, prays to her holy lady that she might deserve her favour and pardon for all offences. She promised that she would carry out this order as swiftly as possible. Then the figure that was the blessed Ethelburga said, 'See that no delay hinders you.' Saying this she was immediately transformed into a little girl. 'Let me', she said, 'rest in your bosom and lay my weary head on you.' Straightway Elfgiva offered herself to the lady with great and befitting joy. With outstretched arms she received the starry maiden into her bosom as though she was very tiny, in truth as a handmaid might receive her lady, or a humble wetnurse might take the royal daughter of her lord. So while she fostered her lovingly in her embrace, behold, there appeared around her the shrines and tombs and reliquaries of the other saints which we believe were also transferred in the same way; sacred relics which, with the blessed Ethelburga, were placed together in the bosom of the new church by this mother, their preserver.

Interpretive Essay

Dead to the World? Death and the Maiden Revisited in Medieval Women's Convent Culture

Jocelyn Wogan-Browne

The nun, like the monk, is supposed to be 'dead to the world', and the letters and other texts in this book all have running through them various themes and preoccupations stemming from this idea. As one interpretive framework for the texts translated here, this essay focusses on the role of death in convent life, both for its gendered representation and for the relation of representation to the social and cultural practices of women religious.

In both medieval and later thought, anxiety that women religious should be strictly enclosed away from the world is much more strongly expressed than concern with monks and their claustration. Purity, as Mary Douglas long ago showed in a famous study, demands separation and apartness:[1] nuns are readily seen as 'requiring' separation and containment in the liminal space beyond the cloister wall in order to be pure. Behind the wall, enclosed women are in a realm imagined as death-like in its purported disconnection from time and history. Here, according to the stereotype, where the nun is in but not of the world, she is dead to the world and hence in the grasp of death; she is contained in a cell which is both a womblike enclosure for her spirituality and the tomb of her life in this world.

Ideas of this kind were expressed in two places important for the image of medieval religious women in our culture. One is the literature and other arts of the eighteenth and nineteenth centuries where nuns were often represented not as citizens leading a communal and institutional mode of life, but through gothic and neo-gothic conventions of enclosure. The other is the letters, regulations and prescriptions of medieval bishops and other clerics, recommending and

---

[1] Mary Douglas, *Purity and Danger: An Analysis of Concepts of Pollution and Taboo* (New York: Praeger, 1966).

enforcing enclosure.[2] Read literally these seemed to confirm gothic and romantic notions of the Middle Ages and to license lurid associations between nuns, enclosure, death, and sexuality. The construction of women as dead to the world has had implications for women's history, helping, for instance, to discourage investigation of the socio-economic and political aspects of nunnery history in much nineteenth- and twentieth-century scholarship.

The power with which notions of enclosure are advocated and imagined for women in religious lives has more to say of the wishes and fears of enclosure's advocates than of the actual lives of conventual women. We can get behind stereotypes to a more nuanced sense of women's lives and culture in medieval convents and also to a better understanding of medieval representations and practices regarding death. More recent scholarship has been concerned to re-imagine the lives behind the wall, not just to see them as shut off from 'normal' humanity. It has placed churchmen's writings on this subject in context and noticed how often enclosure is in practice modified (it was, for instance, quite impossible to run a convent without business travel on the part, at least, of senior nuns and without a range of contact with the outside world).[3] Women behind the wall have been re-imagined with selves, agendas, and social and economic collective lives. In the writings of this volume, women are imaged as enclosed, but they are also seen as athletes running spiritual races, as powerful queens and ladies of heaven, and as heroic martyrs and mothers of martyrs.[4] Indeed the wall itself vanishes to some extent as the fluidity and variety of women's medieval religious lives comes into view. Women did not invariably enter convents once and for all, and once there they were not simply sealed away from life in a living death. Nevertheless, death was very important in convents, death understood through a number of historically

---

2   Jane Tibbetts Schulenberg, 'Strict Active Enclosure and its Effects on the Female Monastic Experience, ca. 500–1100', in John A. Nichols and Lillian T. Shank (eds.), *Distant Echoes: Medieval Religious Women I* (Kalamazoo: University of West Michigan Press, 1984), pp. 51–86: Elizabeth Makowski, *Canon Law and Cloistered Women: Periculoso and its Commentators 1298–1545* (Washington, DC: Catholic University of America Press, 1997).

3   See, for example, Nancy Bradley Warren, *Spiritual Economies: Female Monasticism in Later Medieval England* (Philadelphia: University of Pennsylvania Press, 2001), pp. 65–6.

4   For spiritual athleticism and queenliness in heaven see e.g. I, pp. 22, 38; III, p. 106; for martyrdom see e.g. II, p. 78 and IV, p. 113, and for other role models, see above, Introduction, p. 5.

and culturally specific beliefs and practices which do not always overlap with, or lead to, our contemporary versions of death.

Death and the Middle Ages

We often think death in earlier times was better – more comfortable, more accepted, less disruptive. 'The idea that there was an Arcadian age of death is a constant feature of historical scholarship on the subject', yet practices and understandings of death are chronologically and culturally various.[5] Christianity brought significant changes to pagan death. For the Roman world and for Judaism, the dead body was a site of impurity: honour given to the dead was a form of appeasement, and the dead were kept apart, buried outside city walls, and not to be touched.[6] But in Christianity, with its claim to a final and absolute triumph over death, 'death and the dead were fundamentally re-socialized . . . death re-entered the realm of the living'.[7] In a reversal of classical pagan notions of the underworld kingdoms of the dead, it was now the saints who 'enjoyed the light of reality and the quick who lived in the shadow of life'.[8] As Philippe Ariès has said, 'ever since the risen Christ triumphed over death, the fact of being born into this world is the real death and physical death is access to eternal life'.[9] In Christian culture, links between the living and the dead were stressed, most powerfully so in the figures of the martyrs and saints. These, the very holy dead, were the first to be 'urbanized' by having their bodies brought inside city walls and inside churches for burial.[10] But Christianity's powerful inversion of the traditional opposition between the dead and the sacred meant that

---

5 David Crouch, 'The Culture of Death in the Anglo-Norman World', in C. Warren Hollister (ed.), *Anglo-Norman Political Culture and the Twelfth-Century Renaissance* (Woodbridge: Boydell Press, 1997), pp. 157–80 (158, n. 4).

6 See Paul Binski, *Medieval Death: Ritual and Representation* (Ithaca and New York: Cornell University Press, 1996), p. 11; Philippe Ariès, trans. Helen Weaver, *The Hour of Our Death* (New York: Knopf, 1981), esp. ch. 2.

7 Binski, pp. 11–12.

8 Binski, p. 12.

9 Ariès, p. 13.

10 By some estimates, the first symbolic expulsion of the dead from among the living, foreshadowing the modern 'suppression of death', did not come until the early health reformers in the late eighteenth and the nineteenth centuries demanded removal of cemeteries from the city churches and city centres (Joachim Whaley, ed., *Mirrors of Mortality: Studies in the Social History of Death* (London: Europa, 1981), Introduction, pp. 6–7).

'the dead body of [any] Christian created by its very nature a space if not altogether sacred at least . . . religious'.[11] Not only altars and saints' shrines but churchyards and cemeteries became privileged sites. Death's places were places of holy connection, channels of intercession and negotiation with the sacred. As Goscelin writes of the cemetery at Barking Abbey, 'the whole of this most holy burial place, the treasure-house of this holy dust, overflows perpetually with the grace and glory of spiritual gifts from heaven' (VI [b], p. 147 above). He notes that Ethelburga, first abbess of Barking, 'held it a very sweet thing after Lauds and Vigils to lead the choir not to their beds but to the tombs of the brothers and to commend the souls of the dead to God in sacred hymns' (VI [a], p. 145). Far from being sequestered and uncanny, medieval and early modern cemeteries were important communal places, often functioning as the forum or town square.[12]

Death was not the end, but was followed by resurrection at Christ's return to earth and by God's judgement. As Osbert of Clare writes to Adelidis of Barking, 'whoever has appeared misshapen like Adam will appear beautiful like Christ on the day of judgement' (I, p. 43), while Abelard comments to Heloise that 'the balm of myrrh and aloes which is used to preserve the bodies of the dead signified the future incorruptibility of the Lord's body which all the elect will attain in the resurrection' (II, p. 55). In this ethos, the real threat is less death than sin. 'The entrance of the tabernacle [of eternal life] is the end of the present life', writes Abelard in Letter 7: 'the departure from this mortal life is in sorrow, but the entrance to eternal life is the greatest delight' (II, p. 67). The necessity of penitence and a good death is axiomatic:

> At this entrance those who are full of apprehension about the departure from this life and the entrance to the future are waiting, and they set their departure in order by penitence, so that they may be worthy to enter (II, p. 67).

---

[11] Ariès, p. 41.

[12] Preaching and other public events took place in cemeteries and recluses and those seeking sanctuary might live in them, while the presence of shops and traders until the eventual separation of the bailiff's square from the cemetery in the sixteenth century gives cemeteries some claim to be the ancestors of shopping malls (as with the Palais Royal in Paris). see Ariès, *Hour of Our Death*, pp. 62–71.

The Benedictine Rule of monastic observance enjoined constant awareness of death for all religious.[13] Life on earth was a transient pilgrimage towards and beyond death: but the monastic version of this pilgrimage has, or can have, a particularly direct and powerful trajectory, as in Osbert of Clare's image of the chariot of Ethelburga of Barking taking its fiery path to heaven (I, p. 47). Monastic approaches to death allocated medicine for the body a somewhat conflicted place in the spiritual economy. As Giles Constable points out, Peter the Venerable was a confirmed invalid who frequently took medicines as cure and consolation, yet he writes to his nieces that they should not be too concerned about medicine (III, p. 98). Here he uses a theme frequently found in monastic writings: that too much concern for medical intervention can become impious. In a twelfth-century rule, *The Book of Living Well for a Sister*, nuns are warned that a healthy body may promote excessive fondness for the world, whereas disease purges.[14] In the early thirteenth-century English *Guide for Anchoresses* a story is told where the Virgin refuses aid to one of three sick men who has already taken some medicine: as he has ministered to himself with physical medicine she withholds the more important spiritual healing which should have priority.[15] Spiritual healing offered the best way either to re-compose the body's balance of fluids and vital spirits towards health or to place its distresses in proper perspective. Nevertheless, one important social function of convents was care of the sick, involving knowledge of herbs and the preparation of medicines and potions. Indeed, hospitals in origin are religious houses of a specialized kind, often an outpost of larger convents. Nuns frequently staffed them, es-

---

13 Jean Leclercq, 'The Joy of Dying According to St Bernard', *Cistercian Studies Quarterly* 25 (1990), 163–74 (orig. publ. in Jane H. M. Taylor [ed.], *Dies Illa: Death in the Middle Ages*, Liverpool: Cairns, 1984); A. W. Sipe, 'Memento Mori in the *Rule* of St Benedict', *American Benedictine Review* 25 (1974), 96–107; Sophie Hasquenoph, 'La mort du moine au Moyen Age (Xe–XIIe siècles)', *Collectanea Cisterciensia* 53 (1991), 215–32 (219–21).

14 PL 184:1199–1306; see Anne McGovern-Mouron, ' "Listen to me, daughter, listen to a faithful counsel": The *Liber de modo bene vivendi ad sororem* in Denis Renevey and Christiania Whitehead (eds.), *Writing Religious Women: Female Spiritual and Textual Practices in Later Medieval England* (Toronto: University of Toronto Press, 2000), pp. 81–106 (176–7); Janice M. Pindar, 'The Cloister and the Garden: Gendered Images of Religious Life from the Twelfth and Thirteenth Centuries', in Mews (ed.), *Listen, Daughter*, pp. 159–79.

15 *Ancrene Wisse*, VI; see Anne Savage and Nicholas Watson (trans.), *Anchoritic Spirituality* (New York and Mahwah, NJ: Paulist Press, 1991), pp. 183–4.

pecially the leprosaria which proliferated in twelfth- and thirteenth-century Europe.[16] The figure of the old woman knowledgeable in potions, the woman who knows how to charm, poison and heal, is familiar from romance and somewhat disguises the usefulness and the systematic involvement of women in medicine, both in cloisters and in secular households.[17] (In his rebuke to his nieces, the valetudinarian Peter the Venerable urges concentration on their spiritually aristocratic virginity rather than on the service aspects of convent duties for his nieces – they are young women of slightly lower rank than many other nuns in their extremely aristocratic convent, and their virginity gives them a social and spiritual credential not possessed by all who outrank them).

Anxiety for a good death was common to lay and religious people alike. It was a matter of particular benefit to be present at a saint's death, and accounts of ideal deaths circulated. Osbert of Clare wrote one such in his life of Edward the Confessor, conventionally stressing its calmness and nobility.[18] Holy deaths frequently included signs and portents, as with Abbess Ethelburga, of whom Osbert writes to her successor Adelidis:

> truly the form of her glory was expressed beforehand in her human body, for her own disciple saw her taken heavenwards from the dortor building and raised by ropes of virtues to the joys above (I, pp. 47–8).

For everyone, not just saints, deaths were, ideally, public and anticipated, and allowed the dying person to preside 'over the ceremony of [their] death'.[19] But a good death also needed time for repentance. St Martin of Tours prescribed that dying monks should be laid on ashes on the floor in their last moments as an expression of repentance. Far from regarding these penitential customs as repellent or unnatural, laypeople strove to imitate them, and by the end of the eleventh century accounts of the deaths of royalty and aristocracy often describe such practices. When the son of Henry II of England,

---

16 Roberta Gilchrist, *Contemplation and Action: The Other Monasticism* (London and New York: Leicester University Press, 1995); Carol Rawcliffe, *The Hospitals of Medieval East Anglia* (Norwich: Centre for East Anglian Studies, 1995).

17 See Peggy MacCracken, 'Women and Medicine in Medieval French Narrative', *Exemplaria* 5 (1993), 239–62.

18 R. C. Finucane, 'Sacred Corpse, Profane Carrion: Social Ideals and Death Rituals in the Later Middle Ages', in Whaley (ed.), *Mirrors of Mortality*, pp. 51–2; Crouch, pp. 162–3.

19 Ariès, pp. 18–19.

the younger Henry, was dying in 1183, he was set on the floor with stones placed under his head and a noose around his neck as well. He had recently pillaged some shrines and his death came too suddenly for him to make any form of restitution, so intense ritual practice of repentance was necessary before the dying prince faced his eternal judgement.[20]

The treatment and burial of corpses also had its own elaborate and highly nuanced rituals. As R. C. Finucane has argued, death rituals are not only a question of dealing with a corpse but of 'reaffirming the secular and spiritual order by means of a corpse'.[21] Dead bodies were not removed but displayed and watched over: so, Goscelin tells us, Abbess Ethelburga's body was 'put in the church and was continually attended with holy songs' (VI [a], p. 146). Several, often contradictory (or, at least, heavily context-dependent) strands of feeling appear in the treatment of bodies. On the one hand, intactness was prized as a sign of the whole person due to rise in the resurrection of the Last Day at Christ's return. In the case of saints, incorruption of the corpse was especially valued as a sign of sanctity: thus, when the tomb of Wulfhilda, abbess of Barking is opened,

> the marvellous grace of God was apparent for she was found uncorrupted in the whole body and garments; she seemed as though she was sleeping and not dead after, as has been said, thirty years (VI [d], p. 149)

On the other hand, dismemberment and disembowelling of dead persons were practised. Sometimes this was for practical reasons as in the case, for instance, of crusaders dying in the Holy Land (whose bodies would need to be shipped and carried back to Europe) or, since courts were constantly mobile, of kings and queens dying while travelling. But equally important was the symbolism of the dispersal of the corpse. Directions for burying the heart in one place, the bowels in another, the bones in yet another were frequent, increasingly so in the late twelfth and thirteenth centuries. Basic issues of human existence are involved in these practices – how far does identity depend on the particular body inhabited by a human spirit? – and they were accordingly, as Elizabeth Brown has shown, much considered and debated.[22] Brown suggests, for instance, that,

20 Crouch, p. 168.
21 Finucane, p. 41.
22 See Elizabeth A. R. Brown, 'Death and the Human Body in the Later Middle Ages: The Legislation of Boniface VIII on the Division of the Corpse', *Viator* 12 (1981), 221–70; Caroline Walker Bynum, 'Material Continuity and Personal

in the controversy over dismembering the dead, what had once been felt as core identity enough when some kind of postmortem life was envisaged for all became increasingly tenuous as people felt more strongly the finality of physical death, and that it was this, as well as political considerations, that eventually prompted Pope Boniface VIII's bull of 1299 condemning the separation of flesh and bones.[23]

The dead, far from being hidden away, continue as part of life: not only are visions of the afterlife and reappearances of the dead common occurrences, but the bodies of the dead remain a presence in bids for prestige and power.[24] As noted above, Abbess Ethelburga's body was watched over above ground until a suitable permanent tomb could be organized. This was eventually arranged 'in the church itself where it is, raised above the earth, to this day' (VI [a], p. 146). The raised final position of the body here is important, since it was felt to reflect the spiritual elevation of the virgin abbess saint. Hierarchies of rank and power in death mirrored those in life: the closer to the saint, the closer to the sacred, the closer to successful intercession with God. Both lay and religious people prized being buried as close as possible to the bodies of the holy dead.[25] Osbert of Clare feels that his visit to the tomb of Etheldreda, patron saint of Ely, gives him access to a protection which, through the saint's intercession, is extended by God to him wherever he goes (I, p. 26). Similarly, when Osbert urges devotion to St Lawrence to his niece Cecilia, nearness to the saint as he passes through the

Identity', in her *Fragmentation and Redemption: Essays on Gender and the Human Body in Medieval Religion* (New York: Zone Books, 1992).

23   Brown, pp. 223–5, 248–9. In Letter 7, instead of mapping conventional male/ female hierarchies onto this opposition of bone and flesh (women as body and flesh, men as spirit, reason and bone), Abelard creates an extended metaphor by which to define the special role of women in their loyalty to Christ: Christ is the bones, the disciples the flesh, and the devoted and unwavering women of the Gospels the skin of a human body (II, p. 58 above).

24   See e.g., Jean-Claude Schmitt, trans. Teresa Lavender Fagan, *Ghosts in the Middle Ages: The Living and the Dead in Medieval Society* (Chicago: University of Chicago Press, 1998): Carol Zaleski, *Otherworld Journeys: Accounts of Near Death Experience in Medieval and Modern Lives* (Oxford and New York: Oxford University Press, 1987). For much useful information, see Robert Easting, *Visions of the Otherworld in Middle English* Annotated Bibliographies of Old and Middle English 3 (Cambridge: D. S. Brewer, 1997).

25   Such privileges were granted, in spite of church injunctions against them, to important lay patrons as well as leading ecclesiastic (Ariès, ch. 2). For practices regarding the unholy dead (suicides, excommunicates, heretics), see R. C. Finucane, 'Sacred Corpse, Profane Carrion'.

purgatorial realms of the dead awaiting resurrection is crucial (IV, p. 118). The sacredness and value of dead bodies is most powerfully expressed in the cult of saints' relics, especially in belief in the value, therapeutic and otherwise, of contact with them. Fragments of saints' bodies were often widely dispersed: they were given, bought, or plundered by those with an interest in annexing the saint to their corporate identities or by individuals for their own devotions, protection, and healing. Pilgrimage to relic shrines and the encasing of relics in gold and jewels were practices vigorously engaged in by lay and religious alike. The use of precious gold, silver, and jewels in reliquaries signified the eternity participated in by the saints.[26] The saint's body was a pledge and sign on earth and the focus of negotiations with heaven: it remained an active site of sacred power.

The possession of relics was, especially from the eleventh century onwards, a crucial factor in constructing the identity of a monastic house and embodying its relation with its patron saint. Since they were believed to be alive in heaven, the saints could and did express concern for the care and placement of their own relics: what happened to their bodies was interpreted as expressing their will. When the nuns of Barking are reburying their abbess Wulfhilda, her body cannot be moved until the nuns notice that those praying beside it include a woman whom Wulfhilda herself had condemned to slavery for 'her deceit in heaping up gold' (VI [d], pp. 149–50). Once the saint, 'guided by her maternal feelings', has heard the convent's prayers for forgiveness for the sinner, her funeral procession is able to move onwards (ibid. p. 150). So too, the rebuilding of the Barking Abbey church is understood as the removal of its saints to a more commodious space and expressed as the desire of the founding abbess and patron saint, Ethelburga: 'Learn from this pressure which I put on you how you should take me from this narrow lodging in which I am confined', she is perceived as saying, and Goscelin adds that this is not because the saint wants an inordinate amount of space but because the choir nuns can hardly find room to get to their seats (VI [e], p. 154 above).

The reburial, or 'translation', of saints was a very serious matter. It extended to relic thefts from one monastery to another, in which cases the abstraction of the relics (together with the transfer of shrine

26 Virginia Reinburg, 'Remembering the Saints', in Nancy Netzner and Virginia Reinburg (eds.), *Memory and the Middle Ages* (Chestnut Hill, MA: Boston College, Museum of Art, 1995), pp. 17–33.

and pilgrimage revenues) was not concealed, but, as Patrick Geary shows in a well-known book, proclaimed and celebrated as holy thefts.[27] The movement of relics could happen within as well as between cult centres, as with the saintly abbesses of Barking and the demand for more spaciously arranged tombs. Goscelin repeatedly emphasizes the enormity of what is at stake: 'who would take such a presumptuous deed upon herself?' (VI [e], p. 151). The churchmen of London and Barking and Abbess Elfgiva herself discuss, dispute and hesitate; Elfgiva blames herself 'with most grievous groans' when, in the course of a long and difficult rebuilding, it seems that the saints, after all, do not want to 'change their first position and dwelling' (VI [e], p. 152).[28]

For a successful translation, public witness by the community was required together with a certain amount of stage-management. The Barking community prays and fasts in anticipation of the translation planned by abbess Elfgiva, and Elfgiva herself 'with prudent foresight . . . considered what resources lay hidden in the treasury for the tomb of the bountiful Ethelburga, before it became public consideration and knowledge' (VI [e], p. 152). People sought the opportunity of physical contact with saints during translation and the brief re-exposure of the body as it was carried to its more elevated grave, though in the case of the translation of Barking's abbess Wulfhilda by her successor Lifledis, the same elderly nun, Judith, who testifies to the intactness of the body is also careful to cover the holy remains 'from the unworthy sight of the worldly' (VI [d], p. 149).

Christian attitudes to death do not of course dispense with fear and ambivalence. As Abelard writes in Letter 7, quoting the book of Job, ' "Skin for skin, a man will give all that he has for his life." We all naturally feel such horror of the grip of death that often for the protection of one member we expose another and to save this life we fear no injury' (II, p. 78). Ambivalence and unease is shown in the personifications of Death. In Latin (*mors, mortis*) and French (*la mort*), death is grammatically feminine. In English before the twelfth century it is masculine (*se deaþ*). In an early thirteenth-century homily on the custody of the soul, re-worked for a small female community of anchoresses, Death is feminine and Hell is a house of

[27] *Furta Sacra: Thefts of Relics in the Central Middle Ages* (Princeton: Princeton University Press, 1978).

[28] See Paul Antony Hayward, 'Translation Narratives in Post-Conquest Hagiography and English Resistance to the Norman Conquest', *Anglo-Norman Studies* 21 (1999), 67–93 (81–3).

hers.[29] There is an elderly female death in the magnificent murals of the Three Living and the Three Dead in the Campo Santo at Pisa.[30] In later medieval French literature, ambivalence is explicit in the duality of death as mother and step-mother (*mere/marrastre*).[31] Death is often implicitly or explicitly male, nonetheless, in medieval as well as later conventions: the rider on the pale horse who 'hunts, dances, pounces and eventually rapes'.[32] Representations of death and the maiden – a grim skeletal figure of Death implacably laying hold of a tender young woman – feature still more strongly in post-medieval Western culture.[33]

The move towards the macabre is, however, associated with the later middle ages, the fourteenth and fifteenth centuries. When, in the late eleventh century, Goscelin portrays the nuns of Barking in the plague, death is male and attacks: he is a stormy assault, a 'hostile ambush'. But death is potentially the turning of 'what was expended on earth into the riches of heaven', and it is feared not for the grotesque pounce of a skeleton on female flesh, but for what follows afterwards. The next stage facing the soul is the return of Christ, the judging bridegroom, and Goscelin's account is filled with eschatological references. The abbess Ethelburga strengthens her 'fortress' (i.e., her convent) against the 'hostile ambush' by making sure, in the terms of the parable of the wise and foolish virgins (Matt. 25.4), that her nuns' 'lamps were prepared with an inextinguishable light of oil so that all wakefulness of prayers and good works were made ready against the coming of the Lord' (VI [a], p. 144).

Changes in medieval death are observable after the twelfth century: the carvings of the Last Day on church fronts for instance are increasingly about judgement rather than about the return of Christ; the church itself, and not just its martyrs, is represented as the source of the holy power sought by people in trying to be buried

---

29 'The Custody of the Soul' in Bella Millett and Jocelyn Wogan-Browne (eds. and trans.), *Medieval English Prose for Women* (Oxford: Oxford University Press, 1992), pp. 94–5.

30 Discussed in Ann Turkey Harrison, ed., *The Danse Macabre of Women: ms fr. 995 of the Bibliothèque nationale* (Kent, Ohio: Kent State University Press, 1994).

31 Claude Thiry, 'De la mort marâtre à la mort vaincue', in Herman Braet and Werner Verbeke (eds.), *Death in the Middle Ages* (Leuven: Leuven University Press, 1983), pp. 239–57.

32 Binski, p. 158.

33 Elisabeth Bronfen, *Over Her Dead Body: Death, Femininity and the Aesthetic* (New York: Routledge, 1992).

there;[34] and it is after the twelfth century that a stronger sense of the finality of physical death emerges in a desire to keep dead bodies intact in burial.[35] Changes in attitudes to death are difficult to trace, however, in that older ways persist alongside newer. Distinguishing change from the co-presence of differing views and strands of tradition is often difficult. So, for example, in *Ancrene Wisse*, the early thirteenth-century *Guide for Anchoresses*, long-standing associations of death, hospitality and feasting appear to shift. The *Guide's* regulations about who can be entertained by a recluse are intense: since recluses are dead to the world, they should never have a meal with a guest outside their quarters:

> One has often heard of the dead speaking with the living, but
> I have never found yet that they ate with the living.[36]

But notions of eating, death and hospitality were much more closely intertwined than the *Ancrene Wisse* author is claiming. The custom of eating a funeral meal has an ancestry in Roman appeasement of the dead through ceremonial food taken outside the city and consumed at their tombs. Similarly, one important strand of imagery in the conception of the afterlife sees it as a banquet. The recumbent posture of the dead, although it came to be expressive of the notion of sleeping and waiting for resurrection, is related to the reclining posture of guests at Roman banquets. Part of the power of Christian eucharistic symbolism is that it reclaims a practice associated with the rejection of death and the dead as a way of commemorating triumph over death and partaking in eternal life. *Ancrene Wisse's* concern here is less to dissociate eating and death than to differentiate the life of the recluse from the hospitality which was so important an aspect of contemporary institutional monastic tradition. For Osbert of Clare, writing to the abbess of a great house, there is no such tension. He intensely salutes Adelidis's hospitality, and represents its obverse in the feast of Holofernes, cast by him as a representation of the devil, who feasts his hellish household purely from within itself and without guests (I, pp. 22, 38, 41 above). In opening and closing his epistolary treatise on the purity and authority of professed virginity with the theme of hospitality, Osbert is partly a man thanking an elite institution for very good dinners, and presumably ensuring their continuance. But the underlying resonances of

34 Ariès, pp. 71–2.
35 Brown, n. 22 above.
36 Millett and Wogan-Browne, p. 133.

human community and grace in his lavish paeans on hospitality are not evoked in a merely self-serving way: for Osbert they are part of the ethic of a society in which those who were dead to the world might have a great deal of spiritual and social exchange with the world and in which all were fed by Christ's sacrifice.

The eternal judgement to which death was a prelude in Christian doctrine did not do away with awe and fear at the prospect, although the hope of being adjudged an eternal life offered ways of transcending mortality and the grave. But however fearful or ambivalent attitudes to death itself might be, the dead themselves were neither forgotten nor death denied in this culture, which saw itself as a society composed of the living and the dead.

Death, memory, and religious life

Death and commemoration are central to the existence of monastic houses: intercession and the channelling of spiritual energy between heaven and earth are a large part of their rationale, and this constant interconnection of the two realms makes explicit and continual 'living with the dead' part of the life of monastery or convent.[37] A monastic calendar charts a yearly round of commemorations of different deaths: the deaths celebrated by the whole church (Christ and the universal saints); those of the house's patron saints and their relics; those of distinguished members of the house; those of its secular patrons, prayers for whom were an important aspect of a convent's or monastery's duties.

In monastic calendars, the day but not the year of a death is usually given (the anniversary would come round at the same time each year in the convent's commemorations). Saints' and other people's death days or 'obits' (from Latin *obitus*, *p.p.* dead, or *obiit*, *pa. sg.* s/he died) were fixed and were regarded not as occasions of mourning but celebration: they were birth-days into eternal life. Unlike these anniversaries, movable or 'temporale' feasts such as Easter did not take place on the same date in successive years and had to be recalculated for each year. This combination of fixed and movable feasts, the annual procession of church time, is more important than the linear chronology of historical time, and provides the framework within which the latter is experienced. Each monastic house's calendar

---

[37] Patrick Geary, *Living with the Dead in the Middle Ages* (Ithaca and London: Cornell University Press, 1994); Megan McLaughlin, *Consorting with Saints: Prayer for the Dead in Early Medieval France* (Ithaca and London: Cornell University Press, 1994).

shared a common form, but was also a very specific articulation of identity, of the communal memory of the house.

A calendar from Barking, extant in a late fourteenth- or early fifteenth-century liturgical manuscript belonging to the Abbey, shows a structure of commemoration much of which will have been continuously observed over the centuries. The virgin martyrs such as Agnes and Agatha, often cited as role models in writings for women (as in II, p. 87 and III, p. 99 above), have their feast days marked for celebration, as do some British saints such as Bishop Wulfstan or the virgin Milburga of Wenlock.[38] The house's own saints figure repeatedly: Ethelburga, Hildelitha and Wulfhilda all have double feasts. In keeping with the high value accorded saintly relics, the careers of their relics are also commemorated: the date of the translation – the moving of their shrines within Barking's church which gives Abbess Elfgiva so many problems in extract VI (e) above – is also kept as a feast.[39] Contemporary and recent abbesses and prioresses are also celebrated in this late medieval manuscript as far back as the thirteenth century and perhaps back to Elfgiva herself in the late eleventh century.[40]

The anniversaries felt to be central to the convent's identity could be annually celebrated over centuries, but the calendar could also change over time as feasts and commemorations were abandoned or added. Thus, however fixed death-day commemorations might be, the position of an individual in the hierarchy of death was not stable and remained open to renegotiations of status and changes of fortune much as a living person does.[41]

A second genre of commemoration united the living networks of monastic houses: the mortuary roll or rolls of the dead. These were long scrolls carried between religious houses on which were entered condolences for the honorand together with names of nuns and

---

[38] See J. B. L. Tolhurst, ed., *The Ordinale and Customary of the Benedictine Nuns of Barking Abbey*, HBS 65, 66 (London: Harrison and Sons, 1927, 1928), vol. I, pp. 1–12; for other medieval books extant from the nunnery see David N. Bell, *What Nuns Read: Books and Libraries in Medieval English Nunneries* (Kalamazoo, MI: Cistercian Publications, 1995), *s.v.* Barking.

[39] March 7 (see Tolhurst, I, p. 5).

[40] Mabel de Bosham (resigned 1247; obit 15 October, see Tolhurst, I, p. 10): 'Obiit Aluina abbatissa missa' on 10 May (I, p. 5) perhaps refers to Elfgiva.

[41] Anne de Vere, abbess from 1295–1318, made an ordinance that the anniversaries of previous abbesses of Barking would be commemorated only by solemn masses instead of full feasts, except for those who had given pittances to the convent to fund their services (Tolhurst, II, p. 359).

monks and lay associates of the participating houses for whose souls prayers were also solicited. Sometimes short prose prayers or verses of condolence were also included. Such rolls cross and recross the Channel and include contributions from English and French houses alike, sometimes, no doubt, written by the chaplains of nunneries, but also in some cases by nuns themselves. Heloise was very probably the author of a distinctively good poem on the death (16 September 1122) of Vitalis of Mortain, abbot of Savigny, included in the convent of Argenteuil's entry in one such roll.[42] Later in the same roll, Barking's entry names 'Ælfgyva abbatissa, Lucia priorissa, Petronella priorissa' and the nuns Scholastica, Perpetua, Mathilda, Athelidis, Mabilia and Emma among those of its dead for whom prayers are entreated.[43] From Barking the roll travelled to Westminster (Osbert of Clare's monastery) and around the Midlands, Yorkshire, and the South West, across to Norfolk and Yorkshire again, then once more over the Channel to Dol and Avranches before returning to the houses of the Winchester and Salisbury dioceses, up to Norfolk, and down through Suffolk and London before a last insular entry was made at Arundel on the south coast. This investment of time, energy and messenger's wages may now seem disproportionate, but this commemorative practice is a powerful way of asserting and confirming identities and social cohesion. The scrolls of the dead become places where the living constitute themselves not only as individual communities as in the case of monastic calendars, but as a network, a confraternity or sorority of communities. That one particular roll once physically linked Heloise and the women of Barking is as good an image as any of the shared culture of learning and commemoration in north west Europe at this period, a culture in which Heloise was exceptional, but in which nuns in England have often been underrated or passed over.

The most important death in the church year was of course that of Christ. This was honoured at Barking, as at most other monasteries from the eleventh century onwards, with extra ceremonies elabo-

---

42 For Heloise's authorship see Constant J. Mews, *The Lost Love Letters of Heloise and Abelard: Perceptions of Dialogue in Twelfth-Century France* (New York: St Martin's Press, 1999), pp. 161–3. An anonymous defence of a woman writer's right to compose and of her use of reason is extant in a twelfth-century anthology at Bury St Edmunds and may possibly be by Heloise (Mews, pp. 163–9).

43 Léopold Delisle, *Rouleaux des morts du IXe au XVe siècle* (Paris: Renouard, 1866), no. XXXVIII, titulus 99, p. 315.

rating the events of the Gospels' narrative.[44] After the morning service on Good Friday, a processional cross was ritually buried: the development of a corresponding performance of the resurrection on Easter Sunday is often seen as the origin of Western drama, since it demands dialogue and enactment. The three Marys of the Gospel narrative (Mary Magdalen, Mary Jacobi and Mary Salome) visit the tomb, find it empty and are told by an angel that Christ has risen.

At Barking, as in many convents, the nuns' church was also the parish church, often with various screen arrangements to separate nuns and laity.[45] The three Marys were played by nuns on Easter Sunday before the people in the convent church. The performance began with the whole convent and some of their priests being symbolically released from the chapel of Mary Magdalen (representing the limbo in which the prophets and patriarchs had waited since Adam's fall).[46] After the convent had processed with palm leaves and candles to the 'sepulchre' of the cross (usually the high altar) and removed the sacrament to another altar (that of the Trinity), the drama of the empty tomb was played out by three nuns in white, carrying silver flasks, who approached the 'sepulchre', chanting the verses of the biblical narrative, lamenting and preparing to anoint the corpse. A cleric in a white stole seated before the sepulchre plays the angel who asks 'Whom do you seek?', while the nun playing Mary Magdalen takes the leading role in dialogue with a second priest (representing the risen Christ). She joyfully announces the resurrection to her companions.

In the drama's conclusion the three Marys stand on the altar step and all announce the resurrection to a procession of priests and clerics representing Christ's disciples. Finally, having chanted a hymn of praise, all resume their ordinary vestments in the chapel, and, after a last prayer from the priest by the sepulchre-altar, return to their stations for the rest of the Easter morning service.[47]

---

44 See Karl Young, *The Drama of the Medieval Church* (Oxford: Clarendon Press, 1933, corr. ed. 1962), vol. 1, chs. 9 and 13, esp. pp. 164–6, 381–4; vol. II, pp. 507–13. For comparable celebrations in Northern French nunneries, see Penelope D. Johnson, *Equal in Monastic Profession: Religious Women in Medieval France* (Chicago and London: University of Chicago Press, 1991), pp. 139–40; Diane Dolan, *Le drame liturgique de Pâques en Normandie et en Angleterre au Moyen Age* (Paris: Presses universitaires de France, 1975), pp. 11–13.

45 Margaret Aston, 'Segregation in Church', in W. J. Sheils and Diana Wood (eds.), *Women in the Church*, SCH 27 (1990), 237–94.

46 Tolhurst, I, pp. 107–8.

47 Tolhurst, I, p. 110.

This drama of the defeat of death involves cooperation between men and women, while giving the women of the monastery roles of high status. In announcing the resurrection to the priests representing Christ's disciples, the nuns playing Mary Magdalen and her companions come as close to preaching as medieval orthodoxy permitted women to do. Not all monastic houses had Easter ceremonies as elaborate as those recorded in Barking's late medieval *Ordinale*, but the centrality of Easter celebrations to the Christian year and the importance of the resurrection dialogue makes the representation of women highly significant here. It mirrors the cultural importance of women's roles in death, burial, and commemoration more generally.

Women's cultural roles in death
As Abelard stresses in his Letter 7 to Heloise (II above), Jesus's women followers outstayed the fears of the apostles and followed Christ to the tomb, where they came prepared to anoint his body. Abelard's argument that men give form to the sacraments but Mary Magdalen actually performed the sacral anointing of Christ as king draws on the cultural association of laywomen and the care of the dead. Abelard says that to reject such significance in the Magdalen's act – the pouring of balm on Christ's head as a kingly anointing – amounts to rejection of 'the expression of devotion to the dead' (II, p. 56). If the Magdalen's anointing of Christ's dead body is a valid and significant practice, so too is her anointing of his living head: 'for it is sure that holy women also prepared spices for the Lord's burial; if she had been restrained by bashfulness now [from pouring balm on Christ's head], she would assuredly have been less prepared for the Lord's burial' (ibid.). Abelard here uses the association of women with the corporeal to argue that 'the weaker gender' may anoint Christ with 'as it were, a bodily sacrament': Christ is anointed with the balms of the Holy Spirit as Priest and King from his conception, but the Magdalen 'created [the anointed King Christ] in the flesh' (p. 54). This is the sacrament of 'a heavenly king, not of an earthly one' (p. 56) and so is not a precedent for female sacral power regarding earthly kings. It is also the case that Abelard is here inverting rather than dissolving traditional hierarchies whereby women are flesh and will, and men are spirit and reason. Nonetheless, the pervasive medieval view of death as a sign of heavenly power here allows more power and significance to the Magdalen's acts than might at first seem likely.

Roles of mourning and intercession were traditional, both for lay and religious women. Such roles have the authority of the Gospels and are also widely accepted in social practice. It was through the intercession of Mary and Martha as they mourned their brother that Lazarus was raised from the grave. Stressing the special intercessory power of women, Abelard argues that resurrection miracles occur at the behest of mothers, widows, daughters and sisters in the Old Testament and in the Gospels; that women's mourning and lamenting en route to the crucifixion was most directly responded to by Christ; and that at his own resurrection Christ 'offered most' to those who saw him first (II, p. 85). In medieval women's writing from the twelfth century onwards, as Barbara Newman and Anne Clark have shown, women's concern with suffering and intercession is evident in much reflection on and exploration of the developing doctrine of purgatory as a third 'place' or state in which souls who could not immediately gain Heaven could dwell and hope to be purified.[48]

The value of women's prayer is often suggested in the arrangements made with nunneries for commemorative masses and prayers after death.[49] Prayer was a major form of exchange between the living and the dead, and the work of nunneries was closely associated with intercession, both *for* the dead and *to* the (holy) dead. Writing to his niece Margaret in Barking, Osbert of Clare asks not only for her individual prayers, but that she show his letter to the convent in its chapter meetings and solicit the prayers of the whole community for him on his journey to Rome (IV, p. 113). The communal identity of nunneries as sacred sites of prayer and memory also had a wider political value in sacralizing the politics of regnal and noble houses. (William the Conqueror stayed at Barking, the oldest and most prestigious convent near London, as soon as possible after his conquest of England.)

As suggested by the genres of commemoration discussed above, the tools and practices of intercession and commemoration – the performance of the liturgy (especially the Office of the Dead), books of prayers, psalters, personal and communal devotions, bells, books, candles, incense, and training in the meaning and correct use of these

---

[48] *Elisabeth of Schönau: A Twelfth-Century Visionary* (Philadelphia: University of Pennsylvania Press, 1992); eadem (trans. and introd.), *Elisabeth of Schönau: The Complete Works* (Mahwah, NJ: Paulist Press, 2000); Barbara Newman, 'On the Threshold of the Dead' in her *From Virile Woman to WomanChrist: Studies in Medieval Religion and Literature* (Philadelphia, University of Pennsylvania Press, 1995), 108–37. See also Dinski, pp. 184–94, Takami Matsuda, *Death and Purgatory in Middle English Didactic Poetry* (Cambridge: D. S. Brewer, 1997).

[49] McLaughlin, pp. 184–95, 207–17; Crouch, pp. 166–7.

things – all create a rich culture of intercessory and memorial practice. Although female communities were in a sense specialists (and also themselves the site of holy relics and saintly burials), the links between religious and laywomen in this culture of commemoration are as obvious as the differences. Many convents functioned as family burial houses for their lay patrons, and, in secular households too, much of the work of lineage commemoration seems to have been done by women. Peter the Venerable's mother, the revered grandmother whose example he commends to his nieces (III, p. 106), is elsewhere praised by him for bringing to convent life the skills, such as psalter reading and eloquence, which she had acquired in secular life.[50]

Virginity and death
Death and eternity change in tandem with the needs of the living, and this complex of concerns – mourning, intercession, penance, and prayer – is differently accented in letters to younger women. The Apocalpyse and the New Jerusalem rather than Purgatory and the need to help souls through it supply much of the imagery and themes in such letters. Monastic community is offered to young women as a prelude to an eternal and glamorous heavenly angelic court. Writing to a nun, Ida [?of Barking], Osbert of Clare says that in heaven she will not be called 'Ida' but 'the glorious daughter of the living God'; not 'niece of Queen Adelidis [Adeliza of Louvain, Queen of Henry I]', since greater and more noble domains will belong to her. She will be introduced by St Ethelburga of Barking to the virgin martyrs Agnes, Cecilia, Agatha, Lucy, Faith and Katherine and will be welcomed by St Etheldreda of Ely, the perpetual virgin and queen, before being finally led by the Queen of heaven and earth to her son who will crown her in glory.[51]

The virgin's realm of death was thus the splendid and eternal court of heaven, the very highest and most gracious form of courtly life possible. Osbert paints a glowing picture for his niece Cecilia of her marriage to the heavenly bridegroom there (IV, p. 114). As well as

[50]   Janet Martin in collaboration with Giles Constable (eds.), *Peter the Venerable: Select Letters* (Toronto: Pontifical Institute of Mediaeval Studies, 1974), p. 39. See also *Letters of Peter the Venerable* ed. Giles Constable (Cambridge, Mass.: Harvard University Press, 1967), I, Letter 53, p. 166 where Peter claims that Raingard spoke so well it was more like hearing a bishop than a woman.
[51]   E. W. Williamson (ed.), *The Letters of Osbert of Clare, Prior of Westminster* (London: Oxford University Press, 1929), pp. 139–40.

being socially and spiritually attractive, death to the world as a future high-ranking bride at the eternal court is argued as much preferable to the risk of death in childbirth endured by the wives of mortal men (p. 116). But the heavenly Jerusalem also had mystical aspects: its jewels do not only connote splendour and eternity in the afterlife, but are themselves used in the building of the city of God. A virgin with the gemstone of her virginity is by implication already a part of this supreme courtly existence. Saints might be living stones of God's kingdom dwelling permanently with God and virgin gems also contributed to the construction of God's shining heavenly city. If, then, the professed virgin is living as one dead to the world on earth, it is because she is already a citizen of heaven. In yet another letter (to Matilda of Darenth), one which is essentially a more theological and speculative letter-treatise, Osbert expands on the gems so often associated with virginity. He incorporates discussion of the redemption with exegesis of the precious stones used in building the eternal city of Jerusalem in the manner of the lapidaries, medieval handbooks of the meanings of gems and precious stones.[52] Christ himself is presented as an eternal diamond in the contemporary lapidaries and bestiaries (one of which is dedicated to Ida's aunt, Queen Adeliza).[53] Gems are used by many writers in representing youthful virginity as the 'perfect age of women's life' and as the condition most redolent of eternity: 'precious virginity', Osbert of Clare writes to Margaret, 'is the pearl . . . about which you have already had dealings with the greatest Merchant so that you might obtain palms of dazzling rays in heaven' (IV, p. 111, and see Matt. 13:46).[54] In Peter the Venerable's letter to his nieces, the young women have virginity as the Magdalen does not and consequently will outshine even the glory of the saints (III, p. 102). As a sign of eternity, virginity has powerful associations with origins as well as with endings, with Genesis as well as with Apocalypse. 'It is well-known', Peter writes

---

52 Williamson, pp. 148–53.
53 For Philippe de Thaun's bestiary for Queen Adeliza, see Ruth J. Dean and Maureen B. M. Boulton, *Anglo-Norman Literature: A Guide to Manuscripts and Texts*, ANTS OPS 3 (London: ANTS, 1999), no. 347: for a Latin lapidary with important circulation in England and France in the period, see John M. Riddle (ed.), *Marbod of Rennes (1095–1123): De Lapidibus* (Wiesbaden: Franz Steiner, 1977).
54 See Kim M. Phillips, 'Maidenhood as the Perfect Age of Women's Life', in Katherine J. Lewis, Noël James Menuge and Kim M. Phillips (eds.), *Young Medieval Women* (Gloucester: Sutton, 1999), pp. 25–46.

to his nieces, 'that angels fell from heaven into this world because of their excesses, but virgins have passed from this world into heaven because of their purity' (III, p. 104).

Nuns, cemeteries, and women's history

Memory is not simply a recollection of what happened, but an active making of historiographical tradition. Goscelin writes that

the remains [of Ethelburga] were unknown to all of this generation, but when [Elfgiva] had the shrines of the saints opened, to the great joy of her heart she found them surrounded by the sure evidence of writings, so that you may claim that the blessing of the rejoicing Father smiled upon this devoted guardian. (VI [e], pp. 150–1)

As Elfgiva was intent at the time on clearing away peasant houses from around the churchyard, a re-invention of the convent's collective memory would have been required, whether or not there was uncertainty about Ethelburga's remains. Different times need different memories, and the maintenance of memory and its re-invention is an ongoing process, demanding a range of skills in convents.

Elisabeth van Houts has recently and powerfully challenged the view that although women were chiefly responsible for mourning, both performing and paying for it, it was monks who 'took the initiative in procuring bodies and money and thence . . . monopolized the growth, spread and importance of the remembrance'.[55] Van Houts argues, rather, for cooperation between men and women in the creation of memory, an argument well supported by the texts in this volume. She points to how Goscelin, in his rewriting of the lives of saints at Barking and Wilton, uses the cultural authority of the women at the tomb and the announcement of the resurrection (also cited by Abelard and prominent, as we have seen, in Barking's rituals) to argue that the witness of women should not be rejected in the construction of monastic tradition.[56]

The learning and administrative skills required for nunneries'

---

[55] Elisabeth van Houts, *Memory and Gender in Medieval Europe 900–1200* (Basingstoke: Macmillan, 1999), p. 97: see Geary, n. 37 above.

[56] Like Abelard, Goscelin uses the women of the Gospel as a precedent in the argument 'that the faithful testimonies of this sex should not be rejected is shown by the first Mary [that is, God's mother] and the angel's messenger of the Lord's resurrection [that is Mary Magdalene] and the many saintly female prophets' (see Van Houts, pp. 51–2).

practices of commemoration are obviously not small, though they would be acquired in full only by choir nuns and not by lay-sisters. In Letter 9, Abelard, following the private teaching evolved by Jerome for Paula, daughter of Laeta, stresses reading and memory. These are equally foundational for institutional literacies, and are what Abelard envisages Heloise, as institutional mother, purveying for her spiritual daughters (V, pp. 124–5). This very active conception sees the reading and memorization of Scripture not so much as a technical skill as an entire spiritual formation and way of life, from infancy through to learned theological discussion. A liturgist, poet and song-writer himself, Abelard follows Jerome in concern that the infant Paula is taught good articulation of letters and clear pronounciation in reading. In the adult woman, this becomes long meditation and thorough internalization in study, as in Jerome's praise of Marcella which Abelard also follows (V, pp. 129–30). It is one of the marks of Marcella's moral perfection that she constantly intones the words of Scripture. This meditative reading and learning is, for Abelard, continuous with the liturgical observances of convents: contemplation, song, and penitence are all linked in spiritual formation. The joy, the dancing and singing of the women of the Old Testament prefigure 'in a mystic way' the form of 'holy singing' in conventual communities (II, p. 65).[57] Equipping women for the work of commemoration and communion with the dead was to equip them with the means of self-conscious historiographical and political shaping of their own and others' lives and spirituality.

When we consider medieval death, it is clear that the life of the convent as a death to the world is neither macabre, gloomy or dull. The excerpts in this volume which demonstrate the preoccupation of the Barking abbesses with their cemetery and shrine arrangements give a particularly full representation of the range of death's meanings in the lives of conventual women.[58] Concern with death and

---

[57] On the representation of women's devotions as the holy ring dance of heaven, see James L. Miller, *Measures of Wisdom: The Cosmic Dance in Classical and Christian Antiquity* (Toronto: University of Toronto Press, 1985); Walter Simons, 'Reading a Saint's Body: Rapture and Bodily Movement in the *vitae* of Thirteenth-Century Beguines', in Sarah Kay and Miri Rubin (eds.), *Reading Medieval Bodies* (Manchester: Manchester University Press, 1994), pp. 10–25 (16–18).

[58] Heloise was also concerned with these matters: in 1156, for instance, in the absence of a separate burial ground for lay brothers, she was granted permission to bury them in the nuns' cemetery (see Mary Martin McLaughlin, 'Heloise the Abbess', in Bonnie Wheeler [ed.], *Listening to Heloise: The Voice of A*

burial embraces monastic identity, holy and secular patrons, monastic predecessors, institutional and personal histories and practical and regulatory matters, as well as (in the desire of parishioners to be buried as near the nuns' holy ground as possible) the relations between the convent and the world. The cemetery at Barking was a locus of memory and continuity and an ever-present theatre of events. The dead crowd the living, offer them shelter, share their destruction and burning in Danish raiding, and are sources for renewing the power and prestige of the house (VI [a]–[e]). Moreover the dead are not static: arranging and reordering their hierarchy is as much a part of the culture of the nunnery as its buildings and documents. It is no wonder that the care and arrangement of the cemetery was a recurrent concern for so many of Barking's leaders.

The final extract in this volume offers what could be seen as a supremely 'gothick' moment in Elfgiva's long struggle to expand church and churchyard at Barking while translating the convent's most holy dead, the founding mothers Sts Ethelburga, Hildelitha, and Wulfhilda. Alone in the church at night, praying at the tombs of her predecessors and revisited by the spirit of her dead novice mistress, Elfgiva perceives Ethelburga's tomb moving and fears being crushed to death by it. To the accompaniment of fire, song, and rustling wind, the tomb lid opens, with the tall shining figure of Ethelburga herself rising from it. Then, once the translation of the remains to a more commodious shrine is negotiated and agreed between the living and the dead abbesses, Elfgiva is able to stand, hugging to her bosom her great foremother (who has now become like a little girl and leaps into her arms), while the other tombs open around her and the holy dead of Barking surround her.

Goscelin's account represents this moment as fear overcome: the horror and spectre of financial imprudence and ecclesiastical defiance banished in resolution. At last, after all the anxious discussion, struggles with the bishop of London, prayer, fasting, financial review and directions to architects and crowbar wielders to stand by, Elfgiva sees her way forward. Drawing strength from, and herself perpetuating, the traditions of the house, including (as the appearance of her novice mistress makes plain) her own good education there, she becomes the mother to her foremother, and stands

Twelfth-Century Woman [New York: St Martin's Press, 2000], pp. 1–18 [7]. Abelard's body was returned to the convent of the Paraclete, his foundation for Heloise, a couple of years after his death (ibid., p. 11).

triumphantly protective, surrounded by her monastic family stretching gloriously through and beyond time. No wonder liturgical chant, fiery flames and heavenly radiance grace this moment for Elfgiva. It is one of supreme triumph, of true exchange and continuity in her life with the glorious dead of Barking. The rich memorial and commemorative culture deployed by Elfgiva and her colleagues in the convents of medieval England and France makes them living dead for us too.

Bibliography

Editions of texts in this volume

Abelard, *Peter Abelard. Letters IX–XIV: An Edition with an Introduction*, ed. E. R. Smits (Groningen, 1983), Letter IX, pp. 219–37.

———, 'The Letters of Heloise on Religious Life and Abelard's First Reply', ed. J. T. Muckle, *Mediaeval Studies* 17 (1955), 253–81.

Goscelin of St Bertin, 'Texts of Jocelin of Canterbury which Relate to the History of Barking Abbey', ed. Marvin L. Colker, *Studia monastica* 7 (1965), 383–460.

Osbert of Clare, *The Letters of Osbert of Clare, Prior of Westminster*, ed. E. W. Williamson (London: Oxford University Press, 1929).

Peter the Venerable, *The Letters of Peter the Venerable*, ed. Giles Constable (Cambridge, Mass.: Harvard University Press, 1967).

———, *Peter the Venerable: Select Letters*, ed. Janet Martin in collaboration with Giles Constable (Toronto: Pontifical Institute of Mediaeval Studies, 1974).

Other primary texts of interest

Anon., *The Life of Christina of Markyate*, ed. and trans. C. H. Talbot (Oxford: Clarendon Press, 1959, repr. 1987). Biography of a twelfth-century monastic woman in England.

Goscelin of St Bertin, *The Liber confortatorius of Goscelin of St Bertin*, ed. C. H. Talbot in *Analecta monastica*, series 3, Studia Anselmiana 37, ed. M. M. Lebreton, J. Leclercq, and C. H. Talbot (Rome: Pontifical Institute of St Anselm, 1955), 1–117. Goscelin's treatise for an ex-nun of Wilton, England, after she had become a recluse in Angers, France.

Orderic Vitalis, *The Ecclesiastical History of Orderic Vitalis*, ed. Marjorie C. Chibnall, 6 vols (Oxford: Oxford University Press, 1969–80). Important chronicle of the period.

Peter of Blois, *The Latin Letters of Peter of Blois*, ed. Elizabeth Revell, Auctores Britannici Medii Aevi XIII (London: British Academy, 1993). Includes further examples of letters to cloistered women in England and France.

Savage, Anne, and Nicholas Watson (trans.), *Anchoritic Spirituality*:

Ancrene Wisse *and Associated Works*, The Classics of Western Spirituality (New York and Mahwah, NJ; 1991). Translations of the first major collection of post-Conquest vernacular guidance in England for women.

Tolhurst, J. B. L. (ed.), *The Ordinale and Customary of the Benedictine Nuns of Barking Abbey*, HBS 65, 66 (London: Harrison and Sons, 1927, 1928). Important source for Barking Abbey's rituals and liturgical culture.

Wogan-Browne, Jocelyn, and Glyn Burgess (trans.), *Virgin Lives and Holy Deaths: Two Exemplary Biographies for Anglo-Norman Women* (London: Dent, 1996). Twelfth-century writing for and by religious women in French at Barking Abbey and elsewhere.

Latin letters and women's literary culture

Barratt, Alexandra, 'Small Latin? The Post-Conquest Learning of English Religious Women', in Siân Echard and Gernot R. Wieland (eds.), *Anglo-Latin and Its Heritage: Essays in Honour of A. G. Rigg* (Turnhout: Brepols, 2001), pp. 51–65. Useful study of the current state of knowledge of women's latinity, challenging received notions of its paucity in England.

Bell, David N., *What Nuns Read: Books and Libraries in Medieval English Nunneries* (Kalamazoo, MI: Cistercian Publications, 1995). An indispensable account of the books owned by nunneries in England.

Bond, Gerald A., *The Loving Subject: Desire, Eloquence and Power in Romanesque France* (Philadelphia: University of Pennsylvania Press, 1995). Includes stimulating study of letters between religious men and women in the Loire valley.

Bos, Elisabeth, 'The Literature of Spiritual Formation for Women in France and England, 1080–1180', in Mews (ed.), *Listen, Daughter*, pp. 201–20. Studies religious women and writings for them in England and France. Very useful on the kinds of texts translated in this volume.

Cherewatuk, Karen and Ulrike Wiethaus (eds.), *Dear Sister: Medieval Women and the Epistolary Genre* (Philadelphia: University of Pennsylvania Press, 1993). A pioneering essay collection on women and medieval letters.

Churchill, Laurie J., Phyllis R. Brown and Jane E. Jeffrey, eds., *Women Writing in Latin*, 3 vols (London and New York: Routledge, Taylor and Francis, 2001–). Wide-ranging anthology.

Clanchy, M. T., *From Memory to Written Record: England 1066–1307*

(London: Edward Arnold Ltd, 1979, 2nd edn, Oxford and Cambridge, Mass.: Blackwell, 1993). One of the most important studies available for anyone seeking to understand medieval texts. The second edition pays much increased attention to women and female literacies.

Epistolae (Data Base of Women's Letters in the Middle Ages): http://db.ccnmtl.columbia/edu/ferrante

Ferrante, Joan M., *To the Glory of her Sex: Women's Roles in the Composition of Medieval Texts* (Bloomington and Indianapolis: Indiana University Press, 1997). Deals with many genres and pays special attention to Latin letters and women.

———, 'Women's Role in Latin Letters from the Fourth to the Early Twelfth Century', in June Hall McCash (ed.), *The Cultural Patronage of Medieval Women* (Athens and London: University of Georgia Press, 1996), pp. 73–104. A useful survey.

Mews, Constant J. (ed.), *Listen, Daughter. The* Speculum Virginum *and the Formation of Religious Women in the Middle Ages* (New York: Palgrave, 2001). A valuable collection on continental and insular women's spirituality with particular reference to the ideology of virginity.

Heyworth, Paul, 'Translation Narratives in Post-Conquest Hagiography and English Resistance to the Norman Conquest', *Anglo-Norman Studies* 21 (1999), 67–93. Gives a detailed sense of the monastic and political context of the saints' lives composed by Goscelin of St Bertin, including those for Barking Abbey.

Newman, Barbara, 'Flaws in the Golden Bowl: Gender and Spiritual Formation in the Twelfth Century', *Traditio* 45 (1989–90), 1–46, repr. in her *From Virile Woman to WomanChrist* (Philadelphia: University of Pennyslvania Press, 1995). Elegant and stimulating study of gender in letters and treatises for convent women: important for many of the texts translated here.

Pindar, Janice, 'The Cloister and the Garden: Gendered Images of Religious Life from the Twelfth and Thirteenth Centuries', in Mews (ed.), *Listen, Daughter,* pp. 159–79. Useful study of gender and spirituality in materials comparable with those treated in this volume.

Salter, Elizabeth, *English and International: Studies in the Literature, Art, and Patronage of Medieval England*, ed. Derek Pearsall and Nicolette Zeeman (Cambridge: Cambridge University Press, 1988), esp. Part I, chs. 1 and 2. This famous study is still one of the best accounts of the internationalism of literary culture in the high Middle Ages.

Thiébaux, Marcelle (tran.), *The Writings of Medieval Women* (New

184 *Bibliography*

York: Garland, 1987). Useful general collection, including some letters.

Wogan-Browne, Jocelyn, *Saints' Lives and Women's Literary Culture c. 1150–1300: Virginity and Its Authorizations* (Oxford: Oxford University Press, 2001). Saints' lives, letters, and other documents for and by women in the high Middle Ages in Britain.

———, ' "Reading is Good Prayer": Recent Research on Female Reading Communities', *New Medieval Literatures* 5 (2002), 229–97. Analytic review-essay with bibliography.

Heloise and Abelard

Clanchy, M. T., *Abelard: A Medieval Life* (Oxford and Malden, Mass.: Blackwell, 1997). Important and controversial biography of Abelard.

McLaughlin, Mary M., 'Peter Abelard and the Dignity of Women: Twelfth Century "Feminism" in Theory and Practice', in *Pierre Abélard, Pierre le Vénérable: Les courants philosophiques, littéraires et artistiques en Occident au milieu du XIIe siècle* (Paris: CNRS, 1975), pp. 287–333. Valuable account of Abelard's attitudes to women, especially useful for Letter 7 translated in this volume.

——— (tran.), *Letters of Heloise and Abelard: A Translation of Their Complete Correspondence* (New York and Basingstoke: Palgrave, 2002). New translations by a major scholar in the field: very valuable.

———, *Heloise and the Paraclete: A Twelfth Century Quest* (New York and Basingstoke: Palgrave, 2002). Long-awaited and very important study by a doyenne of scholarship on Heloise and female communities.

Mews, Constant J., *Peter Abelard* (Aldershot: Variorum, 1995) Excellent concise biography of Abelard.

———, *The Lost Love Letters of Heloise and Abelard: Perceptions of Dialogue in Twelfth-Century France* (New York: St Martin's Press, 1999). This well-known study argues for re-discovered letters between Heloise and Abelard and is generally illuminating on their correspondence and its context.

Radice, Betty (trans.), *The Letters of Abelard and Heloise* (Harmondsworth: Penguin Classics, 1974). A pioneering and useful volume, but summarizes Letter 7 briefly and omits Letter 9 (both translated here).

Wheeler, Bonnie (ed.), *Listening to Heloise: The Voice of a Twelfth-Century Woman* (New York: St Martin's Press, 2000). Major collection on a major figure in this volume: copious, rich and various.

Women and monasticism

Berman, Constance H., *The Cistercian Evolution: The Invention of a Religious Order in Twelfth Century France* (Philadelphia: University of Pennsylvania Press, 2000). Major study of a religious order important to women in France (and also in England).

Burton, Janet, *Monastic and Religious Orders in Britain 1000–1300* (Cambridge and New York: Cambridge University Press, 1994, repr. 1997). Lucid history of monasticism in Britain during the high Middle Ages, which (unlike some older histories) includes women.

———, 'Yorkshire Nunneries in the Middle Ages: Recruitment and Resources', in John C. Appleby and Paul Dalton (eds.), *Government, Religion and Society in Northern England 1000–1700* (Stroud: Sutton, 1997), pp. 104–16. An enlightening and detailed account of women's religious houses in the north of England.

Caldicott, Diana K., *Hampshire Nunneries* (Chichester: Phillimore, 1989). Useful, detailed account of southern women's houses.

Elkins, Sharon K., *Holy Women of Twelfth Century England* (Chapel Hill; University of North Carolina Press, 1988). A useful background survey across the range of women in religion in high medieval Britain.

Gilchrist, Roberta, *Gender and Material Culture: The Archaeology of Religious Women* (London and New York: Routledge, 1994). Pioneering and influential study of the gendered distribution of space in monasteries.

———, *Contemplation and Action: The Other Monasticism* (London and New York: Leicester University Press, 1995). Looks at the full range of monasticism, including the para-monastic forms such as hospitals and anchorages with which women were often involved.

Gold, Penny Schine, *The Lady and the Virgin: Image and Experience in Twelfth-Century France* (Chicago: Chicago University Press, 1985). An early and still very important and stimulating study of the culture of women in religion in France.

Golding, Brian J., *Gilbert of Sempringham and the Gilbertine Order c.1130–c.1300* (Oxford: Clarendon Press, 1995). Magisterial history of Britain's post-Conquest monastic double order for women and men.

Johnson, Penelope D., *Equal in Monastic Profession: Religious Women in Medieval France* (Chicago and London: University of Chicago Press, 1991). A fundamental study of women in religion in France.

Kerr, Berenice M., *Religious Life for Women, c.1100–c.1350: Fontevraud in England* (Oxford: Clarendon Press, 1999). Useful study of the important cross-channel order which linked some elite women in England and France.

Leyser, Henrietta, *Medieval Women: A Social History 450–1500* (New York: St Martin's Press, 1995). An excellent one-volume history of medieval women.

Matrix (Database on Medieval Women's Communities, 400–1600): http://matrix.bc.edu/

Power, Eileen, *Medieval English Nunneries 1275–1535* (Cambridge: Cambridge University Press, 1922). Although concerned with a later period than the present volume, this classic of nunnery history remains a generally illuminating, detailed and rich account of women's monasticism.

Schulenberg, Jane Tibbetts, 'Strict Active Enclosure and its Effects on the Female Monastic Experience, 500–1100', in John A. Nichols and Lillian T. Shank (eds.), *Distant Echoes: Medieval Women 1*, Cistercian Studies Series 71 (Kalamazoo, Mich., 1984), pp. 51–86. A pioneering and important study of the gendered nature of monastic enclosure.

———, *Forgetful of Their Sex: Female Sanctity and Society ca 500–1100* (Chicago: University of Chicago Press, 1998). Ranging and fascinating study of nunneries and religious women in early medieval Europe.

Thompson, Sally, *Medieval Women Religious: The Founding of English Nunneries after the Norman Conquest* (Oxford: Clarendon Press, 1991). Fundamental study of women's houses and their patrons and associates in England during the period of this volume.

———, 'Why English Nunneries had no History: A Study of the Problems of the English Nunneries Founded after the Conquest', in John M. Nichols and Lillian T. Shank (eds.), *Distant Echoes: Medieval Religious Women I*, Cistercian Studies Series 71 (Kalamazoo: University of West Michigan Press, 1984), pp. 131–49. Raises important questions about the gendered nature of the history of monasticism and the survival of nunnery records.

Venarde, Bruce L., *Monasticism and Medieval Society: Nunneries in France and England 890–1215* (Ithaca and London: Cornell University Press, 1997). An important argument for separating out the developmental patterns of female communities rather than simply folding them into the history of male monasticism.

Medieval commemoration, death, and intercession

Ariès, Philippe, tran. Helen Weaver, *The Hour of Our Death* (New York: Knopf, 1981). A famous pioneering cultural history of death, still of great interest.

Binski, Paul, *Medieval Death: Ritual and Representation* (Ithaca and New York: Cornell University Press, 1996). Important history of death, scholarly and very challenging and stimulating.

Crouch, David, 'The Culture of Death in the Anglo-Norman World', in C. Warren Hollister (ed.), *Anglo-Norman Political Culture and the Twelfth-Century Political Renaissance* (Woodbridge: Boydell Press, 1997), 157–180. Illuminating study in the social history of death.

Geary, Patrick, *Furta Sacra: Thefts of Relics in the Central Middle Ages* (Princeton: Princeton University Press, 1978). Important study of attitudes to commemorated bodies in medieval culture.

McLaughlin, Megan, *Consorting with Saints: Prayer for the Dead in Early Medieval France* (Ithaca and London: Cornell University Press, 1994). Useful study of monastic intercession.

Reinburg, Virginia, 'Remembering the Saints', in Nancy Netzner and Virginia Reinburg (eds.), *Memory and the Middle Ages* (Chestnut Hill, MA: Boston College, Museum of Art, 1995), pp. 17–33. Lucid and perceptive article, useful for understanding medieval culture of memorialization.

Rouleaux des morts du ixe au xve siècle, ed. Léopold Delisle (Paris: Renouard, 1866). Fundamental source for the commemoration of the dead in the rolls carried between religious houses.

van Houts, Elisabeth M. C., *Memory and Gender in Early Medieval Europe 900–1200* (Basingstoke: Macmillan, 1999). Important argument for women's roles in the transmission of history, despite their more limited access to institutional memory systems.

Subject Index

Note: Page references in italics indicate the text of the letters.

Index of References

Lactantius
Divine Institutes
4.18   82 n.143
Origen
Commentary on the Song of Songs
4.13.191   116 n.23
Pelagius
*Expositions of the Thirteen Epistles
of St Paul II*   70 n.86
In Praise of Virgins   75 n.113
The Praise of Virginity   91 n.188
Pseudo-Jerome
Letter 148.1–2   134 n.37
Pseudo-Hilary
'Letter to his daughter, Abra'   105
n.36
Sidonius Apollinaris
Carmina 24   89 n.176

Medieval
Abelard
Christian Theology
1.127–8   82 n.143
Commentary on Romans
4 (16.2)   70 n.90, 71 n.98
Sermons
8   123 n.3
16   123 n.3
26   123 n.3
29   123 n.3
31   71 n.98

Bede
Ecclesiastical History
4.19   24–5 n.20
4.7   48 n.99, 141
4.9   48 n.99
Gratian
Decretum 2.20.1.4   65 n.69
Gregory the Great
Homilies on the Gospels
2.25   54 n.10
2.33   54 n.10
11.3   68 n.77
17.10   66 n.73
Letters
4.11   70 n.89
Moralia in Job
3.4   78 n.127
14.50   58 n.37
31.34   123 n.3
John the Deacon
Life of Pope Gregory 44   90 n.183
Paschasius Radbertus
On the Assumption   92 n.190
27.69–70   102 n.26
Peter Lombard
Sententiae 4.6.1   54–5 n.12
Smaragdus
*Commentary on the Rule of
St Benedict* 59   65 n.69

Already published titles in this series

Christine de Pizan's Letter of Othea to Hector, *Jane Chance*, 1990

The Writings of Margaret of Oingt, Medieval Prioress and Mystic, *Renate Blumenfeld-Kosinski*, 1990

Saint Bride and her Book: Birgitta of Sweden's Revelations, *Julia Bolton Holloway*, 1992

The Memoirs of Helene Kottanner (1439–1440), *Maya Bijvoet Williamson*, 1998

The Writings of Teresa de Cartagena, *Dayle Seidenspinner-Núñez*, 1998

Julian of Norwich: *Revelations of Divine Love* and *The Motherhood of God*: an excerpt, *Frances Beer*, 1998

Hrotsvit of Gandersheim: A Florilegium of her Works, *Katharina M. Wilson*, 1998

Hildegard of Bingen: On Natural Philosophy and Medicine: Selections from *Cause et Cure, Margret Berger*, 1999

Women Saints' Lives in Old English Prose, *Leslie A. Donovan*, 1999

Angela of Foligno's Memorial, *Cristina Mazzoni*, 2000

The Letters of the Rožmberk Sisters, *John M. Klassen*, 2001

The Life of Saint Douceline, a Beguine of Provence, *Kathleen Garay and Madeleine Jeay*, 2001

Agnes Blannbekin, Viennese Beguine: Life and Revelations, *Ulrike Wiethaus*, 2002

Women of the *Gilte Legende*: A Selection of Middle English Saints Lives, *Larissa Tracy*, 2003

The Book of Margery Kempe: An Abridged Translation, *Liz Herbert McAvoy*, 2003

Mechthild of Magdeburg: Selections from *The Flowing Light of the Godhead*, *Elizabeth A. Andersen*, 2003